MW00574230

## What Oth[illegible]

Nothing lies beyond the reach of prayer because nothing lies beyond the reach of God. In his new book, *Prayer, His Presence, and Intimacy With God*, my friend Scott gives us a cure for a limited spiritual life. Most believers live from measure instead of fullness. This is truly Scott's life message. With so many voices talking about secondary issues, Scott brings us back to ensure the main thing is the main thing.

After the disciples saw the supernatural work of Jesus, they made an important request, "Teach us to pray." They realized that Jesus's intimacy with God was everything. I highly recommend Scott's book to those who desire a deeper walk with God. You will be entrusted with the secrets from the secret place.

**—Dr. Leif Hetland**
President of Global Mission Awareness
Author of *Called to Reign* and *The Love Awakening*

I remember as a young believer in Christ, writing Leviticus 6:9, "*The fire must be kept burning on the altar,*" on the front page of my first Bible. As I embarked on this new journey of faith to rediscover this Jesus of my childhood, the idea of my heart being an altar His presence would enflame, satisfied my seeking heart and guided my pathway forward. In *Prayer, His Presence, and Intimacy With God,* my friend Scott does a masterful job of leading us back to our sacred space of prayer. He not only ignites our passion and purpose for prayer but also trains us in the actual, all-important practice of prayer. Whether you are a seasoned prayer warrior or a brand-new Jesus follower, this book will meet you right where you are on *your* journey of discovery. It will help you build a personal altar of prayer where you will experience God's faithfulness and friendship. Scott has given us a gift, wrapping so many aspects of prayer into one solid presentation of biblical truth. I highly recommend it as the perfect textbook for any school of ministry or home group, as it will truly lay a strong foundation for your individual or corporate house of prayer.

**—Apostle Kathy Bichsel**
Author of *Radical Rising Remnant*
KathyBichsel.com

I love this book! It is full of the heart of God and His gracious keys for going deeper in prayer. The greatest thing you can ever do in this life is move the heart of God through prayer! Scott Tavolacci has given us a delightful handbook on the beautiful realm of prayer. God inspired this book, and you'll feel it as you read it. It will move you to long for more of the Living Water that we drink in as we open our heart and pray. The title says it all—this is what you've been longing for: *Prayer, His Presence, and Intimacy With God*. You'll find this and more in the pages of this book!

**—Brian Simmons**
Passion & Fire Ministries/Author of *The Passion Translation*
www.passionandfire.com

Author Scott Tavolacci offers yet another masterpiece of solid Bible-based content that is sure to propel the reader ahead in his or her desire to truly know God. I urge the reader to especially focus on the vital role speaking in tongues plays in a believer's spiritual life. A second "Pentecost" could be upon us!

**—Dennis Cramer, Prophet/Teacher**
www.Denniscramer.com

A book's stimulation of the heart, soul, and spirit is how we can measure the quality of a person's writing. What I love about Scott is that he embodies what he writes. This book expresses his life's journey, passion, commitment, and love for King Jesus. This book will influence and uplift others.

**—Pastor Lance Bane**
Senior Pastor, Gateway Christian Fellowship
www.yourgateway.com, www.lancebane.com

# *Prayer, His Presence, and Intimacy with God*

SCOTT TAVOLACCI

*Prayer, His Presence, and Intimacy with God*
Copyright© 2023 by Scott Tavolacci
Published by Scott Tavolacci



ISBNs: 978-1-7340053-6-3 (Paperback)

978-1-7340053-4-9 (Ebook)

Printed in the United States of America.

# Contents

# Foreword

Scott Tavolacci is my friend. He is about to become your friend too! A great friend brings out the best in you. He will undoubtedly do that with this book!

Scripture says in the book of Ecclesiastes that God has placed eternity in every human heart. Therefore, as humans, no matter where we are in relationship to God, or what we believe, there is something in us that when things get desperate, we pray. For some, it can be a last-ditch effort just in case Someone is out there listening—a God that might consider helping us. Too often, prayer is like the alarm you pull when your life is on fire. It can be the last resort. It's like the story of the two guys in a desperate life-and-death situation; having tried everything they knew to do to save themselves, one said to the other, "Maybe we should pray." The other man turned to his friend and responded, "Has it come to that?"

If you are a Christian, you know that prayer is foundational to your faith, yet you must be honest and ask yourself if prayer is your first response to the events of your life or your last resort?

Why do so many followers of Jesus struggle to make prayer a part of their daily life? Why do so many Christians find developing an exciting and vibrant prayer life difficult? Even though prayer is essential to the Christian life, many are intimidated or unsure of how to talk to God. Prayer feels awkward, strange, and even old-fashioned to some. Others feel scared and uncomfortable with the idea of talking to God. What is it about prayer that makes it so challenging? What is the issue?

## Prayer, His Presence, and Intimacy with God

Communication is the lifeblood of every relationship. Our relationships are only as healthy as the communication that flows to and from the parties. Communication is the way we get to know someone. Scripture tells us that no one knows another's thoughts unless they are willing to share them. Our thoughts are the most intimate part of our life. It is only when we talk and open our heart to someone that we build intimacy. As the communication in a relationship increases, the relationship grows, and intimacy can be experienced. The depth of any relationship is determined by the willingness to share your thoughts and open your heart to them.

Prayer is simply talking to God. The frequency and sincerity of our communication with Him determines the quality and intimacy of our relationship. The amazing thing that Scripture reveals is that God is a relational Being. God has a name; by the way, it's not God. It's Yahweh. When God revealed His name, He revealed what was most important about Himself. He is compassionate, gracious, slow to anger, and abounding in love and faithfulness. These are relational qualities. Why is that important? Because He wants to relate to us. He is a Person. By Person, I don't mean He's male or female or human. But He is a Person with real feelings and emotions. He desires a relationship with us. He wants to know and be known. It is through prayer that we enter into a relationship with Him.

God is a God who responds. He listens to us and interacts with us, providing wisdom and direction for our life. He cares and is willing to be as intimate with us as we will allow Him to be. Scripture reveals that God has friends. He'd love to be our friend, but like all friendships, it's about how willing we are to be vulnerable, honest, open, share our deepest thoughts and desires, and spend time with Him.

The Bible tells us stories about Moses, David, Jesus, and Paul, along with others, and we think, "That was for them, not for me." But we need to understand that the Bible wasn't written to tell us how others related to God. It is there to inspire us to know how we can develop a relationship with Him like they did. Jesus came, lived, died, and rose from the grave to make possible the kind of relationship that He, Moses, and others had with God.

## Foreword

This is what I love about Scott's book. He shares a profound revelation that our passions and desires are accelerants to God's love. When we embrace that truth, it will enhance our prayer life.

Scott spent years studying and building on this theme. He discovered that it is woven into many of the prayer examples highlighted in Scripture. This book guides those wanting to develop a more intimate prayer life with God. Scott shows his readers how they can spend more time in conversation with God—and enjoy every minute of it!

Let me give you a preview of things you will learn in this book: God's love is the basis of a dynamic prayer life, and when our passions and desires are expressed in complete trust in God, they are divine accelerants. They unleash a powerful force to our prayers.

- Worship is the highest form of prayer. Worship is where we acknowledge God for who He is and express our love and devotion. The more we know Him, the easier it is to trust Him in every area of our life. In worship, we experience His love, and our love grows as we trust in His love.
- God's Word is His thoughts recorded for us. The Word, therefore, is essential to having a dynamic prayer life. We can know and understand His desires and seek to align our desires with His to see our prayers bring results.
- The more we understand our new identity in Christ, the more our confidence grows, and our relational intimacy develops.
- The Holy Spirit plays an important role and helps our prayer life.

This book offers a practical how-to guide for anyone seeking a more dynamic, intimate prayer life with God. Let's get started, experience God's presence, and grow closer to Him. Today is the first day of the rest of your life. It's about to get better!

**—Ken Vance**

Lead Pastor of Vertical Church, West Haven, Connecticut
www.verticalct.com

# Authors Note and Exhortation

As I developed this manuscript, I passed it on to some friends for early reading. One of my spiritual mentors, bible teacher, author, Christian counselor, and a mother in the body of Christ who has served the Lord for sixty years, Shelvy Wyatt, wrote the following to me:

> I would suggest that to get the most from this book, you experience it, not just gain knowledge. Take the six keys and commit to six weeks to savor the richness. Divide the pages of each key into seven sections, and read only one section per day. Take a journal and note what spoke to you and one scripture you want to commit to memory. Make it personal as you enter into His holy presence in prayer. It will change your day and your life.

I could not say it any better. Use the pages and chapters as a study guide, and take your time as you go through the book. Meditate on what is being said, and then put it into practice. If you do this, you are well on your way to understanding why prayer can be the most enjoyable part of your life.

Blessings,

*Pastor Scott*

# Key 1:

# Delight and the Desire for Prayer

## Introduction: The Prayer Journey

Jesus introduced Himself to me in August of 1978, when I was between my junior and senior years of high school. My spiritual life and interaction with church before this amounted to playing CYO (Catholic Youth Organization) basketball and periodic attendance at some Catholic masses.

My dad grew up Catholic and came from Bronx, New York. My mom was from a Jewish family in the Baltimore area. They met at a young age after my dad got out of the Navy following the Korean War. This was the late 1950s—a time when people from Catholic and Jewish backgrounds did not usually intermarry. It was not as socially acceptable then as it is today. I did not grow up in a household that talked much about God, nor did we have any strong spiritual roots, and no one I knew expressed a hunger or desire for spiritual things.

During spring break of 1978, my brother came home from college and told me of the experience he had when he invited Jesus into his life to be his Lord and Savior. He said that he met a man who worked for a campus ministry called Campus Crusade for Christ, and the two of them eventually developed a friendship. The man told my brother that God wanted to have a personal relationship with him, but it was up to him to decide to take Jesus up on His invitation. My brother did, and there was a noticeable change in him—all for the better.

After spring break, my brother went back to college. However, the experience that he shared with me, as I recall, did not make an impact on me. That summer, he was supposed to stay near his college on the eastern shore in Ocean City, Maryland. I thought it would be exciting to spend a summer in a beach town. But lo and behold, about a week or two after he moved to the shore, he called and said that he wanted to come home for the summer. I was a bit perplexed by his decision—spend summer at home in New Jersey or stay in a beach house in Maryland? This would not have been a hard decision for me, at least at that point.

My brother felt like he needed to come home that summer and tell me about Jesus and how Jesus changed his life. This is a Jesus—a God—I had never heard of before. My brother kept telling me about Him. He told me that God was a personal God, and Jesus was a personal Jesus, and that He wanted to have a relationship with me. He told me that Jesus came that I might have life and have it more abundantly, and that in knowing God, I could experience the quality of life that only God could give me (John 10:10). He explained that Jesus came to die for me and to bring me back to God so I can experience eternal life.

Eternal life! What do you mean by eternal life? Is it when you leave your body and hopefully go to a place that Jesus called heaven? Hey, that is part of it! He told me something that Jesus said, which is recorded in the Bible, that profoundly affected me from that day forward. John recorded what Jesus said, which is referred to as Jesus's High Priestly Prayer.

> Now this is eternal life: that they know you, the only true God, and Jesus Christ, whom you have sent. (John 17:3, NIV)

Jesus was referring to something in the present tense. He said, "This IS eternal life," right now! Eternal life starts with knowing and experiencing God now! It is a quality of life followed by quantity of life. This stuck in my mind.

I grew up in a typical suburban home. My family had its own problems; my parents divorced for the third time when I was fourteen (long story). That was rough. But in general, I had things going well. There was something more to this life, and I did have a hunger to know my purpose, but in no way did I feel that God was the answer.

Learning about this Jesus who wanted to give me eternal life was radical for me. I always wanted to get the best out of life. I had a drive to attain, and though God was the One who could satisfy my desires, He did not fit into my equation. Sometimes people say they were searching for God, and then they found Him. I may have also unknowingly said the same, but now I say that God was searching for me, and He sought me out and introduced Himself to me.

One day, after weeks of listening to my brother, I could sense an unseen presence moving on me. It seemed like an unseen force was wooing me and influencing my daily life. I had a consciousness that there was something beyond myself, and that "force" was showing me that He was interested in me. He was urging me to follow Him. It was like I was getting an internal face lift; my passions and desires were changing, and I was seeing the world and my purpose differently. One day, I heard a voice inside of me say something very distinct and clear. The voice said, "I bet you cannot do it." Hmm, does God bet? Some may say He does not. Well, I beg to differ because He bet on me, and He challenged me.

Challenged me to what? He was challenging me to take Him up on His promise to give me life and life more abundantly, and to follow Him on an adventure. I began to understand that God loves me and has a plan for me. It was up to me if I wanted to let Jesus into my life and allow Him to forgive me of my pride—the root of what we commonly call sin, that leads to self-will. I no longer wanted to go my own way and exclude God from my equation. I came to understand that He had a better way, and however much I knew did not matter at all. His way *was* and *is* always better!

In my heart, I said, "Yes! I can." I was and still am a very competitive person. But God knew what buttons to push to get my attention. I can still remember that day; I was walking up the stairs to my room. I can even remember the color of the carpet, the layout of my room, and where my bed was. I went to the left side of my bed, knelt down, and asked Jesus to come into my heart (life) and become my Lord and Savior.

Bam! Something changed! Jesus came into my life, and I started to experience Him. The vacuum that I had felt in my heart from time to time immediately left. I knew that I had found my purpose—God had a plan for my life, and I was going to begin a journey to get to know Him. I like the way the apostle Paul writes about this in 2 Corinthians 4:6-7:

> For God, who said, "Let light shine out of darkness," made his light shine in our hearts to give us the light of the knowledge of God's glory displayed in the face of Christ. But we have this treasure in jars of clay to show that this all-surpassing power is from God and not from us. (NIV)

What Paul wrote in this scripture equates what had happened inside of me with what is recorded in Genesis chapter 1. What happens when God releases His presence over the earth? In Genesis, we read that the earth was formless and void. Then God said, "Light be," and He released light on the earth. Since God is light, His presence was released on the earth. That laid the foundation for God to put the earth in divine order and create man. When we decide to receive the Savior, Jesus, and accept His work of salvation, He comes into our life. In the same way, and I paraphrase, just as God said, "Let there be light in the world," He says, "Let there be light in our spirit." He puts our life in divine order, and Jesus comes in. We get the light of the knowledge of God in the person of Jesus Christ. I received the knowledge of God, and eternal life was imparted to me.

This introduction and experience happened to me in 1978. Now that Jesus and I had been formally introduced, I wanted to learn about Him and understand what it means to know Him. I was not interested in what we call "organized religion," but I wanted a relationship with God. My next question was: How can I grow in this relationship? I learned early on from others who had experienced the same thing I did, that there were a few things I should habitually incorporate into my spiritual life.

The first things were reading, memorizing, and studying the Word of God. The next was the importance and need for prayer. I ventured off into my new adventure with God, and I learned about His Word and prayer through people that God sent into my life. Then I started reading books about God. I learned to pray from those who prayed. The more I did these things, the more I learned and got to know Him. The more I did these things, the more I wanted to experience all of God.

I would spend hours in prayer and reading. As time went on, I realized that it was like a journey down a long and winding road, and at each turn, there was more to learn and more to experience. These times were like God taking His finger and writing the truths of the Word on my heart. They were not just words on the pages of the Bible; it was the living Word inside of me that was transforming my being into the person God created me to be. In Hebrews 5:14, the author writes that by reason of use of the principles of the Word of God, we have our senses exercised to discern the difference between good and evil, discerning what is good and right in the eyes of a righteous and holy God versus what is wrong in the sight of God.

One experience fueled the next, and the next, and the next, and as time went on, I learned to enjoy these times immensely. I continued in them and have habitually kept them for over forty years.

I have studied many wonderful books on prayer and read many others about people who are considered to be prayer giants. Prayer giants are people who have prayed and have had some effect in moving God to manifest His power, which is also commonly referred to as "revival." People like Evan Roberts in the early twentieth century during the Welsh Revival, then subsequently the Azusa Street Revival, where Frank Bartleman and William Seymour's prayers had a profound effect, just to name a few. I often say that revival is like when someone throws so much fuel on a fire that the fire starts spreading and burning out of control—burning everything in its path!

Church history has revealed that, many times, when a revival like these has happened, it was like a wildfire spreading across the land and transforming lives in its great burning path. To some extent, I have seen this fire in many people in my local fellowships. I have experienced microbursts of God's power and fire coming upon people. These experiences are welcome, but our prayer life should not be dependent on—nor should it be sustained by—events like these. In our prayer life, we should be inspired to know God, be known by God, and make God known.

Since these personal experiences, I have had a desire to know God, meaning, to have and experience an intimate and personal relationship with Him. How do I continually do that? I soon realized that there was this thing called prayer, and everyone I met who seemed to have some understanding of God, talked about prayer and spent time in prayer with Him. I had an intense hunger to know God, and as time went on, I found that establishing a personal prayer and communion time with Him was important if I wanted to get to know the God who introduced Himself to me.

What is prayer? Prayer is communication with God. This communication is not one-way. It is not a monologue; it is a dialogue—both talking and listening—and it can have many forms. It can be:

- Worship: acknowledging who God is—His attributes—and expressing back to Him the transcendence and greatness of those attributes
- Praise: acknowledging the greatness of His work and manifestation in this world and in the lives of people
- Thanksgiving: thanking God for what He has done in us, for us, and all that is around us
- Supplication: asking God to do something for us
- Intercession: asking God to do something for others

In the end, all forms of prayer result in communion and communication with the living God. Communion with God is where we become aware of our union with Him—God in us, and us in Him. The purpose of my writing is to tell people what I have learned about prayer and communication with God over the last four decades. These are high-level truths that I have learned and experienced in prayer and how I have learned to enjoy prayer.

Prayer can and should be one of the most enjoyable things in life. I have learned to enjoy prayer and enjoy God. I have also learned that God enjoys me! I came across a verse in Psalm 16:11, and it captivated me. It says:

> You will make known to me the path of life; In Your presence is fullness of joy; In Your right hand there are pleasures forever.

In His presence is fullness of joy! The word "presence" can easily be translated "face." In a face-to-face, intimate relationship, there is fullness of joy. There is something wonderful about a close relationship—it brings fulfillment and joy! Imagine having that kind of relationship with the Creator—the all-knowing, self-existent God (Jehovah)—the God who so loved us that He sent His Son, Jesus, to redeem us and bring us back into relationship with Him!

What I hope to do is lead everyone down that same path of intimate, consistent companionship with God. My experience over the years of walking with God and being a part of many Christian circles and ministries is that most people who call themselves Christians, who attend church, and who have had similar experiences with God, also have a hard time consistently establishing an intimate communion with Him. Many times, we substitute church activity, church doctrine adherence, and church attendance for true relationship and prayer. We are always so busy that we do not learn how to quiet our mind and come to a place of communion with God. We get anxious and do not enjoy prayer and God, so we do not really see this as the highest and most important part of our Christian faith.

This is carnal Christianity. It is having a form of Christianity but not experiencing the essence of Christianity. Also, this is a form of what Jesus dealt with when He started preaching to the Jews and the religious leaders of the day. They adhered to the rules and regulations but had no anointing or relationship with God. Many of Jesus's teachings in the Gospels were directed at correcting this type of religious activity.

My hope in these pages is to express to you what I have learned about prayer, what has helped me establish ongoing communion with God, and how it has sustained me through my walk with Him. I hope you will then use these revelations and principles to experience God for yourself through prayer and meditation.

Learning prayer can be one of the most enjoyable things in life. If prayer and meditation are arduous for you, the principles in this book will help you. Be intentional about employing these principles, and you will experience the fullness of joy that only comes from God and from knowing Him. This will take you from just believing in God to experiencing Him.

King David is an apt example here. As I read about King David in the Psalms, and his statements of hunger and the desire to be in God's presence, they inspire me; they bait me with hunger to know what he knew. David was known for many things, but rarely do people quote what David called himself at the latter part of his life. He did not call himself a great king, a great warrior, or a great prophet. He called himself the "Sweet Psalmist of Israel" (2 Samuel 23:1). He was the chief songwriter and worshipper of God. I can picture David going to the temple to worship God, the people watching him as he worshipped, and the presence of God coming down to him as he poured out the wonderful, inspired words of God. David expresses his desire for worship, prayer, and dwelling with God.

> The one thing I ask of the LORD—the thing I seek most—is to live in the house of the LORD all the days of my life, delighting in the LORD's perfections and meditating in his Temple. (Psalm 27:4, NIV)

Oh, that we would all have the same desire and expression that David had! A psalm is an expression of worship and praise to God, inspired by being in His presence and experiencing Him. Can we not all be like David? Why not? He is still the same God with all the same attributes. In this current age, we have the new covenant and the outpouring of the Holy Spirit who lives in us, not just comes upon us.

My hope is to inspire people through the revelations and experiences I have had with God. Although this book is about prayer, it is also a description of my prayer journey and what God has revealed to me. This book can also be used as a devotional to help you learn how to commune with God. Hopefully, these pages will inspire you to enjoy the same experiences that David had in worship and prayer, and even greater—to experience God in prayer!

## The Desire and Need for Prayer

One of the earliest accounts of Jesus, as recorded in the Gospels, is when He went to the temple in Jerusalem and saw people selling animals for the type of offering and worship that was designated for the Jews to make. They were merchandising the worship of God. So Jesus knocked over the tables of the merchandisers. This incident is recorded in all four Gospels, and it looks like He did it more than once (Matthew 21, Mark 11, Luke 19, and John 2.)

These stories that are recorded in the Gospels signify how important prayer and communion with God are. Jesus knew that the old covenant prescribed methods of worship that entailed the offering of animals. The problem was that they were merchandising the worship of God and doing it within the walls of the temple. I am assuming a few things here, but hear me out. During those days, many Jews may have traveled many miles to worship in Jerusalem, and bringing the animals with them would have been difficult. It would have been much easier to buy them in Jerusalem.

Since people were merchandising inside the walls of the temple, don't you think the religious leaders who were in charge of the temple were getting a cut of the sales? Or charging rent? So they were also merchandising worship. Have you ever been to a sport's stadium to watch a professional baseball or football game? Have you ever compared the price of a souvenir outside the stadium walls to inside? I could buy a baseball cap outside of the stadium for $10, but inside, a similar cap might be $40. I do not think it is a stretch. It was the same back then. People's love for money has not changed.

Now, here comes Jesus, seeing what was going on and having a zeal and love for prayer and communion with the Father (who was also seeing what was going on). He gets upset with them for corrupting such a holy and sacred act as worship of the Father. He turns the tables over and kicks the money changers out.

I want to make two statements here, which I will reiterate throughout this book. The first statement is: Worship is a form of prayer. Prayer is communication with God, and worship is a form of that. I would like to say that worship is the highest form of prayer, which I will explain in a future chapter. It is the place where all intimate communication and effective prayer is birthed. Effective prayer is not just prayer where you are getting God to answer your requests; it is a place where communion and fellowship with God happens, and you receive an impartation of His wisdom and an understanding of His ways and thoughts.

Now the second statement may seem like a contradiction, but it is as true as the first statement. The second statement is: Prayer is a form of worship. Show me someone who prays a lot, and I will show you someone who worships God. In prayer, we express our dependency on God. The act of prayer shows a submission to God and an acknowledgment of who He is, which spearheads us into the position of worshipping the Creator. Worship and prayer are inseparably linked together.

When people have power of any sort, there is usually one of two things that gets them upset. The first is when someone gets in the way of their revenue stream, and the second is when someone gets in the way of their authority. Jesus checked both of those boxes. Now we see even more why most of the religious leaders of the day wanted to destroy

Him. Paul writes to Timothy, his disciple, "For the love of money is the root of all kinds of evil" (1 Timothy 6:10, NLT). The love of money was one of the deceiving forces that drove the religious leaders of the time to try to trap and destroy Jesus. The other was their jealousy because Jesus was disrupting their authority and their power base with the people.

In the new covenant that Jesus brought into being, the temple is no longer built by human hands. Paul writes that our bodies are the temple of the Holy Spirit (1 Corinthians 6:19-20). We read the accounts in the Gospels of when Jesus breathed His last breath as a human being on earth. When He did, an earthquake happened, and the veil of the temple was torn from top to bottom. Did you ever wonder why it was from top to bottom? How did someone get up to a veil that was very high? A big old angel was up there ripping it down! The veil of the temple was a big ornate curtain that separated the holy place and the holy of holies. The holy of holies is where the ark of the covenant rested. It signified the place where the presence of God dwelt. It was where the high priest went in once a year to pour the blood on the mercy seat for the forgiveness of the sins of the nation.

Now, God does not dwell in temples made by people or in buildings. He dwells in the hearts of humans.

> You are his holy priests. **Through the mediation of Jesus Christ, you offer spiritual sacrifices that please God.** (1 Peter 2:5, NLT)

Wow! We are spiritual temples unto God, and through meditation (a part of prayer), we are offering worship to God that pleases Him. In Revelation chapters 5 and 8, we read of a scene in heaven that recognizes these sacrifices: The prayers of the saints—our prayers—rise as incense that fills the golden bowls at the throne of God. This incense is burned as a sacrifice to God before His throne, and it brings fragrance to His nostrils. Imagine that as we pray and communicate with God, He enjoys the offerings and prayers that come before Him.

The above illustration shows us how much it pleases the heart of God when His people pray and commune with Him. It also shows us how He responds to our communion and interacts with us. The Bible describes our God as a consuming fire. So, do you think God throws fire down from the altar of heaven? If so, isn't that a bit scary? The natural and unlearned mind, when it comes to spiritual things, may see it that way. But, one day, as I was thinking about this, the Lord showed me that the fuel to His fire is love. He appears as fire because His love is so pure. God's fire consumes anything that hinders us from experiencing Him. The cross was an expression of God's love, and it consumed the sin that kept us from knowing Him to the fullest. It is the passion of His heart responding to the passion of our heart, and communion comes from that.

These interactions and experiences with God are miracles of the new life that is imparted to us when we believe in Jesus, receive Him, and accept what He has done for us. As the Bible says, we are a new creation, restored to the image and likeness of God. Our spirit is rebuilt in such a way to house a holy and magnificent God who wants to dwell in us, and He wants us to dwell in Him.

Now that we are a holy temple, not built by human hands but built by God Himself through the work of Jesus on the cross, it is more pertinent than ever that we individually and corporately be a house of prayer that offers spiritual sacrifices—prayer and communion, which are pleasing to God.

Jesus knew this to be true, and that is why we read in the Gospels many times that He withdrew, communed, and fellowshipped with the Father. He knew that was the Father's joy—and His also—and it was Jesus's most satisfying act as He walked on the earth. By this, He could say that He only did what He saw His Father doing (John 5:19). He was in constant communion and fellowship with God.

In Mark 1, we read about Jesus getting up early in the morning, while it was still dark, and going to a secluded place to pray. In Mark 6, we read that He went up to the mountain and prayed. We read in Luke that He went up to the mountain and spent the whole night in prayer.

### Key 1: Delight and the Desire for Prayer

Paul, in his writings, is constantly talking about prayer:

- Ephesians 6:18: With all prayer and petition pray at all times in the Spirit.
- Philippians 1:9: And this I pray, that your love may abound.
- Colossians 1:9: And this I pray, that your love may abound still more and more in real knowledge and all discernment.
- 1 Thessalonians 3:10: As we night and day keep praying most earnestly that we may see your face.
- 1 Thessalonians 5:17: Pray without ceasing.
- 2 Thessalonians 1:11: To this end also we pray for you always.
- 1 Timothy 2:8: Therefore I want the men in every place to pray, lifting up holy hands, without anger and dispute.

Early on, I took these verses and illustrations to heart and learned that setting time aside daily to be alone with God was the only way I could learn about Him and commune with Him. This rhythm helped me to grow in Him, learn about Him, and enjoy Him and the relationship He desires to have with me. It has been many years since I started this practice in my life, and I can still tell you that my time with Him is the most enjoyable part of my day.

## Prayer and Dependence on God

When we think of dependence on something, it may not conjure up a good picture for most of us. The issue that man fights all the time is between self-sufficiency or sufficiency found in God. We see this narrative throughout Scripture beginning with Adam and Eve. God provided everything for them, and it was all theirs to have and enjoy. But they thought they found a way to make it even better for themselves, apart from the wisdom and understanding from God. They thought they could have better food than God created for them. They thought they could find things that would be more enjoyable than God. They thought they could find ways to be wiser than the way provided for them by God. All the things they wanted, God had a way for Adam and Eve to have them.

Everything was in their grasp through love and faith in God, knowing and understanding Him, and dwelling with Him and in Him. Despite it all, trying to make things better led them to spiritual death and separation from God, which is the exact opposite of what they tried to attain.

Jesus came to restore man and provide a path back to God. He was God in flesh—the very Author of life. If He was who He said He was, then He would know something about life that we do not know. The Gospels record many wonderful statements about Jesus—especially the Gospel of John. In this book, we find the greatest number of references to the deity of Christ than in any other Gospel. John records Jesus saying, "Before Abraham was, I AM" (John 8:58, KJV). This was a direct reference to what Jehovah-Yahweh called Himself at the burning bush with Moses. Moses was told to go to Pharaoh and tell him to let His people, the Israelites, go. Moses asked God, "Who shall I say is sending me, and by what authority shall I speak?" God said to Moses, "Tell them, 'I AM' sends you." (Exodus 3:14, paraphrase)

John records the seven "I am" designations of Jesus:

1. I am the Bread of Life. (John 6:35)
2. I am the Light of the World. (John 8:12, 9:5)
3. I am the Door for the sheep. (John 10:9)
4. I am the Good Shepherd. (John 10:11)
5. I am the Resurrection and the Life. (John 11:25)
6. I am the Way, and the Truth, and the Life. (John 14:6)
7. I am the True Vine. (John 15:1)

John talks about light and life, often. He gives a wonderful explanation of Jesus when he draws an analogy to the creation of the world and the light of God dwelling in Jesus:

> In the beginning the Word already existed. **The Word was with God, and the Word was God. He existed in the beginning with God. God created everything through him**, and nothing was created except through

> him. The Word gave life to everything that was created, and his life brought light to everyone. The light shines in the darkness, and the darkness can never extinguish it.…**So the Word became human and made his home among us**. He was full of unfailing **love** and faithfulness. And we have seen his glory, the glory of the Father's one and only Son. (John 1:1-5, 14, NLT)

The declaration of these words shows us that God came into the world to bring us back to Himself and to help us walk in the light of His power. But to attain this, we need to make the decision to want it rather than try to live on our own. Dependence on God is a position of humility, admitting that we need His wisdom, power, and understanding, which are greater than ours.

Like any close relationship, communication is necessary in order to grow and learn about one another. Humility is a place of entire dependency on God, and prayer is the way we express it. The New Testament records numerous times that whoever exalts himself shall be humbled, and he who humbles himself shall be exalted (Matt 23:12, Luke 14:11, Luke 18:14, James 4:10, 1 Peter 5:6). Being exalted means being given the highest state of opulence and prosperity. There is no higher state of opulence and prosperity than being in God's presence.

In the book of Revelation, we read about seven churches and the commendations, directions, promises of reward, and corrections that Jesus gave them. Let us focus on one specific church: the Church of Laodicea. Laodicea did not receive any commendations. It is commonly known as the lukewarm church. I remember preaching numerous times on the term "lukewarm" and encouraging those around me to be fervent in their service to God. The term "lukewarm," in retrospect, does not really take the context of what was being discussed about Laodicea.

We need to ask why they were called lukewarm. Well, let us read exactly what was written:

> Write this letter to the angel of the church in Laodicea. This is the message from the one who is the Amen—the faithful and true witness, the beginning of God's new creation: "I know all the things you do, that you are neither hot nor cold. I wish that you were one or the other! But since you are like lukewarm water, neither hot nor cold, I will spit you out of my mouth! You say, 'I am rich. I have everything I want. I don't need a thing!' And you don't realize that you are wretched and miserable and poor and blind and naked. So I advise you to buy gold from me—gold that has been purified by fire. Then you will be rich. Also buy white garments from me so you will not be shamed by your nakedness, and ointment for your eyes so you will be able to see. I correct and discipline everyone I **love**. So be diligent and turn from your indifference." (Revelation 3:14-19)

The reference to Jesus spitting the Church of Laodicea out of His mouth gives a picture that is not very pleasurable. One time in prayer, I was thinking about this scripture, and the Lord gave me an understanding of what this is: I saw a picture of two people kissing each other; one was very passionate, and the other was distracted and not very passionate. Then I saw the face of the one who was being distracted and not very passionate. She was the bride. Relating this to Jesus being the Groom and the church being His bride, I realized that Jesus was kissing the church—His bride. The bride, being distracted, not passionate about the love, and lacking in response to the Groom's passion, left an unpleasant taste in the Groom's mouth—a distraught taste that made Him want to spit it out.

Jesus points out that the Laodicean church thought they did not need the Lord or His help. Why? Because they thought they were rich and self-sufficient. Yes, Laodicea, at one time, was known to be a very wealthy city. They were geographically in the path of a trade route, which made them very important. They were rich in gold and clothing and were known for medical ointments used to treat people's eyes. These ointments were very important to the people in that region, since the region was dusty and dry, and the people who lived there experienced problems with irritation of their eyes.

Since prayer is a place where we express dependency on God, we can easily conclude that the Church of Laodicea was prayerless and did not realize how God saw them. They thought they were wealthy and needed nothing, but God said that they were wretched, miserable, poor, blind, and naked. Let us give some description to these terms: "wretched" means to endure toils and troubles; "miserable" means to be pathetically pitied; "poor" means to be a beggar; "blind" means to physically and/or mentally lose sight, "naked" means to walk around exposed and not even know it. Imagine walking around naked in public and not knowing it, while everyone walking by knows it! What a stark contrast to the way man and God see the same situation. This type of deception comes from pride, which is the principal tool that deceives our heart and mind and keeps us from seeing things the way God sees them.

We will never see as God sees unless we turn our heart and mind to prayer and communion with Him. First, we must acknowledge who He is. Then, acknowledge His wisdom, acknowledge our inability to understand truth without Him, and express our desire to understand Him. Jesus advised the Church of Laodicea to buy pure gold of very high value—gold refined and purified in God's fire and formed by His hand. Pure gold represents divinity. A goldsmith purifies gold by melting it in intense heat. When melted, the impurities in the gold separate from the gold itself. As the gold cools, it hardens. Now, this is pure gold. This is exactly what God's presence does for us. God is a consuming fire, and when He shines the light of His presence on us, it separates all of the impurities from us. We are the gold refined in the fire of God's presence, and that exposes our sins that separate us from Him. It exposes the selfishness of our heart and the evil within. This adjusts and aligns our spiritual vision and hearing. Once we acknowledge that spiritual vision and hearing and allow God to do His work in us, He will do it.

Another way to describe this process is with the term "nakedness." The term "nakedness" goes all the way back to Adam and Eve. Genesis records that Adam and Eve were naked but not ashamed of being naked in public. Why would that be? Because they were clothed with God's garment—the garment of the glory of God! This garment covered their spirit, soul, and body, and it perfected them. When they sinned, they immediately realized they were naked, and they were ashamed. Then they tried to clothe themselves with leaves to cover their nakedness. Shame brings exposure to our shortcomings, which causes us to hide. We hide to protect ourselves from the pain of our faults and the shortcomings that expose us. The Bible says that Adam and Eve hid themselves among the trees of the garden, which were given for their pleasure. Similarly, when we are in shame and fear, we tend to try to hide under everything in life that can give us pleasure or make us feel better. The pleasure we seek is to make us look good on the outside.

Have you ever worn a nice suit or dress and felt pleased because of how beautiful those clothes were? Or have you experienced a feeling of satisfaction after a success at a job, obtaining money, or gaining prestige? That is the same feeling I am talking about. God's creation is for us to enjoy, but these pleasures will always be secondary to the pleasure of enjoying God.

We will run from God until He shows up and we see the reality of our state. God spoke to Adam and Eve about what they had done, and when they turned to Him and felt exposed for their nakedness and shortcomings, God took their coverings of leaves and made garments for them—He clothed them again.

No matter how much we try to clothe ourselves, it will never feel the same as being clothed by God. This brings new meaning to the scripture:

> For all have sinned, and come short of the glory of God. (Romans 3:23, KJV)

Similarly, Jesus was inviting the Laodicean church to come to Him—to come into His presence so He could cleanse them and show them how to see. He wanted to show them pure gold and true wealth, and the way to real life. He wanted to anoint their eyes and clothe them with the same garment of glory that He clothed mankind with when He created us.

Jesus says:

> Look! I stand at the door and knock. If you hear my voice and open the door, I will come in, and we will share a meal together as friends. Those who are victorious will sit with me on my throne, just as I was victorious and sat with my Father on his throne. (Revelation 3:20-21, NLT)

From my early days of hearing the gospel and sharing the good news with others, as far as I can remember, most people I knew would quote the above scripture to try to make people understand that to receive what Jesus did for us, we must open the door of our heart and let Him in. Many years ago, I remember reading a little tract called "Four Spiritual Laws," published by Campus Crusade for Christ and its founder, Bill Bright. I will be forever indebted to them for their deposit of spiritual truths and discipleship in my life. At the end of law four in the tract, which states that we need to individually receive Jesus Christ as our Lord and Savior, Revelation 3:20 is quoted. I cannot tell you the number of times I have used that scripture—in the same context—to explain the realities of a personal relationship with Jesus.

The reality of this scripture is that Jesus is not talking to someone who has not met Him before. He is talking to the Church of Laodicea. They knew Him and used to believe in Him. I do not want to disrupt much of your current thinking. Not that you cannot relate to what is being said here in the context of first inviting Jesus into your life—I believe you can. But the context of the scripture goes deeper—Jesus is asking those He has met before—His beloved—to open the door of their heart so He can come in and do His work in them and through them. He then talks about us dining with Him, and He with us. To me, that cries intimacy, communion, and fellowship with God through prayer.

This is not a one-time event; it is a process. It is a lifestyle of prayer, communion, and communication with Him. Our spiritual heart is the center of all our passions and emotions; it is the womb of the spirit. It is where Jesus deposits the seeds of His words of life. This has been my experience, and I believe it needs to keep evolving and progressing.

I want to point out that there is more to Jesus talking about opening the door of our heart. As we open the door and welcome Him in, He will come in and dine with us. This points to the intimate fellowship of friends and family sharing a meal and communing with one another.

What do we dine on? Throughout the New Testament, we read several instances of dining and eating. Jesus said that man shall not live by bread alone but by every word that proceeds out of the mouth of God (Matthew 4:4). In the Gospel of John, Jesus said that He is the Bread of Life and the Word made flesh. The Lord Himself, when teaching us how to pray, using what we commonly refer to as the Lord's Prayer, tells us to ask God for our daily bread. Our daily bread is the Word that proceeds out of His mouth each day to personally commune and communicate with us.

For the Jewish people, the reference to daily bread was an analogy to draw their attention to how God fed them in the wilderness—daily, with manna from heaven. John 6:47-51 is a beautiful recollection of what Jesus said about this:

> Truly, truly, I say to you, he who believes has eternal life. **I am the bread of life.** Your fathers ate the manna in the wilderness, and they died. This is the bread which comes down out of heaven, so that one may eat of it and not die. **I am the living bread that came down out of heaven; if anyone eats of this bread, he will live forever; and the bread also which I will give for the life of the world is My flesh.**

Jesus promised us, the church, that if we open the door, He will come in and have communion and fellowship with us, and speak His Word to us. Jesus's exhortation was an invitation to intimacy with Him, communion with Him, learning from Him, and trusting Him. The place where this starts and ends is continual and purposeful communion and prayer.

So now the practicality: how do we do this? It starts by willingly and intentionally setting aside consistent time with Him each day to commune and talk with Him. But until we purposefully and consistently make the time to do this, are we not like the Church of Laodicea—dependent on ourselves and not on God? Are we what Jesus calls lukewarm? Are we the ones He has a distaste for because of our lack of attention to Him?

## Simeon's Secret Place

In the Gospels, we read about three people who lived in a secret place of prayer and communion with God: Simeon, Anna, and Mary of Bethany. Their lives of faith and prayer are very endearing, and they all caught my attention and the intimate attention of God.

Many of us have read or heard of Psalm 91 at some point in our life. Most often, in times of trouble, we tend to mention something about this psalm, regardless of whether or not we have a relationship with God. Psalm 91 starts with the following verse:

> He who dwells in the **secret place of the Most High** shall abide under the **shadow of the Almighty**. I will say of the Lord, "He is my refuge and my fortress; My God, in Him I will trust." (Psalm 91:1, NKJV)

Most commentators attribute this psalm to either Moses or King David. We will talk about both men and their intimate relationship with God in this book. Both knew about *the secret place of the Most High*. In the phrase, "*He who dwells in the secret place,*" I would like to highlight the word "dwells." It means a place of habitation. I like to translate this phrase as follows: *He who lives in the house of Elohim (the Most High God) will lodge under the defense of the protection of El Shaddai (God Almighty).* This means that one must make a conscious effort to enter the house of God and be with Him. Earlier, we talked about how God's house is a house of prayer, communion, and fellowship with Him. Now, how do we do that?

Let us think about that for a minute. Think about the place you live in today. You usually open the door, walk in, and you are very familiar with your surroundings. When you walk into your house, you notice details that other people might not because of your ongoing familiarity with your surroundings.

Not only do you become familiar with your surroundings, but you also become familiar with the people you live with as well. When you dwell with someone, they are a part of your family. They communicate with you in ways they do not communicate with others. You learn their secrets and the most intimate thoughts of their heart. They will tell you things they would tell no one else. Hmm, is it any different when we learn to dwell with God?

Also, we will protect those we live with. What would you do if an intruder broke into your house? What would you do with someone who wants to bring harm to you and your family? Is God, our Father, any different? I would think not. The psalmist says in verses 2-7:

> This I declare about the Lord: He alone **is my refuge, my place of safety**; he is my God, and I trust him. For he will **rescue you from every trap and protect you from deadly disease**. He will **cover you with his feathers**. He will **shelter you with his wings**. His faithful **promises are your armor and protection**. Do not be afraid of **the terrors of the night, nor the arrow that flies in the day. Do not dread the disease that stalks in darkness, nor the disaster that strikes at midday. Though a thousand fall at your side, though ten thousand are dying around you, these evils will not touch you**.

I am not sure if any passage in the Bible can draw a greater description of God's protection and care for those who co-habitat with Him.

## Key 1: Delight and the Desire for Prayer

So, what and where is this "secret place"? Men and women who are passionate for God, through prayer experience a place of inner heartfelt communion with Him, where secrets are shared or perceived—an experience that others may not have. Have you experienced that secret place? If not, then why not? Why not now? Why not today? Why not me?

In Luke 2:25-35 (NLT), we read about Simeon:

> At that time there was a man in Jerusalem named Simeon. He was **righteous and devout and was eagerly waiting for the Messiah to come and rescue Israel. The Holy Spirit was upon him and had revealed to him that he would not die until he had seen the Lord's Messiah. That day the Spirit led him to the Temple**. So when Mary and Joseph came to present the baby Jesus to the Lord as the law required, Simeon was there. **He took the child in his arms and praised God**, saying:
>
> "Sovereign Lord, now let your servant die in peace, as you have promised. I have seen your salvation, which you have prepared for all people. He is a light to reveal God to the nations, and he is the glory of your people Israel!"
>
> Jesus' parents were amazed at what was being said about him. Then Simeon blessed them, and he said to Mary, the baby's mother, "This child is destined to cause many in Israel to fall, and many others to rise. He has been sent as a sign from God, but many will oppose him. As a result, the deepest thoughts of many hearts will be revealed. And a sword will pierce your very soul."

Here is the context of this Scripture passage: Israel was under the rule of Rome, and the Israelites had not heard the voice of the Lord through any prophet for hundreds of years. At that time, a devout and righteous man named Simeon, who was of old age, lived in Jerusalem.

Because of his devoutness and righteous standing with God, and because he lived in Jerusalem, I think he would have gone to the temple often to offer prayers and sacrifices to God. Since Jesus said that His house, which was the temple, was a house of prayer, I infer that Simeon made his human body a house a prayer and presented it (himself) at the temple to have communion and fellowship with God.

Simeon knew the promises of God regarding the coming Messiah, which had been spoken hundreds of years before—since the time of the patriarchs, Moses, and David. As he was waiting for the coming of the Messiah, the Comfort of Israel, he heard the Lord say to him that he would not die before he sees the Messiah. Wow! Talk about a secret that everyone would want to know! Can you imagine the depth of his relationship with God—first, for him to hear God and recognize His voice, and then, to believe the message and tell others what he had heard? I imagine that Simeon would go to the temple and have an audience as he spoke about Elohim, and at times, share what he heard from Elohim to encourage the people. Some may have thought that he was crazy; some may have been intrigued. But then, there were others who had an intimate communion with God the way Simeon had; they were inspired, and they stood together with him in prayer for the people of Israel and for the fulfillment of the promise.

There is no timeline recorded of when Simeon heard this promise or for how long he waited for its fulfillment. But knowing God and how He operates, there was a period of waiting between the promise and the manifestation. I like to say that God slow walks things and is perfect in His timing. He does things in His own time and in His own way—and they are perfect!

One morning, Simeon was prompted by the Holy Spirit to go to the temple. To him, that could have felt like a usual prompting, and as he had obeyed many times before, he could have gone to the temple. Or, he could have felt that it was an extra ordinary prompting, and he could have shown up at the temple that day with a sense that something special was going to happen. Obviously, he found it to be the latter. While at the temple, he saw Mary and Joseph, who had come to present their newborn son in dedication to God, as was the custom and requirement of the law.

Simeon saw Mary and Joseph with the child, Jesus, and immediately knew the baby was the Messiah. This alone is a demonstration of the secret place that Simeon had access to and was familiar with. He was told that he would see the Messiah before his death. By such a word, I imagine it would be a man preaching or a man leading as a king, like David. But, seeing a baby of everyday Jewish parents, and knowing by the Spirit the baby was the One, is amazing and shows that he knew the voice of the Father in the house where he dwelt.

I can picture Simeon taking the baby in his hands, and with great joy, looking at Him and understanding that the fulfillment of the Father's joy, and the deliverance of the nation of Israel, was in his hands. Simeon must have prayed about the coming of the Messiah and discussed it with the Father many times. There were times when he would have felt the Father's presence and assurance that the Messiah would come soon, and then the Father told him that he would see the One before he dies.

As soon as Simeon finished blessing the Christ child, Anna came in. She is also one of those who lived in the secret place. Luke calls her a prophetess. Luke records that she never left the temple and was there praying and worshipping God day and night for over sixty years. Anna saw Simeon talking to Mary and Joseph and immediately recognized who the Child was. She began praising God and telling everybody about Him.

There were hundreds of people there, but Anna knew who the baby was, and what He was supposed to do. She lived her days prophesying to everyone who would hear about the Child.

Now Simeon and Anna were people who knew the secret place, dwelt with God, were familiar with God's voice, and understood His ways. They did not just believe in God; they experienced Him, and God experienced them. They knew some of the secrets that can only be learned in that secret place. So, why not you? Why not me? Why not now?

## Mary of Bethany and the Secret Place

Mary of Bethany experienced God and lived in the secret place. She knew the secrets that very few understood. She is mentioned three times in the Gospels as the woman sitting at Jesus's feet, listening to Him, worshipping Him, and ministering to Him.

The first time was when Jesus was invited to Mary's house with her sister, Martha, and brother, Lazarus, for dinner. Yes, the same Lazarus whom Jesus raised from the dead. While Jesus and the disciples were at Lazarus's house, Martha was in the kitchen making dinner, but Mary was sitting at Jesus's feet and listening very intently to Him instead of helping Martha. She was entering the secret place with Jesus. Martha was getting upset because she felt that Mary should be helping her. In her defense, cooking a meal for fifteen or so people was no easy feat. I am sure that Jesus was aware of what was going on.

Martha could not take it anymore, and she came barreling into the room and asked Jesus to tell Mary to help her. Martha was solely thinking of herself, saying to Jesus, "Don't you care that I am working so hard, and Mary is just sitting there?" Her statement had an accusation, and if you picture the verbs, it gives the connotation that as she burst in upon them, her face was twisted in anger. Have you ever been in a situation where you were so angry and frustrated that every word that came out of your mouth was emphasized by a twisted look on your face? The look on her face emphasized the depth of anger and emotion coming out through her words. That right there was Martha.

Jesus did not respond harshly to Martha, but in a compassionate, direct tone, He let her know that her worry and troublesome thoughts were not helpful to her. It did not serve her or help her attain spiritual growth and intimacy. He told her that there was only one thing that is most important, and because Mary engaged in that one thing, He was not going to take it away from her. Mary, intently listening to Jesus's words, was engaged with Him. She was enjoying His presence, and He was enjoying her. Mary and Jesus had an intimate communion and communication going on.

### Key 1: Delight and the Desire for Prayer

This one-thing pursuit leads us to the secret place. Now I understand that we all have things that we have to do to live in this world, but learning, understanding, and prioritizing the one thing is a conscious decision we need to make.

The second time we read about Mary at the feet of Jesus was at the death of Lazarus. Jesus was sent word that Lazarus was sick and that He should come and pray for him. Jesus, led by the Spirit, delayed His visit by a couple of days. When He arrived at Bethany, Lazarus was dead. As soon as Martha and Mary saw Him, they approached Him and said the same thing to Him.

John 11:21-27 (Martha's discussion)

> **Martha then said to Jesus, "Lord, if You had been here, my brother would not have died.** "Even now I know that whatever You ask of God, God will give You." Jesus said to her, "Your brother will rise again." Martha said to Him, "I know that he will rise again in the resurrection on the last day." Jesus said to her, "I am the resurrection and the life; he who believes in Me will live even if he dies, and everyone who lives and believes in Me will never die. Do you believe this?" She said to Him, "Yes, Lord; I have believed that You are the Christ, the Son of God, even He who comes into the world."

John 11:32-35 (Mary's Discussion)

> **Therefore, when Mary came where Jesus was, she saw Him, and fell at His feet, saying to Him, "Lord, if You had been here, my brother would not have died."** When Jesus therefore saw her weeping, and the Jews who came with her also weeping, He was deeply moved in spirit and was troubled, and said, "Where have you laid him?" They said to Him, "Lord, come and see." Jesus wept.

Note how differently the two women interacted with Jesus and how He responded to the one who lived in the secret place (Mary) versus the one who was trying to live in the secret place, but because of worries and troubles, had a hard time hearing what the Lord was saying (Martha). Worry is like a static background noise that makes it difficult to hear, comprehend, and walk with God. It is also like a door that blocks the light from coming in and makes it difficult to see where you are going. It brings confusion, doubt, and fear, and causes us to react based on those emotions instead of our experiences in the secret place, God's Word, and our relationship with Him.

Jesus responded to Martha by telling her that her brother will rise again. Martha, thinking that Jesus was talking about being raised in the resurrection, responded to Jesus that she believed Lazarus will be raised on the last day. Jesus, perceiving that she really did not understand what He was going to do, told her that He was going to raise Lazarus and then asked her if she believed that. Her answer revealed that she believed Jesus was the Christ, but she had no idea what He was talking about or what He was about to do. I call this the religious response. It has an element of spiritual truth; it shows that the person believes in God and has some association with Him, but they do not have an intimate relationship with Him or communion with Him in the moment.

We can hear scriptures, we can hear people talk about God, we can attend church, we can serve in the church and serve other people, and still not have a personal understanding of God or intimacy with Him if we do not learn to live in the secret place. Many times, we respond to God and other people with brilliant answers to their questions without really understanding our answers because we are mimicking others or just saying things that make sense to us.

Now let us contrast Martha's response with Mary's. When Mary came to Jesus, she first fell at His feet as an act of worship. Worship is the first and foremost thing that brings us into God's presence and connects us with Him. Worship leads us to the secret place.

Next, Mary said the same thing that Martha said. Mary was emotional, and she was weeping because of her love for her brother. Jesus saw her and those around her weeping. Mary—the beloved who had the one-thing connection with Him and dwelt with Him—was distraught. Jesus's connection with her moved Him to have compassion on her. Jesus groaned in His Spirit because He was deeply moved and troubled by the distress that Mary and those around her were feeling. But make no mistake, it was Mary's distress that was most important to Him.

Have you ever deeply loved someone—a husband, a wife, a daughter, or a son—who was distraught and crying? What would your response be to them? You would do anything to stop their crying and remedy their situation. Is that not what Jesus was doing?

Jesus asked the people where they had laid Lazarus and told them to move the grave's stone away. Martha, still not understanding the moment, responded that Lazarus had been in the grave for a few days and that, because his body was decaying, the odor would be strong. Her response showed that she still was not in the moment and not in the secret place with Jesus and Mary.

Then Jesus, with one of His most powerful recorded statements, told Lazarus to come forth. As Lazarus came forth, Jesus told the people to loose him and let him go. Oh, the power of the secret place of prayer with God!

Have you ever been in a situation where you groaned because of the stirring of emotions inside of you? Not that Martha did not have a connection with Jesus, but it was Mary's deep devotion and love for Him, and her ongoing dwelling in His presence, that moved, inspired, and added fuel to the faith Jesus was going to release when He raised Lazarus from the dead. Now the question to ask, would Jesus have raised Lazarus if both Mary and Martha were not in faith and agreement? I think the answer would be yes, but when we are in the one place with God, we can add our faith to what we see is His will in the situation. It was noted in the Gospel of Matthew that when Jesus was in His hometown, he could not do many miracles or works of power because of their unbelief (Matthew 13:57-58). Mary's intimacy with Jesus allowed her heart to intertwine with the will of God and become a participant in what He was doing rather than a hindrance.

This connection led Mary to a place of understanding the secret of why Jesus was headed to the cross. The New Testament records several instances of Jesus speaking to His disciples about going to Jerusalem, being betrayed and handed over to the religious leaders, being killed by them, and then rising from the dead. The first time He mentioned this, Peter's head blew up! He could not fathom it and started to rebuke Jesus, saying it would never happen. Then Jesus sternly rebuked Peter and told him that he was more interested in himself and his position than the plans and purposes of God. His motives were off. When our motives are off, we have a challenging time living in the secret place, abiding with God, and hearing His voice.

Not so with Mary though. In John 12, we read that about a week before the Passover and Jesus's ultimate death on the cross, Jesus and His disciples were in Bethany at Lazarus's home. After Martha made them dinner, they reclined at the table. Then Mary came to Jesus with some costly perfume, which was valued at a year's wages for the common man. Mary, understanding that Jesus was going to die as He had said to them many times before, poured the perfume on His feet and then wiped His feet with her hair. Note, she did not wipe His feet with a cloth, but with her hair. This shows her deep devotion to Jesus. We read in the New Testament that a woman's hair is a glory given to her. I liken this to the elders in Revelation 4 worshipping and throwing their golden crowns before the throne—giving back to God all the glory that was given to them.

Mary did this in preparation for Jesus's burial because she understood what Jesus was saying about His impending death. As we read on, it is apparent that the disciples did not understand what was going on. But Mary did. Why? Because she understood the secrets and dwelt in the secret place. It took a while for the disciples to understand what Jesus was talking about; it was not until after His death, resurrection, and subsequent experiences though. But Mary understood well before they did because she dwelt in Jesus, and He dwelt in her. They had an understanding and were clearly communicating with each other.

The week before Passover, Jesus went back and forth between Jerusalem and Bethany. The Gospel of John records that this happened six days before the Passover, but in Mark and Matthew, we read of a woman anointing Jesus in Bethany before this timeline. Mark's timeline indicates that this anointing was done two days before the Passover. In John's Gospel, we read that Mary poured the perfume over His feet and wiped His feet with her hair. In Matthew 26:6-13 and Mark 14:1-9, we read that two days before the Passover, at the house of Simon the Leper, a woman broke the vial and poured it over Jesus's head. The only similar act recorded in both narratives was the reaction of Judas and the disciples to what the women did. Mary of Bethany did this two times, and there was also another woman. But it is clear to me that Jesus was still trying to get across to the apostles what was going to happen; He was trying to draw them into the secret place, but they were not ready. They were still clouded by their own ambition and misunderstanding of how the kingdom works. These worldly things get in the way and blur the road to the secret places of God.

## Human Passion and Desire: the Divine Accelerant

Too often, we try to separate emotion and passion from our relationship with God. My question is, how can we separate emotion and passion from any intimate relationship? The answer: if the relationship is intimate, you cannot; otherwise, the relationship is not growing and active. God is passionate for us! How else can we explain what He did? He sacrificed His Son for us by death on a cross. We call this the "Passion of Christ."

We are commonly taught to separate emotions from our relationship with God because emotions can lead us in wrong directions. Humans are emotional beings. God made us that way because He is an emotional Being. One cannot read the Old and New Testaments without coming to that conclusion. Let me add more color to this conversation: Emotions are like catalysts to our passions and strengths. If we are walking in fellowship and unity with God, He uses our emotions to strengthen our faith and our walk with Him. It makes our life more vivid, animated, and colorful—not just black and white. Jesus taught that the greatest commandment is to love the Lord with all our heart, soul, mind, and strength. The heart is the source of passion and emotion; it is the joining of the spirit to the soul. That is why the Lord tells us to love Him with our heart, because to whatever we engage the passions of our heart, we will direct our soul (our thinking mind and intellect) and the actions of our body. This process can work on both sides; it will either enhance our relationship with God or get in its way. It just depends on where the passions of our heart lie. They can be with God, first and foremost, or with other things that take our attention from Him.

I want to make a statement here, and it is one of the most profound statements that the Holy Spirit said to me in all the years I have known Him.

**"Human passion and desire are like divine accelerants for My presence."**

These words caught my attention and captivated me. I have never heard anyone say that before. I heard this when I was at a Friday night service at a fellowship I was attending. My family had been a part of that fellowship for a while, and we helped grow that church from a congregation of one hundred or so to 1,500 members. Soon after, we knew that it was time for us to move on. The night I heard those words, I knew that it would be my last night at that fellowship as a member and leader. I would usually participate in the service and be prompted to move in the gifts of the Spirit, but that night, I decided to just be and keep to myself.

I have learned that telling God what you are going to do and how you plan to do it just sets you up for a change of plans. As we started to worship that night, the Holy Spirit rested upon me strongly. It felt like every part of my body was vibrating with the power of God. It seemed like everything else around me went quiet, and God and I had this clear and intimate communication. Then, as I closed my eyes in worship, I saw a fire burning in front of me, and it had the likeness of a human presence. My experience was relatable to Moses's experience in Exodus 3:2, where we read, "*There the angel of the Lord appeared to him in a blazing fire from the middle of a bush.*" At that point, the Lord said to me that the fuel to His fire is His deep love, and it is so deep and strong toward man that it appears as fire. Then He said that human passion and desire are divine accelerants for His presence. I got the impression and understanding that when we are in worship, expressing a heartfelt and single-focused desire for Him, we are flooding the atmosphere with this human passion accelerant. When God shows up in our midst, the accelerant gets lit up by His presence. The place and atmosphere we inhabit become infused with His presence. When this happens, we experience a divine interaction and exchange with Him; we experience His nature and character, His power, and His presence. The Word is made flesh, and it is no longer about Scripture written on a page but what He does to write it on our heart and reveal truth to us.

As I was having this experience and revelation, the Lord moved me to speak forth and prophesy about what I was seeing. I remember prophesying for a few minutes, and then I sat down. The Spirit of the Lord rested on me very strongly, and I continually felt His presence for several days after that. The weight of His presence and glory was so strong that the world could have blown up around me, but it would not have affected the resident peace within me.

This was a period in my life when God was constantly revealing things to me. Over time, I learned that when I get these revelations, I need to take them back to God and ask Him to explain them to me. I started praying, meditating, reading, and studying the Bible regarding these revelations, and God began laying out the interpretations and meanings for me through various scriptures and instances from the Bible. Then the Lord started to bake these revelations inside of me as I meditated on them over time. In recent years, He has led me to teach and preach on them.

One day, the Lord led me to Deuteronomy 4:24:

> For the Lord your God is a consuming fire, a jealous God.

And also to Hebrews 12:29:

> For our God is a consuming fire.

As I was aware of God's presence and experiencing it as a consuming fire, I heard a still small voice inside me say, "The fuel to My fire is My love." I continued worshipping God and contemplating this, and I began to realize that God appeared as fire because His love burns so passionately for us—so passionate that it emerges as a burning fire. Can you imagine a love so pure and powerful that it burns and appears as fire? Although this sounds terrifying, it is attractive and draws us to itself, just like Moses was drawn to the burning bush. God's love is comforting and safe. It is astonishing, stunning, and amazing. It purifies everything it touches. It purifies us of sin and anything else that separates us from Him. This fire draws us into God and purifies us by His love. It consumes all things that are not love, so we can experience God, and He can experience us.

> "Who can live with this devouring fire?" they cry. "Who can survive this all-consuming fire?" Those who are honest and fair (righteous and sincere), who refuse to profit by fraud, who stay far away from bribes, who refuse to listen to those who plot murder, who shut their eyes to all enticement to do wrong— these are the ones who will dwell on high? (Isaiah 33 :14-16, NLT)

Sometimes the immediate and carnal interpretation of "The God who appears as fire" is that He is coming to judge and require retribution from us. This is the same thought that most of Israel had when God came down on Mount Sinai to visit them after Moses led them out of Egypt. Let us go through the accounts that are given in Exodus and Deuteronomy. I will tell you how God took this revelation and explained it to me through different scriptures and experiences people had with Him throughout the Bible.

In past times, when people had to make a covenant with each other, they would cut an animal and walk between its pieces saying, "Let what happened to this animal happen to me if I break the covenant with you." As per this practice, in Genesis 15, we read how Abraham made a covenant with God. When Abraham cut the animal to make a covenant with God, he saw a "Smoking Oven and a Flaming Torch" walking through the animal pieces. This signifies that the old covenant with Abraham was cut by God the Father (The Smoking Oven) and Jesus (The Flaming Torch). God established a covenant with Abraham that Jesus was going to come through his lineage. This is the first narrative in the Bible of the presence of God as a fiery Being.

Moses's first experience with God as fire was at the burning bush. Then, when Moses and the children of Israel left Egypt, they came to Mount Sinai, where the God of fire revealed Himself to them in ways they never imagined.

You can read these accounts in Exodus 19-24 and Deuteronomy 4-6. Both accounts were recorded at different times. In Exodus, they were recorded as they happened, while in Deuteronomy, they were recorded after Moses led Israel for forty years. During those forty years, as Moses fellowshipped, worshipped, and dwelt in the presence of God, he must have gotten God's perspective of the account—what was in God's heart and how the people responded. Exodus gives an account of the Law, while Deuteronomy explains the spirit of the Law and gives more understanding to what happened and the significance of it.

Israel traveled through the wilderness for a few days and came to Mount Sinai (Horeb)—the place where Moses met the God of fire and love. God sent Moses to Egypt to deliver His people and judge Egypt for how they mistreated Israel. The heart of the matter is that God wanted to deliver His people so they could go into the wilderness and worship Him (Exodus 7:16, 8:1, 20, 9:1, 13, 10:3, 7). Worship is a form of prayer, while we are in our earthly bodies, that sets the table for God to reveal Himself to His people.

Now the Israelites arrived back at Mount Sinai, and Moses went up the mountain again to talk to God. God instructed Moses to tell the people about His invitation.

> Then Moses climbed the mountain to appear before God. The LORD called to him from the mountain and said, "Give these instructions to the family of Jacob; announce it to the descendants of Israel: 'You have seen what I did to the Egyptians. You know how I carried you on eagles' wings and brought you to myself. **Now if you will obey me and keep my covenant, you will be my own special treasure from among all the peoples on earth; for all the earth belongs to me. And you will be my kingdom of priests, my holy nation.' This is the message you must give to the people of Israel."** (Exodus 19:3-6, NLT)

God proposed a wonderful offer here—an offer of engagement for Israel to become His special treasure that would worship Him, interact with Him, and learn to get to know Him. Moses took God's proposal, went down the mountain, told the people about it, and their response was yes! Then Moses went up the mountain again. God told Moses to go back to the people and prepare them because He wanted to go down to meet them in three days; He wanted to interact with His people and speak to them.

Moses went down the mountain to the people and prepared them to meet God by consecrating them. People meeting their God and God meeting His people is what happens when we worship. Moses led the people to Mount Sinai to worship, and the Lord descended as a great fire. The mountain quaked when the Lord spoke, and it sounded like thunder. Exodus 19 recounts that the presence of the Lord descended on the mountain as fire and smoke. The mountain was like a "Smoking Oven," and it trembled constantly.

### Key 1: Delight and the Desire for Prayer

We read that Moses went up and down the mountain a couple of times to meet with God and carry His instructions before God spoke the ten commandments to the people as they stood down the mountain and listened. The people became fearful hearing the voice of God and told Moses to tell God to communicate with him alone rather than with all of them. They were so fearful that they thought they would die from hearing the thunder of His voice. But they did not die. They heard God and lived. They could obey God's Word as He spoke to them. They did not have to wait to hear it from Moses. One of the starkest realities we must learn is that only if we hear God ourselves, and interact with Him personally, will our encounters have a lasting impact on us and transform and empower our lives. How can we love someone and have a relationship with them when we have no personal experience with them? If all the knowledge we have of the one we love is from the information others gave us, and we do not experience them personally, then the intimacy of the relationship will not last. That is how we all personally learn the ways of God and learn to love Him. Psalm 103:7 says that Moses knew the ways of God, and the children of Israel knew His acts. Sadly true, the children of Israel never knew the God of Israel. That is one of the reasons they had so much trouble obeying His commandments.

But why did God appear in such a way to the children of Israel? Why did He appear as fire, thunder, and an earthquake? Did He want to scare them into love and obedience? Just think about what happened: God delivered His beloved Israel and made an offer of engagement. They accepted the offer, and they met God. Do you remember when you first met that person who made your heart pound with desire and passion? Weren't you excited to meet your beloved? If the fuel to God's fire is His love, and He is going to meet His beloved, He will not scare them—He will come to them and reveal Himself to them. God was excited to meet His beloved, and He could only react the way He did because human passion and desire are divine accelerants for His presence. The God of fiery passion, whose fuel is love, is wanting to meet His beloved who expresses passion and desire for Him.

Moses recalls this incident in Deuteronomy 4:10-11:

> Remember the day you stood before the LORD your God at Horeb, when the LORD said to me, "**Assemble the people to Me, that I may let them hear My words so they may learn to fear Me all the days they live on the earth, and that they may teach their children**. You came near and stood at the foot of the mountain, and the **mountain burned with fire to the very heart of the heavens: darkness**, cloud and thick gloom.

Note that this recounting was forty years after Moses led the children of Israel—spending forty days in God's presence, not once but twice, and then establishing a lifetime of living in His presence for another forty years. As those years progressed, Moses got closer and closer to God and learned and understood more and more about His character and nature.

Moses said that the fire burned to the very heart of the heavens (Deuteronomy 4:11). The word "heart" in Greek comes from a group of words that center around core, heart, understanding, inner man, and the seat of passion and emotion. I can imagine the greatness of the appearance and burning of that fire that touched the very heart of God, which was pounding in desire for His people. He longs to have fellowship with His people. Similar words are also used to describe how the fire burned to the heart of the heavens. We read in Song of Solomon 4:9 about how the groom's heart flutters and pounds when he sees his bride:

> You have made **my heart beat faster**, my sister, my bride**; You have made my heart beat faster with a single glance of your eyes**, With a single strand of your necklace.

We need to see the situation on Mount Sinai through the lens of a God who is passionate for His beloved. God invited the Israelites to the mountain to worship Him. They accepted His invitation, prepared themselves for worship, and finally met Him and heard Him speak. God's passion was released, and it met man with a literal bang!

**Key 1: Delight and the Desire for Prayer**

Many of the readers of this book may have heard about the three-and-a-half-year revival that took place from April 1906 to November 1909 in Los Angeles, California, which is commonly referred to as the Azusa Street Revival. It was one of the greatest outpourings of God's presence in the church age. If you go to Azusa Street today, you will see a plaque in the place where the old mission was, commemorating the revival. I have read many books about the revival, but one fairly recent book gives an account that really got my attention.

The book by Tommy Welchel, *True Stories of the Miracles of Azusa Street and Beyond*, is a compilation of eyewitness accounts of what happened at Azusa Street. On page 18, the author makes the following statement:

> This same glory cloud dwelled within the walls of the Azusa Street mission and even hovered around the outside of the building during the revival, every day and night for three-and-a-half years. On certain nights, **flames could be seen shooting from the rooftop of the mission converging with flames shooting from the sky into the mission.** This, too, is the Shekinah Glory described in Exodus 13 as the "pillar of fire" that led the Israelites by night. Also, in Exodus 24:17, "...the glory of the LORD appeared at the summit [of Mount Sinai] like a consuming fire."

In the above statement regarding the happenings at the Azusa Street Revival, what he describes was human passion and desire ignited by the presence of God and the presence of God coming to meet it. This account talks about how the fire went up from the Mission and, at the same time, came down from heaven—they met together with converging flames. I was beside myself after reading that. God came down in the fire, and the passionate desire the people expressed to Him was so intense that it went back up to Him as fire. The atmosphere was so infused with passion for God that it burned back up. What an explosion! This was a similar reaction to what happened on Mount Sinai. The people of Israel said yes to God's special offer. The God of passionate love showed up. He appeared as fire, and the fire and passion were so great that the earth quaked. Let us go on and explore this phenomenon more.

## Human Passion and Desire—Effects in Heaven

The more I prayed, worshipped, and discussed this revelation with God, the more He revealed to me what it meant. He said that He wanted to show me how passionate worship and prayer touches Him in heaven and how it reflects down on the earth. He led me to the book of Revelation, which talks much about scenes in heaven and earth. To really understand this book, one needs to know that it is not just the revelation of Jesus the Christ, but also the revelation of the Lamb of God. The book of Revelation refers to the Lamb of God over thirty-five times!

Let us look at two scenes in Revelation 4-5 and 8. Both scenes are centered around worship. Revelation 4-5 talks about John being taken into heaven where he sees a throne. From that throne were flashes of lightning and thunder, and seven lamps of fire were burning around it. A common theme we see when the presence of God manifests is lightning, thunder, and fire. The living creatures around the throne see the glory of God with their eyes and do nothing but cry, "Holy, Holy, Holy."

Why do they do that? Does God have a button up there, and when He wants to hear someone tell Him how great He is, He presses it, and they cry, "Holy?" First, God does not need anyone to tell Him that He is holy. He knows that He is holy. He is not insecure. Those around the throne cry, "Holy" because, as they look at God, they perceive something about Him that is holy, and the perception never gets stale because they constantly see something new that they have never perceived before. Their perception fascinates them, and God fulfills them.

What do those around the throne mean when they cry, "Holy?" They mean that God's character (His nature) is transcendent and infinite in its measurement. If we were to measure God's love, mercy, kindness, wisdom, or power, it would far exceed anything we can imagine. So as those around the throne keep perceiving this, they keep crying, "Holy" as an expression of awe and wonder. That is why worship and prayer are so important. During worship and prayer, God reveals Himself to us, and we become an expression of Him.

As the living creatures worship God, the twenty-four elders join in the worship. Notice what they do: first, they cast the crowns that the Lord gave them, before Him, giving Him glory for all things. The scene goes on, and John finds out that only Jesus, the Lion of the tribe of Judah, the Root of David, and the Lamb of God, is worthy to open the book. This is the picture of the Lion and the Lamb. The authority of the Lion was released into the world through the finished work of the Lamb of God.

We see three groups of worshippers here:

1. The living creatures and the elders around the throne
2. The angels around the throne
3. Every creature in heaven and on earth and under the earth and in the sea

The elders worshipped with harps. Harps represent music. So they were using music to worship God. The purpose of music ministry is to help us worship God. In addition to the harps, the elders had golden bowls full of incense. Incense is used to worship God in many cultures. It represents the prayers of the saints. As the elder's worship God, their worship, prayer, and devotion bring a fragrance to the throne of God. I think this fragrance would be delightful and aromatic because it is infused with the passion and desire for man to know, love, and worship God. Not only is human passion for God a divine accelerant, but it is also a fragrant offering to His nostrils. This divine accelerant has a certain fragrance that brings pleasure to the heart of God.

The living creatures and the elders worshipped, saying the Lamb is worthy to open the seals because of His great sacrifice on the cross that redeemed all of mankind and made them a kingdom of priests to reign on the earth.

Hosts of angels joined in saying, "*Worthy is the Lamb to receive power and riches and wisdom and might and honor and glory and blessing.*" (Revelation 5:12)

Every creature in heaven and on earth and under the earth and in the sea joined in and said, "*Blessing, honor, glory, and dominion forever.*"

Thus, the Lamb of God was continually worshipped for His great sacrifice, and because of His sacrifice, every level of human and heavenly authority rests on Him.

Let us explore another scene of worship in Revelation 8:2-5:

> And I saw the seven angels who stand before God, and seven trumpets were **given to them. Another angel came and stood at the altar, holding a golden censer, and much incense was given to him, so that he might add it to the prayers of all the saints on the golden altar which was before the throne. And the smoke of the incense, with the prayers of the saints, went up before God out of the angel's hand**. Then the angel took the censer and filled it with the fire of the altar, and threw it to the earth; and there followed peals of thunder and sounds and flashes of lightning and an earthquake.

This heavenly scene is a perfect representation of what happens when the saints worship and pray. Their prayers go up to heaven with a fragrance of passion for God, and an accelerant gets mixed with the divine incense at the altar. The smoke from the offering and the incense go before the throne of God. Then an angel takes the censer, fills it with fire from the altar, and throws it down to earth. This represents God's presence coming down and responding to His people. The divine accelerant meets the divine fire. Once this happens, thunder, lightning, and earthquakes follow.

Now I realize this process can happen in varying degrees, and there can be times when we see its manifestation and how it affects the world. But God responds to pure worship to Him in one way or another. His presence does come, and we do experience—to some degree—the God whose passion burns so great for us that it appears as fire.

As I was contemplating why the Bible records God's presence along with thunder, lightning, and earthquakes, God gave me an analogy of a thunderstorm. In a thunderstorm, a warm front rises and forms cumulus clouds. It then hits the upper atmosphere, which is cooler, and a reaction happens. When the two fronts collide, it has all it takes to cause a thunderstorm. Electrical charges are produced and released as lightning, the lightning creates the sound that we call thunder, and the earth seems to quake under the sound of the thunder. Hence, a thunderstorm. Since the beginning of the world and the fall of man, creation has been suffering the penalty of sin, and it groans for the revelation of the divine order for which it was created. Similarly, any time God manifests Himself on earth, the same happens. When God's burning presence and His fiery love collide with a world that is still subject to sin and the effects of it, it reacts just like a thunderstorm. We have the God of all creative ability, who lives in a realm of complete spiritual order, colliding with a realm that suffers from spiritual disorder. Thus, there is a reaction.

## Human Passion and Desire—Effects on Earth: The Day of Pentecost

Now that we have an understanding of the scene in heaven—of man worshipping and expressing his desire for God, and God responding to the passions and desires of man's worship and prayer—let us take a look at the historic day of Pentecost to understand its effect on earth. The day of Pentecost is recorded in the book of Acts. Before we go any further, we need to understand the extent of the manifestation of God's presence. I have learned that God's movement on the earth is a combination of man's desire and his heart cry for God, and the sovereignty of God's response and how He manifests Himself. Sometimes it is broad with a large societal change in scope, and other times it is more personal and hidden. Usually, one leads to the other and vice versa.

After Jesus had risen from the dead and manifested Himself to His disciples, He told them what happened at the resurrection and the significance of it, and He shared with them matters concerning the kingdom. He then told them to wait in Jerusalem for the Holy Spirit—the Holy Spirit that was going to come and live within them, after which, they would receive power and become His witnesses in Jerusalem, Judea, Samaria, and the rest of the world (Acts 1:8).

The disciples then returned to Jerusalem and went to where they were staying. This place had an "upper room." An upper room is a room set aside on an upper floor, where people would go to pray. In Acts 1:14, we read:

> These all continued **with one accord in prayer and supplication**, with the women and Mary the mother of Jesus, and with His brothers. (NKJV)

I like to say that they were feeding fuel to the furnace and infusing the atmosphere with passionate prayer and supplication, which reached heaven—very much like the scene recorded in Revelation 8.

We read that the disciples were in one accord. The word "accord" is used eight times in the book of Acts and is particular to the book of Acts. It is a word that means to rush alongside in unity. Imagine a band of musicians coming alongside each other to play a piece of music. They may have different instruments with different tones, which produce different sounds, but they come alongside in unity to harmonize together and produce an exceptional sound for all who hear.

I can picture each disciple rushing to Jesus's side, being passionate about Him, and adding their own part—not being concerned about their position or rank but looking to produce a wonderful sound and fragrance for God. Each one added something very important to the passion by being in one accord. As I meditated on this years later, I received another revelation of great importance. The Lord spoke to me and said, "Unity, or being in one accord, is like what oxygen is to a fire." Oxygen is very important for a fire to burn. If oxygen is sucked out of the atmosphere, even the biggest raging fire would immediately go out. Not only do we need passion for God to infuse the atmosphere, but we also need unity. The easiest way to make dormant the presence of God in your life, family, or assembly is to get into constant strife and dissention.

Avoiding strife and dissention does not mean that everybody agrees on everything; it is also how we treat others when we disagree. We can disagree without being disagreeable. If we choose to honor one another, respect one another, and not tear down those we disagree with, then, by following the path of love, we can move toward the path of unity.

If unity is not cultivated, no matter how much passion you have for God, the movement of God in and through you will be limited. We can have all the gasoline vapor in the air and come in with a blow torch to light the fire, but nothing will happen if oxygen is not in the atmosphere. Unity is a key ingredient for the spiritual combustion process. Do you remember reading about God saying that the fuel to His fire is love? That same God appears as a flaming fire because His love is so great. We cannot take a key ingredient out of the combustion process and think it is going to burn.

Paul wrote a beautiful description of this in his letter to the Colossian church:

> So, as those who have been chosen of God, holy and beloved, put on a **heart of compassion, kindness, humility, gentleness and patience; bearing with one another, and forgiving each other**, whoever has a complaint against anyone; **just as the Lord forgave you, so also should you**. Beyond all these things put on love, **which is the perfect bond of unity**. (Colossians 3:12-14)

Paul talks about putting on or being clothed and endued with a heart of tender virtues that allow the power of God to work in and through us. These virtues are imparted to us by the grace of God. Humility and meekness (gentleness) are at the center of these powerful qualities. God gives grace to the humble. But beyond this, Paul says to put on love as a garment that forms and fits our body; it is the perfect bond of unity. I like to say that love holds everything together.

We can liken this concept of unity to our human body. Our body has bones, but unless those bones are held together by ligaments, they cannot fulfill their designed purpose. Ligaments connect the bones together and allow the joints to move. They give stability and strength to the skeletal structure. Then, we have tendons. Tendons attach the muscles to the bones. Tendons hold everything together. They strengthen the muscles so they can perform tasks. Love can be likened to ligaments; tendons can be likened to joy. The joy of the Lord is our strength (Nehemiah 8:10). Joy is an overflow of our love relationship with God, and we are joyous because we are known and accepted as the beloved of the Father. Joy is a catalyst to our faith; it makes it stronger and more enduring.

We are the body of Christ. If we do not clothe ourselves with love, we will have no mobility or strength to perform the tasks needed. The body will be weak and immobile.

Imagine each of us rushing along at Jesus's side, keeping our eyes on Him, and getting direction from Him—not being concerned about who is more important or who has the biggest role, or judging one another. There is something about keeping our eyes on Jesus that sharpens our sight and our ability to love one another.

Let us move on to the day of Pentecost. This prayer furnace had been going on for forty days. In Acts 2:1, we read:

> When the Day of Pentecost had fully come, they were all with one accord in one place. And suddenly… (NKJV)

The day of Pentecost had come, and the disciples were praying in one accord. They were all in one place, not just physically, but also spiritually. The atmosphere was infused with passion and unity of spirit. It was like when a propane or natural gas leak is infused in the atmosphere—all it takes is the littlest spark to cause an explosion. The disciples were in a place of perfect unity, all with one passion, and that combined with the sovereignty of the moment. How was God going to respond to that and manifest Himself? With a spiritual explosion, of course! The day of Pentecost happened, and the world has never been the same.

I am going to paraphrase what happened in Acts 2:2-4:

When the day of Pentecost arrived, they were together in one accord, in fervent prayer, in one place physically and spiritually in their desire for God. Suddenly they heard a loud noise, like a violent tornado or a speeding locomotive. Then the sound burst into their room. There appeared a pillar of fire in the center of the room, and then the fire disseminated into each of them. This fire then appeared to be coming forth from within them with flames above their head. They were baptized with the Holy Spirit and fire, and they started speaking in different languages as the Spirit inspired them.

When the children of Israel were in the wilderness, there was a pillar of fire that went before them by night and a cloud by day. Both the fire and the cloud were manifestations of God's presence—the God of glory whose fuel to His fire is love. I can picture this fire coming down from heaven swiftly and burning greatly like a fire tornado. Have you ever seen a raging forest fire where the fire got so hot that the flames flew off the large trees and created a loud sound like a fire tornado? Such a fire sucks the fuel from the atmosphere around it and burns and consumes everything in its path.

On the day of Pentecost, instead of a natural fire tornado that destroys everything around it, a spiritual one formed. God came down to meet His people again. This time, it was not Mount Sinai, which represents the old covenant; it was Mount Zion, which represents the new covenant. God can now come and dwell in the heart of man. Just think, man was separated from God for thousands of years, but now, a way has been paved through the sacrifice and offering that Jesus made on the cross. Do you think God is excited that He can dwell in man again? Our God who is full of passion and compassion for His people can now dwell in man.

The disciples were baptized with the Holy Spirit and fire. They created a spiritual greenhouse of passion for God, passion for His Word, and unity with Him and one another—the furnace was prepared! Now all that was needed was for the God of fire to show up and create an explosion. And God did! This explosion was heard from the depths of hell to the very throne room in heaven.

On the day of Pentecost, the one hundred and twenty disciples in the upper room were set on fire, and the fire spread and changed the world they knew. One thing I have learned about spiritual fire is that it is not like natural fire. Natural fire accelerates the destruction of matter, while spiritual fire accelerates the destruction of sin and the results of sin in this world. It creates life and life more abundantly in the lives of people who accept it. It is the creative force that forms the structure of God's kingdom within us, which results in us living life abundantly.

We have pictured the scene of what prayer does in heaven, and the response of prayer on earth on the day of Pentecost.

Now that man is redeemed by the work of the cross, God has come to dwell in him once again. He is a new temple, not made by human hands, but by God Himself so He can dwell in man and in unity with man. In the New Testament, Paul writes a number of times that we are the temple of God.

> For we are the **temple of the living God**. (2 Corinthians 6:16)

> Do you not know that you are a temple of God and that the Spirit of God dwells in you? (1 Corinthians 3:16)

> Or do you not know that your **body is a temple of the Holy Spirit who is in you**, whom you have from God, and that you are not your own? For you have been bought with a price: therefore glorify God in your body. (1 Corinthians 6:19-20)

## Key 1: Delight and the Desire for Prayer

The people in the upper room were filled with the Holy Spirit, and as a result, they spoke in other tongues. All the people around them could hear them in their own language singing of the mighty deeds of God. We could describe this as speaking the wonderful works of God. What could they have actually said? They were speaking of the love of God poured out through His Son and the work of the cross that brought man back to God and God to man. God could dwell in man again as it was in the beginning.

The disciples were so happy, jubilant, and joyful in the upper room that the people around them thought they were drunk with natural wine. But not so! They had the supernatural wine of the Holy Spirt living inside of them.

The day of Pentecost was the fulfillment of so many promises and plans that God talked about in the Torah and in the Old Testament. It was the fulfillment of what Jesus talked about in John 4 and John 7. John 4 talked about the Holy Spirit springing up within us a well of everlasting life, the knowledge of God the Father and Son being revealed by His Spirit to our spirit within us, and the power of the Holy Spirit flowing out of us like rivers of living water to refresh and bring this life to man.

Rivers of living water started flowing immediately on that day. Peter stood up in boldness, not in timidity or in the fear that gripped them several days before at Jesus's arrest and crucifixion. He expounded on the Old Testament scriptures by revelation. The Holy Spirit was springing up everlasting life within him. He explained the plans of God that were foretold and how Jesus fulfilled them. He quoted the prophet Joel about the pouring out of the Holy Spirit and that men would prophesy and have visions and dreams, and that we all are a part of how God reveals Himself to us. He explained how Jesus fulfilled the prophecy that David was talking about in Psalm 16:10:

> For you will not leave my soul among the dead or allow your holy one to rot in the grave. (NLT)

Peter's sermon was so powerful that day because the rivers of living water were flowing through him, and it is said that the Word pierced their hearts. Three thousand men gave their heart to Jesus that day. The well of life sprang up in them, and the rivers started to flow.

## Human Passion and Desire—Effects on Earth: Dedication of the First Temple

The day of Pentecost was not the first time something like this happened. There was a significant foreshadowing of this in the Old Testament when Solomon dedicated the Temple.

God is so good about how He reveals His words to us. After meditating on the day of Pentecost, I started thinking about the dedication of Solomon's Temple in the Old Testament. David desired to build God's Temple, but God allocated that task to Solomon. So David collected money and set it aside, and put everything in place for Solomon to build the Temple. After David died, Solomon became king, and he took up the task of building the Temple and completed it in seven years. We can read this narrative in 2 Chronicles 3-4. In 2 Chronicles 5, we read that once the Temple was completed, all the sacred instruments of worship were put in place. Lastly, the ark of the covenant, which signifies the presence of God dwelling among the people, was put in place.

> When the priests came forth from the holy place (for all the priests who were present **had sanctified themselves, without regard to divisions**), and all the Levitical singers, Asaph, Heman, Jeduthun, and their sons and kinsmen, clothed in fine linen, with cymbals, harps and lyres, standing east of the altar, **and with them one hundred and twenty priests blowing trumpets in unison when the trumpeters and the singers were to make themselves heard with one voice to praise and to glorify the LORD,** and when they lifted up their voice accompanied by trumpets and cymbals and instruments of music, and when they praised the LORD saying, "He

> indeed is good for His lovingkindness is everlasting," **then the house, the house of the Lord, was filled with a cloud, so that the priests could not stand to minister because of the cloud, for the glory of the Lord filled the house of God.** (2 Chronicles 5:11-14)

Now that everything was in place, the people came to worship God. Each priest had a certain rank and assignment, but not one of them seemed to care about their position. Together, they filled the Temple with worship. Some of the Levites who were designated as priests in the current order of worship were also worshipping, singing, and playing various instruments such as cymbals, lyres, and harps. They were joined by one hundred and twenty priests who were playing trumpets. The trumpeters and singers unified in their praise and adoration for the Lord. They were recalling and expressing gratitude to God for His faithfulness and lovingkindness. They were recalling the character and the nature of the One they were in covenant with, and the One they were in union with, as a holy nation and a royal priesthood.

Do you see a similar picture here as in the day of Pentecost—another temple being prepared as a dwelling place for God? The Israelites were working as one to dedicate the Temple—the place where the Lord would dwell among His people and meet with them to fellowship and interact with them. They sacrificed so many sheep and oxen they could not be counted. They were all in one accord, in a symphony, harmonizing in one direction, and worshipping God. They filled the atmosphere with a divine accelerant of human passion and desire. They abandoned focus on their position, rank, and order; they were only about worshipping God together and being in unity and harmony with God and one another.

Heaven was filled with worship by God's beloved sons and daughters. The incense from the altar of heaven burned, and a sweet fragrance was inhaled by the God of heaven. Then, fire came down to earth and lit the earth's atmosphere with God's presence. God came, and the Temple was filled with His glory in the form of a cloud. The glory of God sometimes manifests as a cloud. We read that when the Israelites were in the wilderness, they followed a pillar of fire by night and a cloud by day. The cloud filled the Temple so densely that the Israelites could not stand any longer. They were overcome by God's presence and glory, and they fell to the ground. We call that being "slain in the Spirit." The presence of God is so strong that our natural bodies cannot function normally. A divine interaction and exchange happens between God and man. I have experienced this before, and it felt like I was glued to the ground. I could not move.

So, where was the fire then? I think it must have been there because where there is smoke, there is FIRE!

As this happened, Solomon bowed down, worshipped, and prayed to God. He prayed a wonderful prayer of dedication to the Lord God (2 Chronicles 6). Then the glory of God came down again. Read 2 Chronicles 5-7 to get the entire context of what happened at the dedication of the first Jewish Temple.

Once Solomon finished his prayer of consecration and dedication to God, the glory, fire, and smoke came down again and enveloped everybody.

> **Now when Solomon had finished praying, fire came down from heaven and consumed the burnt offering and the sacrifices, and the glory of the LORD filled the house.**
>
> The priests could not enter into the house of the LORD because the glory of the LORD filled the LORD's house.
>
> **All the sons of Israel, seeing the fire come down and the glory of the LORD upon the house, bowed down on the pavement with their faces to the ground, and they worshiped and gave praise to the LORD, saying, "Truly He is good, truly His lovingkindness is everlasting."** (2 Chronicles 7:1-3)

## Key 1: Delight and the Desire for Prayer

There were many more days of worship with thousands of sacrifices and several feasts. Once those days ended, God appeared to Solomon and answered his prayer. The words God spoke to Solomon in 2 Chronicles 7:13-14 are some of the most commonly used scriptures in the Christian church regarding prayer and God's presence:

> If I shut up the heavens so that there is no rain, or if I command the locust to devour the land, or if I send pestilence among My people, and My people **who are called by My name humble themselves and pray** and **seek My face** and **turn from their wicked ways**, then I will **hear from heaven, will forgive their sin and will heal their land.** (2 Chronicles 7:13-14)

When we read these scriptures in context of what was going on at the time, it exposes a larger picture of our relationship with God. This invitation to prayer is a picture of man seeking the face of God with passion and humility. We express our desire and passion for God, filling the atmosphere with a divine accelerant. When we do this, we get ourselves to a place where we can see what in us is evil before God, and we give the Lord space to consume it so we can have the divine burn of His presence.

Can you see the parallels between 2 Chronicles 5-7 and Acts 2? There are so many. First, they both involve dedication of a temple. A temple is a place where we meet and interact with God. In the Old Testament, the Temple was a physical building erected with prescribed ways to worship God because man was separated from God because of sin. When the Temple was dedicated, God's presence came and dwelt in it. It was represented by a cloud of glory. In the New Testament, Jesus paved a new way to God—a living way into His presence. He taught us the way by saying, "I AM the WAY." God no longer dwells in temples made by human hands. He made a way to dwell in us—in our bodies. We are His temple, not made with human hands, but made by God Himself. The day of Pentecost represented God coming and living in His temple—us.

In the Old Testament, during the dedication of the Temple, the people were worshipping God for several days. They were in one place expressing their desire for God. They prepared the Temple so God could come and dwell in it. Then God came; His fire came, and His glory came. In the New Testament, the people were praying and seeking God for forty days, waiting in Jerusalem as Jesus told them to. They were expressing their desire and passion for God, filling the atmosphere with the divine accelerant.

In the Old Testament dedication of the Temple, we see that the people were in one accord. The singers and the musicians were in unison. They were not concerned about their position but just wanted to interact with God. On the day of Pentecost, again we see that the people were in one accord. Not only was the atmosphere filled with the divine accelerant, but the atmosphere was filled with unity as well—unity—the spiritual oxygen to fire. The atmosphere was set for a perfect burn. The only thing needed was fuel. The Consuming Fire (God in the Person of the Holy Spirit) came, and the explosion happened. The fire came, the glory of God manifested, it collided with the people's passion, desire, and unity, and a spiritual explosion happened that changed the course of human history.

## Blessed Are Those Who Mourn—For His Presence

Let me tell you about another interaction I had with God during prayer, which reinforces what we have been discussing so far. Several years ago, in the assembly that I was attending, I was in what we called "pre-service prayer." I was walking around and talking with God. While we were fervently praying and asking God to manifest Himself during the service, I was drawn to a scripture from the Sermon on the Mount:

> Blessed are those who mourn, for they shall be comforted. (Matthew 5:4)

As I reflected on this scripture, my immediate thought was to put on a state of continual mourning before God because of my sins and the things I do that grieve Him and separate me from Him. This sin consciousness continues to invade most of the Christian church. Most commentators interpret this scripture saying that people should mourn because of their sin; express an intense sorrow for their sin, for themselves, and their nation; and come before God in heartfelt sorrow and conviction for the overturning of the result of sin in our life and community. So, considering what I thought, I was trying to put on my best mourning prayer, repentance tone, and solemn face.

I was doing this in hope that God would move in our service that day. By "move," I mean that people would experience a tangible presence of the Lord—maybe healings, conviction of hearts unto repentance, manifestation of the gifts of the Spirit, the glory cloud descending on people, revival breaking out—all or any of these would suffice.

In the midst of prayer, God interrupted me. I heard a voice inside of me saying, "What are you mourning for? Have you ever been transformed from just being sorry for your sins?" I stopped and thought about those two questions. Then I heard God say to me, "What you need to mourn for is My presence, just as much as you mourn for the sins that you committed, because when My presence comes and you interact with Me, you will be changed and transformed." Through these statements, I realized that just feeling sorry for my sins could not change me. What I needed to be sorry for and grieve for are my actions that separate me from God's presence and from the ability to interact and fellowship with Him. There is a fine line here, but that line makes all the difference in experiencing God.

Now putting two and two together, this concept perfectly fits the statement: Human passion and desire are like divine accelerants for God's presence. The Greek word for "mourn" is the strongest form of its verb. It is used to describe mourning for the death of the person who was the closest to you emotionally. It is the kind of grief that takes hold of a man and cannot be hidden. That type of emotion comes from a deep passion and desire for being with the person you lost and can longer be with because of death. The scripture in Matthew says, "*Blessed are those who mourn.*" "Blessed" means happy or joyous—the joy that is completely independent of all the chances and changes in life.

As I kept contemplating this, the Holy Spirit drew my attention to James 4:6-10:

> But He gives a greater grace. Therefore it says, "GOD IS OPPOSED TO THE PROUD, BUT GIVES GRACE TO THE HUMBLE." Submit therefore to God. Resist the devil and he will flee from you. **Draw near to God and He will draw near to you. Cleanse your hands, you sinners; and purify your hearts, you double-minded. Be miserable and mourn and weep; let your laughter be turned into mourning and your joy to gloom. Humble yourselves in the presence of the Lord, and He will exalt you.**

Before we dive into this scripture, I want to give you some perspective to reinforce that the root cause for our mourning is the loss of a relationship and the sadness of not being able to be in the presence of the other person. Do you remember the first time you ever experienced an intimate relationship with someone special like a boyfriend or girlfriend, and something detrimental happened to the relationship that made you break up? How did that feel? Did it hurt? Did you feel intense pain that caused you to mourn? Why? Because you experienced the loss of an intimate relationship and a fulfilling emotional companionship. If you were the cause for the break-up, then yes, you would be sorry for what you did. But you would mourn more because of the emptiness in your heart than for the fact that you caused the break-up.

Now in light of those thoughts, think of what James says: "*Draw near to God.*" Approach Him. When you want to approach someone, you are looking to be in their presence. As you draw near to God and express your desire for Him, He draws near to you and expresses His desire for you. Cleansing and purifying happens in God's presence because He is a Consuming Fire. He consumes all things that hinder our relationship with Him. Your misery, mourning, and lack of emotional connection to God will be changed when you are in His presence. James goes on to say, "Humble yourselves in the presence of the Lord, and He will exalt you." Humility is a place of complete submission to God—a place where God is everything and you are nothing. It is a place where we accept and digest the truth about ourselves and the truth about God. Yes, it is a place where we acknowledge our sins and the ramifications of those sins. As we continue dwelling in that place, God exalts us. This begins with enjoying the presence of God and being in union with Him. Paul writes in his Epistles:

> But God is so rich in mercy, and he loved us so much, that even though we were dead because of our sins, he gave us life when he raised Christ from the dead. (It is only by God's grace that you have been saved!) For he raised us from the dead along with Christ and seated us with him in the heavenly realms because we are united with Christ Jesus. (Ephesians 2:4-6, NLT)

> So let us come boldly to the throne of our gracious God. There we will receive his mercy, and we will find grace to help us when we need it most. (Hebrews 4:16, NLT)

The throne of grace is God's throne. God's grace is His unmerited favor toward us. To expound on it even more, I would say that grace is God's willingness to use His power on us to bring on us that which we cannot bring on ourselves. Grace brings change in us. Grace comes from God's presence and from His response to our humility when we submit ourselves to Him, seek Him, and acknowledge Him in all that we do.

King David's life, as expressed in Psalm 51, is a classic example of God's grace. The prophet Nathan confronted David about his adulterous ways, premeditated murder, and abuse of power. In 2 Samuel 11, we read that David who was actually supposed to be out with his troops in battle, decided to stay home. He woke up from his afternoon nap and walked on the roof of his palace, which overlooked the city. There he saw beautiful Bathsheba bathing. David lusted after her and took an immoral direction—he decided to worship the creation instead of its Creator. He substituted human passion for the passion and love of God. He sent for her and had sex with her that night. Together they committed adultery, and Bathsheba got pregnant.

This caused significant problems since Bathsheba was already married, and not just married to anyone, but to Uriah the Hittite. At the end of his life, David recalled the thirty mighty warriors who served him (2 Samuel 23). These were the ones he counted on the most. We know David as the greatest king in Israel, but it was not just David building the kingdom. God raised up a whole group of men to help him.

Uriah was one among David's thirty mighty warriors. David kept his mighty warriors and associates close to his palace. That is why Uriah's house was so close that David could see beautiful Bathsheba as she bathed that evening. David keeping his mighty warriors and associates close to his palace became a potential for a major scandal in the ranks of leadership in the kingdom.

Bathsheba got pregnant, and David tried to hide his sin. He hid his sin by authoring more sins. David sent word to Joab, the captain of his troops, to send Uriah back home. Uriah's integrity and selfless devotion to David and his troops highlighted David's selfishness and the evil that David was in the midst of committing. Here is the summary of the acts of David and the evil he authored, as recorded in 2 Samuel 11:

1. David slept with Bathsheba, the wife of Uriah, one of David's most trusted warriors.
2. David called for Uriah to come home from battle so he could get Uriah to sleep with his wife, and the conceived baby would be attributed to Uriah.
3. David urged Uriah to go down to his house and enjoy his wife. But Uriah refused to go to his house and instead slept by the palace door. His integrity and loyalty would not allow him to enjoy his wife while his men were at battle in an open field and the ark of the Lord was in a temporary place.

4. David called for Uriah the next day, and got him drunk, hoping he would go down to his house and sleep with His wife. But again, Uriah did not sleep with his wife.
5. David sent Uriah back into battle and ordered Joab to set Uriah up to be killed in battle. He told Joab to put Uriah on the front-lines of the battle and withdraw the men before him.
6. Joab did not actually obey David's orders but found a way to have Uriah killed in battle. As a result, many other men were also killed in battle. David's sin did not just cause Uriah's death but the death of other servants in the kingdom as well.
7. After Bathsheba finished mourning for Uriah, David took her as his wife.

Today, we would call this premeditated murder. David ordered the execution of someone in his ranks and hid his ulterior motive for doing what he did. He abused his power, leadership, and anointing to get what he wanted at the expense of others. It was pure selfishness. This is the core of all evil—the opposite of good.

I am sure there was murmuring in the kingdom about the things that David did, especially from his close associates. God sent the prophet Nathan, exposed David's sin, and pronounced judgment on him. From then on, major issues and calamity struck the house of David just as Nathan had spoken from the Lord. Notice what David said when he was exposed by Nathan:

> Then David said to Nathan, **"I have sinned against the LORD**." And Nathan said to David, "The LORD also has taken away your sin; you shall not die." (2 Samuel 12:13)

David knew that his sin separated him from God who was the most important Person to him. David was mourning for the presence of God to come back into his life. This is the scenario behind David's writing of Psalm 51.

*A psalm of David, regarding the time Nathan the prophet came to him after David had committed adultery with Bathsheba.*

Have mercy on me, O God,
because of your unfailing **love**.
Because of your great compassion,
blot out the stain of my sins.
Wash me clean from my guilt.
Purify me from my sin.
For I recognize my rebellion;
it haunts me day and night.
**Against you, and you alone, have I sinned;**
**I have done what is evil in your sight.**
You will be proved right in what you say,
and your judgment against me is just.
For I was born a sinner—
yes, from the moment my mother conceived me.
But you desire honesty from the womb,
teaching me wisdom even there.

Purify me from my sins, and I will be clean;
wash me, and I will be whiter than snow.
**Oh, give me back my joy again;**
**you have broken me—**
**now let me rejoice.**
Don't keep looking at my sins.
Remove the stain of my guilt.
**Create in me a clean heart, O God.**

**Renew a loyal spirit within me.**
**Do not banish me from your presence,**
**and don't take your Holy Spirit from me.**

Restore to me the joy of your salvation,
and make me willing to obey you.
Then I will teach your ways to rebels,
and they will return to you.
Forgive me for shedding blood, O God who saves;
then I will joyfully sing of your forgiveness.
Unseal my lips, O Lord,
that my mouth may praise you.

You do not desire a sacrifice, or I would offer one.
You do not want a burnt offering.
**The sacrifice you desire is a broken spirit.**
**You will not reject a broken and repentant heart,**
**O God.**
Look with favor on Zion and help her;
rebuild the walls of Jerusalem.
Then you will be pleased with sacrifices offered in the right spirit—
with burnt offerings and whole burnt offerings.
Then bulls will again be sacrificed on your altar.
(Psalm 51, NLT)

David was in deep mourning for what he had done. He knew his sin was first against God. He highlights this in verse 4. He knew that it was God who had entrusted and anointed him with the position and authority he had. He used that position and authority for his own benefit and caused death and destruction to the people who were entrusted to him.

He was truly sorry for what he did, but the separation from God was his greatest pain.

David knew that his sin was forgiven, and that the ramification of his sin would have a profound effect on the kingdom and his household.

Let us highlight some of the statements that David made. In verse 8, he asks God to restore his joy. Joy can come from many sources, but the main source is the presence of God. David experienced what only few people experience—the joy that comes from being in God's presence. The word "presence" can be translated as "face" or "having an intimate face-to-face relationship." When you are face-to-face with someone, you experience the depth of who that person is. Being face-to-face with God—the presence of God who is all love, light, and life—will have a profound effect on you. Since we were created to fellowship with God, that experience of being in God's presence causes us to connect with our very purpose of being. The joy that we experience is an overflow of our relationship with God, and that causes us to experience the very pleasure of life that has been destined for us. Experiencing the presence of God is one of the most fulfilling and transforming experiences in life. It is self-perpetuating. It fuels the desire to experience the Creator even more. It puts all the pieces of the puzzle together. It causes all the gears to work as they were created to work and brings into being the best of you and what you can be.

In verse 10, we see that David pleaded with God. He did not plead with God to take away the retribution for his sins, but he pleaded with God to create a clean heart in him and renew a loyal spirit within him; he wanted a heart that was not bent on abusing his power for personal gain. Jesus said that out of the abundance of the heart, the mouth speaks. David allowed his position, power, authority, and success to influence him and change him. There is a fine line that we all walk; it is around our dependence on God and acknowledging His control and influence over our lives, and us taking that control back and allowing our success to go to our head. Many times, we are not even aware that this is happening to us until we are presented with a situation that draws these evil actions out of us. Obviously, David's lust for another man's wife, and the ability to fulfill his lust because he was king, overtook him. David had several wives and hundreds of concubines. Concubines were a group of women set aside for David's pleasure. They would have sex with him any time he wanted. But he had to have Bathsheba. He was taken over with the lust for pleasure. This can happen to anyone. If you think that you would never have done that, then clearly pride has won inside of you.

A heart clear of pride and self-seeking uses power for good and good alone. David was asking for a renewal and restoration of that loyal heart that would seek God, and in all its doing, it would prioritize spreading the goodness of God. This reminds me of the power of what Paul talked about in his second letter to the Corinthians. In chapter 5, Paul reminded them that everyone must appear before the judgment seat of Christ and be judged for all the deeds they do in their body. Paul was saying that it is the love of Christ that constrains us to do good. The power of acknowledging and understanding how the love of God was manifested to us through the cross, works in us so we do not live unto our own desires but unto the One who died and rose again for us.

In Psalm 51:11, David makes a statement that highlights all that I am trying to express here: "Do not banish me from your presence, and don't take your Holy Spirit from me." David was mourning for the presence of God, which led to intimate fellowship with Him and the rebuilding of the integrity of David's heart. He knew that whatever happened as a consequence for his actions, his comfort and sustaining power would come from the intimate fellowship of the holy presence of God and help him get through the situation.

Now let us go back to Jesus's statement in the Beatitudes, "*Blessed are those who mourn, for they shall be comforted*" (Matthew 5:4). What are we comforted with? We are comforted with His presence. But in the New Testament, it took on a more expanded personal meaning. Jesus's work on the cross ushered in a new age in which the Holy Spirit can dwell in the hearts of men again. Notice what Jesus said to His disciples in John 14-15, and then later what John said in his first letter:

> And I will ask the Father, and he will give you another **Advocate (Comforter, Helper Paraclete)**, who will never leave you. He is the Holy Spirit, who leads into all truth. The world cannot receive him, because it isn't looking for him and doesn't recognize him. But you know him, **because he lives with you now and later will be in you…**But when the Father sends the **Advocate (Comforter) as my representative—that is, the Holy Spirit**—he will teach you everything and will remind you of everything I have told you. (John 14:16-17, 26, NLT)

> But I will send you the Advocate (Comforter)—the Spirit of truth. He will come to you from the Father and will testify all about me. (John 15:26, NLT)

> My dear children, I am writing this to you so that you will not sin. But if anyone does sin, we have **an advocate** (comforter) who pleads our case before the Father. He is Jesus Christ, the one who is truly righteous. He himself is the sacrifice that atones for our sins—and not only our sins but the sins of all the world. (1 John 2:1-2, NLT)

The root word used throughout the New Testament for comfort/comforted/comforter is the same in all the above scriptures. This is the word that was used when Jesus said, "*Blessed are those who mourn, for they shall be* ***comforted***." John, in his gospel, records Jesus referring to Himself as a Comforter, and the Holy Spirit as a Comforter as well. It means: the One you can call to assist and help you in whatever you need. This Comforter advocates, brings encouragement, exhorts, consoles, comforts, instructs, and admonishes.

These verses highlight the trust that we are discussing; when we mourn, we are comforted by the Comforter's presence. Today, the Comforter is in the Person of the Holy Spirit. He is the One who brings all truth to us—God's reality and God's ways and understanding. As our soul mourns and we experience Him, He brings comfort of restoration, forgiveness, healing, and deliverance.

I love what John says in his first letter above. If we sin, we have that Advocate who comes alongside of us and pleads our case, atones for our sins, and rewards us with His presence.

Let me end this chapter with a prayer:

> *God, manifest in us a clean heart. Renew a right spirit within us. Take not Your presence from us. God, fulfill Your Word in us as You said You will, and never leave us or forsake us. Please be with us forever. We mourn and desire You. Comfort us with Your presence. Bless us in our mourning with Your presence. Substitute our mourning with the fullness of Your joy and the pleasures of Your presence. Amen.*

# Key 2:

# Worship and Prayer

## Worship and Prayer Introduction

One of the most important things I learned about prayer, communication, and intimacy with God is that worship is the doorway to God's house, and that intimacy, prayer, and communion with God happen within its rooms. I personally know some fervent and committed believers, and I have witnessed how they live and express kingdom life. Something deeper and more intimate happens though, when they loosen themselves and begin to worship God freely and passionately. Sometimes they raise their hands; sometimes they are contemplative and quiet; sometimes they dance; or sometimes they shout. But the common denominator is that they freely and passionately express their worship to God. They do not consider what people around them think of them or their worship; they focus on God, considering what God would think of them and their worship, and what He would experience from their communion with Him.

Prayer is communication with God, and worship is a form of prayer. In worship, we are communicating with God. Worship shows submission to God—an acknowledgment of who He is and our need for Him. Worship is a form of prayer in which there is no focus on us, but the focus is on God only. It is the highest form of prayer because, in worship, we are at a place of humble submission to God. The Bible has a recurring theme about humility—the humbler you are, the higher you go. In this context, "higher" means to go deeper into God's presence and experience a greater intimacy with Him. Jesus said that we are raised up with Him and seated with Him in heavenly places. That means we get to experience daily what Jesus has given us through His work on the cross.

All throughout my journey with God, I have been involved with numerous organizations and various denominations. Although the songs sung, instruments played, and types of music used in worship varied across the board, the core outcome was always the same—worship amidst music would bring a tangible presence of God. My first experience with worship was at an outdoor camp meeting called "Jesus 78" in Mount Union, Pennsylvania. Thousands of people came and camped there and attended different meetings each night. Back then, I had just decided to receive Jesus and follow Him. I was a brand-new believer. At that camp, I experienced a strong presence of God, received the baptism of the Holy Spirit, and spoke in tongues. I experienced corporate worship that night. The presence of God was so strong that I felt Him influencing the atmosphere and the hearts and minds of many people.

A few years later, I was part of an evangelical college fellowship. During our fellowship meetings, we used to sing and worship. One song that we sang often was, "Worthy is the Lamb." The lyrics to this song are from Revelation 5. Every time we sang this song, we strongly felt the presence of God. We would worship at our meetings and, to some degree or another, God's presence would fill the room. Later on in college, we started our own Christian fellowship. In this fellowship, we gave greater emphasis to the baptism of the Holy Spirit, gifts of the Holy Spirit, and healing. We emphasized worship accompanied by music and passionate intimate prayer times. We experienced many wonderful manifestations of God and personal transformations.

Early in my Christian experience, I attended a few Catholic charismatic services, and I felt the presence of God in worship as we were singing. The type and style of the music was different from what we used in our fellowship, but the outcome of worship was the same. The same can be said for Presbyterian and the non-denominational Evangelical church that I attended in college. When I went home from college, I attended an Assemblies of God church and various other denominational meetings. Most of them had a time of worship and praise, and music was involved. All types and forms of worship had the same outcome in one degree or another—a strong presence of God when we worshipped corporately accompanied by music. During most of these worship times, I felt the influence of God on me, I heard the voice of God talking to me, and a greater understanding of God was revealed to me.

I found myself constantly attracted to places that had a strong emphasis on worship. In the midst of worship, I usually experienced God's presence, the gifts of the Holy Spirit working in and through me, and a divine revelation and understanding of God.

There is something about music that helps one enter into a place of worshipping God. Music is one of the most powerful forces in the world. I do not know of anyone who does not like music. Now, we all may have our preferences on the style of music, but when someone plays or turns on music and worships God, it creates a more direct on-ramp to the presence of God. Music is a ministry of helps; it helps us worship God. You do not need music to worship God, but it sure turns the light on in the room faster and brighter!

It is not just a musician's or a singer's talent that matters; it is the heart behind the worship. I have seen and heard many highly talented musicians and singers perform, but there is something glorious when they express their passion for God through singing or playing; it brings a distinct quality of purity into the room—one that God meets abundantly. Like any other gift one may have, musical ability can be corrupted by pride that says, "Look at me and how good my gift is." The heart behind using one's gift matters.

There is a prayer movement that started in the late twentieth century called International House of Prayer. They highlighted what we call the harp and bowl prayer model inspired by the twenty-four-hour prayer model described in Judges and 1 Chronicles that David set-up, as well as some other people in church history. It highlighted the importance of prayer, and this led to starting prayer rooms across the world.

The original prayer room of this movement is in Kansas City, Missouri. They have been hosting twenty-four-hour prayer for seven days a week since it started in 1999, and it still continues at the time of this writing in 2023. Here, musicians play, and people pray and interact with God. I have visited and attended their prayer room sessions numerous times and have been enormously blessed by God. Let us look at Scripture for a few examples of worship, music, and prayer together.

We will look first at Revelation 5. John was taken up to heaven, where he saw the living creatures around the throne worshipping God. He then observed a scroll, and a strong angel asked loudly, "Who is worthy to receive the scroll?" The Lion of the Tribe of Judah, the heir to David's throne, was worthy. He stepped forth and was counted worthy to open the scroll. John then saw a "Lamb that had been slain," which is Jesus, the glorified Christ.

> He stepped forward and took the scroll from the right hand of the one sitting on the throne. And when he took the scroll, the four living beings and the twenty-four elders fell down before the Lamb. **Each one had a harp, and they held gold bowls filled with incense, which are the prayers of God's people.** (Revelation 5:7-8, NLT)

When the Lamb stepped forth, the twenty-four elders around the throne worshipped Him. They each had a harp and a gold bowl filled with incense, which are the prayers of the saints. A harp is a musical instrument, and incense represents prayer. The above scripture paints a picture of heaven's worship service, and music is used to help combine worship and prayer. I find that when something that is practiced in heaven is practiced on earth as well, then heaven invades earth. Earth, meaning our bodies, because we are made from earth, and we globally affect the planet Earth we live on.

In Revelation 8, we read how worship and prayer created a fragrant burning incense that pleased God. The smell reached God's nostrils, and He was so pleased with the passionate worship, prayer, and communion of His people that He responded by sending His fiery presence. We described this in much detail in the previous chapter when we discussed human passion and desire. The major point here is that music helps you worship and pray, and these work in unison to bring the presence of God.

Years ago, I had an experience that helped me put the pieces of the puzzle about music, worship, and prayer together. In our fellowship, after each Friday night service, we had an all-night prayer meeting. We would do this periodically, and that led to a history of a very strong prayer emphasis in the church.

To give you some context, work weeks were very long for me personally, and at the end of the work week, we had our Friday night service that lasted two hours, and then we had our all-night prayer meeting. At the all-night prayer meeting, each leader in the fellowship took a half-hour slot and led a specific prayer topic. My topic was repentance. I was supposed to bring this up at about midnight.

There were about a hundred people at the meeting. We started out in fervent prayer, but it was apparent after the first hour that we were running out of steam. Prayer seemed like breaking rocks; we had no unction to function, partly because we were tired, and partly because there was no presence. We can produce great biblical topics for prayer and pray through all the wonderful prayers in the Bible, but without the presence, anointing, and leading of the Holy Spirit, prayer can feel like breaking rocks. Have you ever tried to break rocks using a sledgehammer? If you did, you would know how hard it is.

It was getting close to midnight, and my time to lead on the topic of "repentance" was approaching. The topic was definitely not a recipe for inspiration and enthusiasm at that point. So I went to the leader of the prayer meeting and asked if we could have someone come up and play worship music. He agreed.

Then I went to the front of the congregation and told the people that the topic for the next half hour was "repentance," and that we were going to worship God as the musicians played. I told them that once we got into worship, we would start experiencing the presence of God. I told them not to start digging up things religiously to repent for—things like not praying, or Christian compromise, or not going to church. Those things may be true, but I refer to them as mechanical repentance, and that kind of repentance rarely leads to change without God's anointing, voice, and presence bringing it to our attention. Instead, I told the people to ask God if there was anything He wanted to bring to their attention that they needed to repent for, and to give them the grace to repent for it and change from it. I also said that if God does not show them anything, they should not do the religious digging but continue to worship Him.

We started out worshipping, and after a few minutes the atmosphere started to change. It changed from breaking rocks and tiredness to a refreshing and revitalizing river of living water springing up and flowing out of us. People began engaging with God, and passion was flowing from their lips. It was as if we got the infusion of glory from heaven stuck into our arms with heavenly electrolytes. People kept praying, repenting, and they also began praying for one another.

What made the difference? We were worshipping with the assistance of music. As stated before, worship is the highest form of prayer because it demonstrates humility and meekness. This act or form puts us in a place where we can interact with God, hear His voice, and experience His Word and presence together.

Now, how do we experience this in our personal time with God? Rather than starting prayer with supplication, start prayer with worship. Well, how do we do that? The easiest way is to play worship music and start engaging and signing along or reading scriptures that describe worshipping God with music—take the substance of what is being said and make it your own. Read the psalms that express God's greatness and those centered around worshipping Him, and make them your own.

I like reading 2 Chronicles; the people were worshipping God, dedicating His Temple, and meditating on Him. I enjoy envisioning myself as part of that group of worshippers.

Sometimes I read Revelation 5 and imagine the worship scene in heaven, and I begin to worship God in the same way by calling out His holiness.

Sometimes I sing and ask for inspiration as Paul wrote, "*Speaking to one another in psalms and hymns and spiritual songs.*" (Ephesians 5:19)

I like listening to other people pray and worship. I like listening to their passion, desire, and words, and letting that inspire me. You can catch the flame, inspiration, and passion from those around you.

There was a pastor in our fellowship who had been in the ministry for a long time—an older gentleman called Pastor Ben. A group of us would meet with him for prayer on Wednesday nights. Pastor Ben would worship God and then start praying. He would say, "Oh, God," with such passion and emotion. It brought such an atmosphere to the prayer meeting. I made sure I always sat next to him. If there was no room next to him, I would ask the others to kindly move over so I could sit next to him.

> *Father, give us grace to catch the fire of worship and prayer. Draw us into Your presence and help us worship You in spirit and truth. Amen.*

## God Desires Worship

In the earlier sections of this book, we discussed man seeking and desiring God and how that attracts God. In this chapter, let us discuss how worship fits into this equation. If there is one thing I can point to that is core to experiencing God, it is learning how to worship Him and partaking in worshipping Him.

Why did God send Moses to deliver the children of Israel from the enslavement that was happening in Egypt? Was it to answer their prayers? Was it to fulfill His covenant with Abraham? Both are reasonable explanations. God would have delivered the children of Israel because they were His firstborn and His covenant children of Abraham. But the real reason He wanted to deliver them is so they could go into the wilderness and worship Him. God telling Moses this reason and asking him to announce it to Pharoah is recorded in Exodus 7:16:

> Then announce to him (Pharoah), 'The LORD, the God of the Hebrews, has sent me to tell you, "Let my people go, so they **can worship me in the wilderness**." (NLT)

Each time Moses went to Pharaoh to announce a plague, the first thing he told Pharoah was what God said, *"Let my people go, so they* ***can worship me in the wilderness.*** *"* This is recorded about seven times in the scriptures. It is clear that the reason God delivered the children of Israel was because He wanted them to go to the wilderness and worship Him.

Why does God want us to worship Him? Is it because He is insecure and needs someone to tell Him how great He is so He can feel superior and be God? Is God a controlling dictator who needs the people under Him to worship Him so He can feel in control? These are all reasonable questions, but the answer is NO!

God wants us to worship Him so He can reveal Himself to us. Worship is a direct manifestation of our passion and desire for God. There is something about worship that allows us to get beyond our weaknesses and frailties and focus on Him. When we get to that space, God then reveals Himself to us. That revelation allows us to see and understand who He is to us and who we are to Him. This cycle produces a continuous flow of love and affection between us and Him, and that drives us to worship Him more and more. This is how we go from glory to glory.

Imagine the living creatures around the throne as described in Revelation 4; each had six wings and eyes within and all around. Now, recall Jesus praying that we would have eyes to see and ears to hear. This representation in Revelation 4 is the perfection of spiritual insight. Once these creatures saw something about God, they immediately cried, "Holy, Holy, Holy." God was not making them do that. They kept doing it because they were completely captured by God's beauty.

"Holy" means transcendent in measurement; nothing can compare or measure up. If we could measure love, wisdom, kindness, mercy, justice, or patience, and compare them to God's love, wisdom, kindness, mercy, justice, or patience, we would find nothing even close to God's generosity toward us in all these categories. His capacity is beyond human measure. Imagine this: in each moment of eternity, the living creatures saw something new about God, and they cried, "Holy." Then the next moment, they would see something else new to them, and guess what they would say, "That is even holier." And the next thing, and so on. Their worship was a constant divine interaction that led to more worship, appreciation, and love for the Creator.

When the children of Israel reached Mount Sinai after their deliverance from Egypt, God called Moses up the mountain and gave him an offer, and told him to announce it to the children of Israel.

> Then Moses climbed the mountain to appear before God. The LORD called to him from the mountain and said, "Give these instructions to the family of Jacob; announce it to the descendants of Israel: 'You have seen what I did to the Egyptians. **You know how I carried you on eagles' wings and brought you to myself. Now if you will obey me and keep my covenant, you will be my own special treasure from among all the peoples on earth; for all the earth belongs to me. And you will be my kingdom of priests, my holy nation.' This is the message you must give to the people of Israel."** So Moses returned from the mountain and called together the elders of the people and told them everything the LORD had commanded him. **And all the people responded together, "We will do everything the LORD has commanded." So Moses brought the people's answer back to the LORD.** (Exodus 19:3-8)

The children of Israel were the children of a covenant that God had made with Abraham. God considered them His firstborn. This points to birthright though, and not to voluntary love and affection. God wanted to take His relationship with the children of Israel to another level—a place of voluntary submission, love, and affection that comes from a human passion to worship a holy God who is devoted to them.

When the children of Israel accepted God's offer, they had no idea what was going to happen. The God of Israel was coming down to visit them at Mount Sinai. God told them to prepare themselves before He could visit them. Then, on the third day, as we read in Deuteronomy 4, Moses led the children of Israel to the base of Mount Sinai, and the fire on the mountain, which was the presence of God, burned to the very heart of heaven. At first glance, it may have looked like God was trying to scare them. But no. God had given them an offer of betrothal, and the children of Israel accepted it. God was coming to meet His bride. The term "heart of heaven" does not just mean the middle of heaven or the center of heaven; it means the center of passion and emotion. The center of heaven is the center of God's heart. The mountain burned and quaked because God was excited to meet His beloved bride. Remember, as we stated in previous chapters, the fuel to God's fire is His love. When we worship God with a voluntary heart of submission to Him, He will reveal Himself to us.

Unfortunately, the children of Israel were afraid of the fire and quaking, so they told Moses to hear God for them, and they would obey what God wanted them to do. But that did not work out because what God wanted to do in them never got into their heart. So, sadly, that generation was not able to receive what God intended for them to have. We all need to worship God for ourselves and receive our own revelation. We need to acquire our own fire and not just be satisfied with the fire of others.

> *Lord, light the fire of our heart with passion for You, and reveal Yourself to us. Let the fire of heaven burn bright in our heart as we worship and seek You. Amen.*

## God Seeks Those Who Will Worship Him in Spirit and Truth

Let us continue down the path of God wanting us to worship Him so He can reveal Himself to us. In the New Testament, Jesus took His relationship with us to a whole new level through a new covenant.

There are two narratives in the New Testament where Jesus said that God seeks after something specific. The first is recorded in Luke 19 in His interaction with Zacchaeus. Zacchaeus was a rich chief tax collector in the region of Jericho. He was very short in stature. The Jews classified him as a notorious sinner. When Jesus had come to Jericho, a large crowd gathered around Him. Zacchaeus, desiring to see Jesus, ran ahead of Him and climbed a tree that was along the path Jesus took and was going to pass by. As Jesus came by the tree where Zacchaeus was, He stopped and looked up at Zacchaeus, called him out by name, and asked if He could have dinner at his house. Jesus did not know Zacchaeus prior to this meeting. This was God seeking out the lost by supernaturally stopping and calling out Zacchaeus's name. Zacchaeus responded to Jesus's invitation, had Him over at his house for dinner, and in response, he committed to change from his sinful ways. Jesus taught us that God comes to seek and save the lost, and Zacchaeus's story is a perfect example.

The second narrative of Jesus saying that God comes to seek and save the lost is recorded in John 4 where Jesus met the Samaritan woman at the well. This is one of my favorite stories. It is amazingly perfect how Jesus interacted with her, engaged her, revealed Himself to her, and then radically affected her and that whole Samaritan town. Here is the situation: Jesus arrived in Samaria. It was not common for Jews to go to Samaria; they would instead walk around Samaria because it was considered much like a gentile world. Samaria was home to a well of one of the Jewish patriarchs—Jacob. Jesus and the disciples were on a long walk, and Jesus was tired. It was around noon, and the place was getting hotter. He and His disciples grew hungry. So the disciples left Him at the well and went into the town to get food.

While Jesus was waiting, a Samaritan woman approached the well to draw water. When Jesus saw the Samaritan woman, He asked her to draw out water for Him to drink. She was taken back since He was a Jew, and Jews did not talk or interact with Samaritans. Samaritans were considered half-breed Jews and were looked down upon by the Jews. And she was a woman; women were considered very low in the social order at that time. Lastly, she was an outcast among the people. Why else would she be going to the well alone at midday?

It was unusual for someone to draw water at midday. Carrying heavy containers of water in the midday sun is not the most pleasurable thing to do. Most people went early in the morning to draw water because it was much cooler then. This Samaritan woman had five husbands, and the one she was living with then was not her husband. So she was considered an outcast in society—a loose woman. She chose to go to the well at noon so she would not have to hear the verbal abuse of the other women for her lifestyle, faults, and moral failings. She was insignificant to everyone based on societal norms, except to God.

When Jesus asked her for a drink, she responded in a very surprised manner. She asked Him why He, being a Jewish man, would ask a Samaritan woman for something. Then Jesus replied to get her attention and to see if she would respond to a personal offer from God to experience something more.

> The woman was surprised, for Jews refuse to have anything to do with Samaritans. She said to Jesus, "You are a Jew, and I am a Samaritan woman. Why are you asking me for a drink?" Jesus replied, **"If you only knew the gift God has for you and who you are speaking to, you would ask me, and I would give you living water."** (John 4:9, NLT)

Reading this scripture, one cannot help but ask this question: How do you go from asking the woman for a drink of water to responding to her question by saying, ***"If you only knew the gift God has for you and who you are speaking to, you would ask me, and I would give you living water?"*** By the way, she had to wonder: *What the heck is living water? So, I would never have to go back to the well again?* She must have thought, *Okay, so here is a well, and to draw water from it, you need a bucket or vessel. This guy has nothing with Him. So how does He plan to draw out the living water? He must be another arrogant Jew* *thinking He is better than us and is making fun of me. He may say that the well is not as good as the wells the Jews have in Israel.* She verbalized her thoughts as a reply to Jesus, saying, "*Do you really think that you are greater than our ancestor Jacob who dug this well and drank from it himself, along with his children and livestock?*" (John 4:12, TPT)

Now since Jesus had her interest, He replied radically, knowing it would get her attention. He told her that He was ready to give her a drink of water that would keep her from thirsting again, and that it would spring in her everlasting life. Well, who would not want that water, especially if she did not have to go at midday and carry heavy jugs of water back to her house? She respectfully asked Jesus for it!

As the conversation progressed, Jesus totally changed the subject. She asked for this living water, and Jesus asked her to go and bring her husband. Why was Jesus asking for her husband? Was she not worthy to receive this water because she is a woman? No, not at all.

Jesus's question was a test to see if she was serious about really wanting the water. It was the test of "truth." Jesus met her at the heart of her greatest pain and wanted to see if she was going to tell the truth. She was living with a man but was not married to him. That was a source of pain for her; it was why she was ostracized and considered an outcast, and why she was going to the well at midday when no one else was going there. She was looked down upon for many reasons. She was a Samaritan, a woman, and a loose woman. She was not only rejected by the Jews but also by the Samaritans for her lifestyle and decisions.

She told Jesus the truth that she had no husband. Jesus commended her for telling the truth and then prophetically narrated her past.

> You have correctly said, "I have no husband"; for you have had five husbands, and the one whom you now have is not your husband; this you have said truly. (John 4:17-18)

When I read this, I wondered why Jesus went from talking about a drink of water from the well to living water, and then to asking her to get her husband. The conversation was just getting good, and then Jesus changed the subject. I have learned that when the Lord asks a question, there is always a good reason. Jesus's question to the Samaritan woman was a test. He wanted to see if she would tell the truth and not hide her past, no matter how much it embarrassed her or hurt her. She passed the test with an honest and good heart. From then on, she was released to experience her calling and future.

Jesus saw into her heart and knew that she was broken, and He recognized her desire to love and worship God. The woman realized that Jesus was more than just a common Jew asking for water. She went on to ask Him the questions that were at the heart of the rift between the Jews and the Samaritans. *Where should we worship God? Who are the true worshippers? Who are the people chosen to worship God?* These questions demonstrated her hunger and desire for God.

Jesus answered her, saying that salvation came through the Jews because Jesus had come through a Jewish lineage, and God had chosen the Jews for that purpose. But God is Spirit, and He seeks after ALL who are willing to worship Him in spirit and truth. He is seeking us. He is zealous for us and is craving for all who are willing to open their heart to Him, be honest and truthful with Him, and worship Him. Jesus's original request to the woman was for a drink because He was thirsty. He not only thirsted for water in His humanness, but being God in the flesh, He thirsted for fellowship and communion with His people. God thirsts for us more than we can ever thirst for Him.

The Samaritan woman demonstrated a thirst for God. She did not run away with her shame, guilt, and fear after being confronted with her weaknesses; instead, she was willing to stay and linger in the presence of God. She asked Jesus about the Messiah, and He plainly told her that He was the Messiah. Nowhere else in the New Testament was Jesus that plain and direct with someone about who He is. This is powerful! The Samaritan woman worshipped God in spirit and truth, and Jesus revealed Himself to her.

It is one thing to want to worship God, but it is another thing to start interacting with Him. That is when you realize that all things are open, naked, and bare before Him. Will you run away in fear, shame, guilt, and pain, or just because you think it is too hard for you? God is a consuming fire, so His nature is to consume anything that keeps Him from us. He does not expose us to hurt us but to transform us so we can know who He is and what He has made us to be.

This is what happened to the Israelites at Mount Sinai, as we discussed earlier. They were overcome with fear; they feared that when they came into the presence of God, they would be exposed, and God would kill them as punishment for their sins. They did not know the heart of a compassionate God who just wanted them to worship in truth.

Jesus took a woman of insignificance and made her significant. He took a woman of no influence and made her a woman of influence. She influenced her town for Jesus. How? By showing that she worshipped God in spirit and truth. God sought her out, healed her, and made her an evangelist.

Let us explore deeper what it means to worship God in spirit and truth. What does it mean to worship God in spirit? The only other place a reference is made to worshipping God in spirit is Paul's letter to the Philippians. In this letter, Paul talks about people who preach out of selfish ambition, and in chapter 3 verse 3, he talks about people who are requiring others to live under the circumcision and the law. By doing this, they were putting confidence in the flesh and not in the work of God through the cross of Christ. Worshipping God in spirit has several elements. First, it shows a dependence on God and not our own works. Second, it is a place of complete openness to God and a willingness to be exposed before Him, giving Him access to the depths of our heart. Jesus is always knocking at the door of our heart. It is up to us to open that door and let Him in. Sometimes we think this is a one-time choice to invite Him to be our Lord and Savior. But no! From what we read in Revelation 3; Jesus is asking the church to let Him in. It is not just a one-time experience; it is a lifestyle of allowing God to have access to our heart with its passions and emotions. It is the place where all things are birthed within our innermost being.

Coming back to the Samaritan woman at the well, we see that she opened her heart to Jesus in the conversation. She was willing to expose her innermost being and the hurts of her heart to the Lord. She did not whitewash her past; she knew who she was.

So the question: What is the truth? The conversation Jesus had with Pontius Pilate lives on even today. Jesus told Pilate that He was a King and that He had come to testify of the truth. Pilate asked, "What is the truth?" The truth that Jesus was talking about is not truth corrupted by our selfish ambition and desire to get what we think is best for us. The truth that Jesus, the Christ, was talking about is exposing the thoughts and intents of the human heart that He discerns. Truth is examined under the light of God's presence and deemed good and not evil. It does not hide from right and wrong. It does not make excuses for human frailty but admits shortcomings and faults, and accepts responsibility for the ramifications of our actions. It does not point to the faults and frailties themselves or blame others for their actions. It encapsulates humility because humility accepts the truth about us and God.

That is what the woman at the well did. She did not run from who she was or what she had done. The Lord has His way of touching the deepest hurts and wounds in our heart. It feels like having a broken rib and someone jabs you right there. I remember breaking a rib playing football in high school, and the doctor came in and showed me the X-ray. He then showed me where it was on my rib cage by poking me right on that spot and saying, "It should hurt right there." I jerked in pain and thought to myself, "Really! Did you have to do that?" The only thing worse was a sneeze coming on!

Jesus does not poke us to hurt us. He pokes us to help us—to show us the way to healing and then heal us. He exposes the thoughts and intents of our heart, shows us the results of them, and then leads us to the throne of grace. He does not reject us; He helps us. He brings us to Himself so we can receive His mercy. He keeps us from what we really deserve. Then He points us to His grace, and His grace changes us and gives us the good things we do not deserve.

God gives grace to the humble. God's grace is more than unmerited favor; it is His willingness to use His ability and power on our behalf to do for us what we cannot do for ourselves.

The woman at the well, received grace. She received living water so she would not thirst anymore. She received the real Bridegroom—all because she worshipped God in spirit and truth. She changed, and then she changed the world around her.

> *Lord, we desire to worship You in spirit and truth. We open our heart to You and invite You into the deepest parts of our heart. Give us revelation and understanding of how we can worship You in spirit and truth. Take us from the shame and insignificance of our past, to the future of our significance in Christ. Amen.*

## Worship and Eternal Life

Jesus told the woman at the well that living water would spring up in her as a well of everlasting life. So what is this everlasting life or eternal life? I ask this question when I teach, and I am always amazed at the answers I get from Christians in church. They usually say that eternal life means to live forever. Our spirit will live forever after we pass away from this earth physically. Eternal life is not about quantity, it is about divine quality.

Jesus taught us what eternal life is in His wonderful High Priestly Prayer, as recorded in John 17:3:

> **This is eternal life**, that they may know You, the only true God, and Jesus Christ whom You have sent.
>
> **And this is the way to have eternal life**—to know you, the only true God, and Jesus Christ, the one you sent to earth. (NLT)

> **And this is the real and eternal life: That they know you**, the one and only true God, and Jesus Christ, whom you sent. (MSG)

There are a few things to point out here: the verb "is" appears in the present tense. "Is" implies the time as now. Eternal life comes through knowing God the Father and His Son, Jesus Christ. Eternal life comes through personally revealed knowledge of God. The more we experience God for ourselves, the more that well springs up within us and satisfies our true thirst to know Him.

If we put two and two together here, we conclude that worship leads to God revealing Himself to us. That revelation brings the living water, and the living water results in us experiencing the abundant eternal life that Jesus came to give all of us. This is the New Testament form of what we discussed in the previous chapter: why God wanted to deliver the children of Israel. He delivered them so they could worship Him, and He could reveal Himself to them so they could receive the precursor to what would come through the cross of Christ.

Worship brings an intimate time of interaction with God so He can reveal Himself to us. It leads us to a place of intimacy with God.

To know God personally means to gain knowledge about Him, understand who He is, and be known by Him. Just as we learn about a person by spending time with them, we can know God personally and intimately by spending time with Him. God wants us to worship Him so He can reveal Himself to us.

If we look at all the people in the Bible who had an intimate knowledge of God and a revelation of Him, there is a common thread of personal prayer and worship. I would say they all had this one-thing mindset that David writes about in Psalm 27:

> One thing I have asked from the Lord, that I shall seek: That I may dwell in the house of the Lord all the days of my life, to behold the beauty of the Lord and to meditate in His temple. (Psalm 27:4)

When you behold Him, you cannot but worship Him, and then the revelation happens. The best example of this process is the narrative of Moses at Mount Sinai. Moses spent forty days and forty nights in God's presence, not once, but twice. The first time, his time with God was interrupted when the Israelites sinned by making a golden calf and worshipping it. Moses had to leave the presence of God, go down the mountain, and clean up the mess that the Israelites had created. Being in the presence of God was a continual habit for Moses.

The story starts in Exodus 24 as Moses and the priests and elders of Israel came to the mountain to worship God. Aaron, Nadab, Abihu, and the seventy elders of Israel worshipped from a distance, while Moses approached the cloud of glory.

> Then Moses went up with Aaron, Nadab and Abihu, and seventy of the elders of Israel, and they saw the God of Israel; and under His feet there appeared to be a pavement of sapphire, as clear as the sky itself. Yet He did not stretch out His hand against the nobles. (Exodus 24:9-11)

After this, God called Moses to come up the mountain and remain with Him. Moses went up the mountain, and God covered the mountain with a cloud of glory. The glory of the Lord dwelt on the mountain. Israel, watching the cloud from a distance, said that it looked as if a consuming fire was on the mountain. The cloud rested on the mountain for six days.

Imagine watching a cloud for six days. What would Moses have thought during those six days? He was there for six days as the glory of God fell around him as a consuming fire. What were he and God doing? Most of us have a hard time sitting still for even a few minutes. What Moses was doing was beholding God. He was beholding the beauty of the Lord. He was beholding God's glory and His holiness. Like the living creatures around the throne, Moses beheld God and saw something about His character and nature that could only be described as holy.

This type of communion and interaction transforms us. It is why the living creatures continually cry, "Holy," and the elders continually throw their crowns before Him and worship Him. They have a revelation of who God is and can do nothing but worship Him. The more they worship Him, the more they see of Him. They are going from glory to glory.

For six days, Moses beheld the glory of God. That may sound like a long time, but for Moses, it went by like a few seconds. When you see God clearly, all aspects of time fade away. Moses beheld God, and God beheld Moses. It was a two-way relationship. Moses enjoyed God, and God enjoyed Moses. At the end of the six days, God spoke to Moses. When we start to behold God and have that similar intimate interaction with Him, God starts a heavenly heart surgery in us that we may not even be aware of. Paul writes in 2 Corinthians 3:15-18 (NLT):

> Yes, even today when they read Moses' writings, their hearts are covered with that veil, and they do not understand. But whenever someone turns to the Lord, the veil is taken away. For the Lord is the Spirit, and wherever the Spirit of the Lord is, there is freedom. So all of us who have had that veil removed can see and reflect the glory of the Lord. And the Lord—who is the Spirit—makes us more and more like him as we are changed into his glorious image.

When we turn to the Lord, the veil and covering of our heart is removed, and transformation begins. Beholding Him opens our heart to Him and brings us to a place of spiritual nakedness and openness before Him.

One subject that is not clearly understood or discussed much, or rightly discerned, is the subject of the heart. I do not mean the physical heart but the spiritual heart. We are all triune beings—we each have a spirit, a soul, and a body. Your spirit is the real you—your essence. It has multiple related essences, as does the soul. The heart is the part of the spirit that communicates with the soul. It is the joining place of the spirit and the soul.

Let us take a look at the parable of the Sower from Matthew 13:1-23, Mark 4:1-20, and Luke 8:4-15. The seeds that the Sower sowed signify the Word of God. The ground (or soil) signifies the heart of man. The devil comes to steal the Word of God out of man's heart. The heart is the source of man's passion. Passion fuels emotion. Emotion fueled by passion, combined with faith and love for God, can be one of the most powerful forces in the world.

The presence of God softens the soil of our heart. It prepares and tills the soil for the seeds—the Word of God—to be planted.

Here is a pattern of prayer that I think can be helpful for us: For six days, Moses beheld God. As he beheld God, something happened in his heart. The more we behold God, the more our heart softens and opens to Him and His deep love for us. And then, God begins to speak to us. As we hear Him, our heart begins to receive His words. This is why, for six days, Moses beheld God before God spoke to him on the seventh day.

By the seventh day, Moses's heart was prepared for God to write on it. The Old Testament refers to the heart of man as stone because man was spiritually dead, but God showed man that He can write on stone. That is why the ten commandments were written on stone. The stones were a representation of the heart of man. God promised, as part of the new covenant, that He would give man a new spirit and a new heart, and take that heart of stone and make it a heart of flesh.

New birth brings forth a new spirit in the image and likeness of God. And when that happens, the heart is no longer stone; it is a heart of flesh. The heart becomes softer and more receptive and responsive to God. When we behold God, worship Him, and interact with Him, our heart is prepared to receive His Word. It is like tilling the soil, turning it over, and preparing it before planting a garden. The more the soil is prepared, the easier it is for the seeds to germinate, grow up, and bear fruit.

After six days, God spoke to Moses. On the seventh day, Moses's heart was in a place to receive God's Word and for it to take root. When the Word of God, which is God Himself, speaks, He brings revelation. Revelation brings a deeper knowledge of God. This knowledge springs within us wells of everlasting water. Everlasting water brings the experience of eternal life now and forever. This is the God-type of life—the abundant life that Jesus meant when He said, "*I came that they may have life, and have it abundantly.*" (John 10:10)

I have put this principle to the test. Most of the revelations I teach today come directly from my times of worship and prayer with God. I could be in a time of meditation and prayer, enjoying the presence of God, and all of a sudden, a picture would form in my mind and God would start talking to me about it. Then, things I have read in His Word and experienced in Him would start coming together in ways I never imagined. It is like an unseen hand putting all the pieces of the puzzle together.

## Worship—The Highest Form of Prayer

Prayer is a concept or action the seems to be limited to the believer while on earth. Since we live in a different realm than God, He has given us prayer to commune and communicate with Him. Once we leave our body and go to be with the Lord, we do not see the concept of prayer in the Scriptures. We see a direct communication with God. But whether in heaven or on earth, we do see the action of worship going on. Worship in heaven must be the most fulfilling thing in our existence. But while on earth, I would still classify worship as prayer because we are communicating with God. Now this leads to the subject that, while on earth, worship is the highest form of prayer.

Over the past several years, I have repeatedly emphasized that worship is the highest form of prayer. That thought just keeps coming back to me when I talk about worship. I know this is inspired by God, but I have never really given much thought to it. One day, as I was in prayer, I started thinking about it. In the end, I realized it is very simple but profound, and it fits into a biblical theme of understanding, communing, and interacting with God.

My first thought with that statement is that if I could measure to determine the best form of prayer, it would be worship. If I had to rate the forms of prayer on a scale from 1-10, worship would be a ten. In that case, why not always worship? Would that be the best way to go for my spirituality and my life?

I came to realize that worship is not the highest form in a rating system, but it is the highest form of prayer that allows me to experience God from my position as a believer in Christ. Scripture tells us that we are raised up and seated with Christ in heavenly places:

> I also pray that you will understand the incredible greatness of God's power for us who believe him. This is the same mighty power that **raised Christ from the dead and seated him in the place of honor at God's right hand in the heavenly realms...**But God is so rich in mercy, and he loved us so much, that even though we were dead because of our sins, he gave us life when he raised Christ from the dead. (It is only by God's grace that you have been saved!) **For he raised us from the dead along with Christ and seated us with him in the heavenly realms because we are united with Christ Jesus.** (Ephesians 1:19-20; 2:4-6, NLT)

The theme of many of Paul's letters is what Jesus, as the Christ, accomplished for us through the work of the cross. Jesus was crucified, died, buried, quickened, made alive, raised, and then seated with the Father in the heavenlies. In his writing, Paul emphasized that through faith in Jesus, the Christ, we will receive the same. I encourage you to spend some time reading the following portions of Scripture: Romans 6:1-12, Ephesians 1:19–2:1-12, Colossians 2:11-13, Colossians 3:1-14, and Galatians 2:19-20.

By faith in Christ, and because of all the things that Jesus did through identification of the cross, we are in Him. God considers and treats us the same as His Son, Jesus Christ. The English translation of the New

Testament states this in the past tense, but the Greek language calls this the aorist tense. The English translation does not articulate exactly as the Greek language, but it means that it has been done in the past, present, and future. We are in Him forever, sealed by the work of the cross.

Jesus was fully man and fully God. He was the manifestation of God dwelling in Him, and He in God. The same can be said of us. We are in God, and He is in us. We must allow God to dwell in us so we can experience Him from the position and place of being seated in the heavenlies and be acknowledged by Him.

God dwelling in you is present tense. There is another half of the equation here: you dwelling in Him, present tense. When Paul writes about Christ dwelling in us, he always uses the present tense. The present tense is our part. Paul says in Ephesians 1:22-23 that we are being built into a dwelling place for God. In Ephesians 3:16-17, he prays that we will be strengthened with power through His Spirit, in our inner being, so that Christ may dwell in our heart. In Colossians 1:27, Paul talks about Christ in us the hope of glory. The New Testament has plenty of references about Christ dwelling in us. Jesus's discussions in John 14, 15, and 16 were all about abiding and dwelling in Him. He said that in His Father's house are many dwelling places. It is unfortunate that the King James Version translated the term "abiding place" as "mansions." The exact translation is "abiding places." Jesus did not mean physical mansions in heaven, but spiritual temples, and a dwelling place for God in us now and Christ in us now. In John 15:4, Jesus says:

> "Abide in me and I in you."

I like to call this the duality of existence: God in you, and you in Him. When we learn this, we learn to pray from our position and calling. Paul writes a prayer to the church at Thessalonica. Read this text carefully:

> To this end also we pray for you always, that our God will count you worthy of your calling, and fulfill every

> desire for goodness and the work of faith with power, so that the name of our Lord **Jesus will be glorified in you, and you in Him**, according to the grace of our God and the Lord Jesus Christ. (2 Thessalonians 1:11-12)

Paul is praying for the reality of Jesus being glorified in each of us and each of us being glorified in Him—the duality of existence.

How does worship help us experience God from our position and calling? Jesus said that God seeks after those who will worship Him in spirit and truth. That is why it is vital for us to understand the importance of worship being a form of prayer—the highest form of it. Here are some thoughts that should bring this together. First, worship expresses a reverence for who God is and how holy He is. That immediately puts God in a place of highest importance to us.

Worship expresses and feeds into a desire and passion for God. It helps us shed any inhibition about expressing our intimate desire for Him. The more we experience Him in worship, the more we express our desire and passion for Him and, in turn, we receive the same from Him. That is His desire for us, and it will always outshine and transcend our desire for Him.

Worship leads us to a place of realization that there is something greater than self and selfish desire. Selfishness and being self-absorbed will always lead in directions opposite the ways of God. Self-seeking will always lead to all kinds of evil, strife, and derision. It is a cancer that will lead to darkness, death, and destruction.

Worship demonstrates a voluntary submission to God. It shows an understanding that God's ways are better than ours, and it brings us to a place of submitting to His will. That is what Jesus taught us in the Lord's Prayer—to first hallow and reverence His name is to worship. Second, He taught us to ask for His kingdom to come and His will to be done on earth as it is in heaven. I see this in a different light than what I have heard. Since Jesus said the kingdom of God is within us, and we are made from earth, I pray for God's kingdom and His will to be done in "this earth," which is my body, as it is in heaven. This is a perfect example of how worship leads to voluntary submission to God. It is a prayer of committal of your will and your body to Him. It is presenting your body as a living sacrifice to God so He can work through you. Paul says that we are to offer every part of ourselves to God as an instrument of righteousness for God's glory.

> But present yourselves to God as those alive from the dead, and your members as **instruments of righteousness** to God. (Romans 6:13)

The last and most important characteristic that worship brings out in us is humility! Humility demonstrates submission to God. Humility is when we voluntarily become entirely dependent on Him. It is when we exhibit unwavering faith in God by responding to His loving grace. We come to a point where we begin to realize that this grace makes God worthy of our submission to Him and our dependence on Him.

Humility is when we learn what the truth is, and we voluntarily submit to that truth which comes from God alone. We do not argue with God about what is truth, but whether we understand it or not, we know that He is right. Humility is when our human pride is exposed, and we understand that pride is a satisfactory cause of every human fault and weakness.

There are many discussions in the Bible about the concept of humility. One that stands out to me is if you humble yourself, you shall be exalted, but if you exalt yourself, you shall be humbled. Let us start with Jesus. In Luke 14, we read that while Jesus was at a Pharisee's house for dinner, He gave some advice to all those who were there. He noticed that everyone was trying to sit at the place of highest honor at the dinner table. So He told them to sit at the lowest place instead, and to let the host of the feast move them to a higher place of honor. He goes on to say:

> For those who **exalt themselves will be humbled**, and those who **humble themselves will be exalted**. (Luke 14:11, NLT)

I know no higher place than God's presence—to dwell with Him and be seated with Him in heavenly places.

Let us take a look at a couple of other examples from the Gospels. In Matthew 18, we read that the disciples started to argue about who would be the greatest in God's kingdom or who will have the highest rank. The seeds for this argument were sown a little earlier in Matthew 16 when Jesus told the disciples they were going to be leaders in His kingdom with authority to rule. It immediately went to their heads.

There were three arguments on this topic as recorded in the Gospels. Matthew 18 was the first. The second was when John and James came with their mother who asked Jesus if her sons could have the highest position by sitting at His right and left hand in His kingdom. And the third was at the last supper.

Jesus's response to this argument in Matthew 18:3-4 (NLT) was:

> I tell you the truth, **unless you turn from your sins and become like little children, you will never get into the Kingdom of Heaven**. So anyone who becomes as humble as this little child is the greatest in the Kingdom of Heaven.

Jesus told them that unless they **humbled themselves like a child**, they would not enter His kingdom, let alone become a leader in it.

Let us hit a few spots in the epistles:

> Humble yourselves before the Lord, and he will lift you up in honor. (James 4:10, NLT)

> And all of you, dress yourselves in humility as you relate to one another, for "**God opposes the proud but gives grace to the humble**." So humble yourselves under the mighty power of God, and at the right time he will lift you up in honor. (1 Peter 5:5-6, NLT)

In the above verses, both James and Peter repeat the same thing. Peter adds that God opposes the proud. The word "oppose" has a very strong meaning; it means to stand resolutely against. You are not in a good place if God is standing against you.

Isaiah wrote about dwelling and abiding with God. The two most revealing statements he made are in the following scriptures:

> **But to this one I will look, To him who is humble and contrite of spirit, and who trembles at My word**. (Isaiah 66:2)
>
> For thus says the high and exalted One Who lives forever, whose name is Holy "**I dwell on a high and holy place, And also with the contrite and lowly of spirit In order to revive the spirit of the lowly And to revive the heart of the contrite**. (Isaiah 57:15)

In both scriptures, we are reminded of God's regard for the humble. I love the statement in Isaiah 57 that says God inhabits eternity, and His habitation is holy, and there, He dwells in a high and holy place with the humble. I could not have said it any better. He dwells. He has His being with us on high to breathe life into us. That is the place we experience God from our position and through our relationship and communion with Him for the unity of dwelling in Him and He in us.

When you pray from your position and communion with God, prayer no longer becomes wrought and arduous. We learn to enjoy the communion and relationship, and prayer flows from that. We learn to understand what to pray for, how to pray, and where to pray.

The Bible has numerous examples of great prayers and the people who prayed them. We can easily mimic and pray all of Paul's wonderful apostolic prayers from Galatians, Ephesians, and Colossians. We can pray for those in authority. We can have supplication, thanksgiving, and intercession through our prayer. But the form of prayer that I am talking about combines all of those things; it comes to us prompted by the desires of God's heart and lives continually in His heart and mind.

## King David's Worship and Prayer

King David was known for many things. When you think of David's accomplishments, what comes to your mind first? He killed Goliath as a young man. He was one of the greatest kings of Israel. He united both Israel and Judah. He was a great warrior. He was a king, priest, and prophet. He righteously dealt with Saul when Saul was trying to kill him out of jealousy. On the other hand, David also had some faults and failings. He premeditated murder and adultery. Similarly, we too may do many good things as well as evil things. We are all mixed bags. Only God can take a mixed bag and make it righteous and holy through the work of the cross.

David was also known for his musical abilities. As he played the harp, the presence of God would come and calm Saul when he was vexed by the evil spirit preying on his insecurities and fears.

> One of the servants said to Saul, "One of Jesse's sons from Bethlehem is a talented harp player. Not only that—he is a brave warrior, a man of war, and has good judgment. He is also a fine-looking young man, and the LORD is with him. (1 Samuel 16:18, NLT)

> And whenever the tormenting spirit from God troubled Saul, David would play the harp. Then Saul would feel better, and the tormenting spirit would go away. (1 Samuel 16:23, NLT)

One day, as I was reading from 2 Samuel 23 about David's life and accomplishments, I came across the last words of David.

> These are the last words of David: "David, the son of Jesse, speaks—David, the man who was raised up so

> high, **David, the man anointed by the God of Jacob, David, the sweet psalmist of Israel.** The Spirit of the LORD speaks through me; his words are upon my tongue. The God of Israel spoke. The Rock of Israel said to me: 'The one who rules righteously, who rules in the fear of God, is like the light of morning at sunrise, like a morning without clouds, like the gleaming of the sun on new grass after rain.'" (2 Samuel 23:1-4, NLT)

David acknowledged that it was God who raised him and anointed him, and then he called himself the sweet psalmist of Israel. He did not draw attention to the fact that he was the most successful king in Israel's history, nor about his great exploits on the battlefield, nor that he was a prophet. But instead, he drew attention to his psalms and worship songs that he wrote and worshipped God with. No wonder God called David a man after His own heart. Here are some wonderful verses from the book of Psalms:

> O God, you are my God; I earnestly search for you. My soul thirsts for you; my whole body longs for you in this parched and weary land where there is no water. I have seen you in your sanctuary and gazed upon your power and glory. Your unfailing **love** is better than life itself; how I praise you! I will praise you as long as I live, lifting up my hands to you in prayer. You satisfy me more than the richest feast. I will praise you with songs of joy. (Psalm 63:1-5)

> For a day in Your courts is better than a thousand outside. I would rather stand at the threshold of the house of my God than dwell in the tents of wickedness. (Psalm 84:10)

David set up a tent to keep the ark of the covenant. In 1 Chronicles, we read how the Levites brought the ark of the covenant into Jerusalem and how David led them in dancing for joy as they brought it into the tent. David was worshipping God with dance. Then, he goes on to do something that I believe was inspired by his love and worship for God. He appointed singers and musicians to worship continually before the Lord. Their job was to worship God 24/7. There is nowhere in the law where God commands this. So why did David do this? He did it as an expression of his love and desire to worship God. Let us read this account in 1 Chronicles 16:4-6:

> David appointed the following Levites to lead the people in worship before the Ark of the LORD—to invoke his blessings, to give thanks, and to praise the LORD, the God of Israel…They played the harps and lyres. The priests, Benaiah and Jahaziel, **played the trumpets regularly before the Ark of God's Covenant.**

Later, in 1 Chronicles 16:37-38, we read:

> David arranged for Asaph **and his fellow Levites to serve regularly before the Ark of the LORD's Covenant, doing whatever needed to be done each day**. This group included Obed-Edom (son of Jeduthun), Hosah, and sixty-eight other Levites as gatekeepers.

This group of people worshipped continually before the Lord. They had continual worship going on, and David was the chief songwriter. David was the sweet psalmist of Israel, or we can say that he was the number one songwriter in all Israel. All of David's songs had to do with worship to the Lord. I like to say that David was the "Boss." Ah, why do I say that? I am just drawing an analogy to a current performer in secular society; when he goes on stage to sing and perform, people call him the "Boss" because of the musical show he puts on.

Not that David was trying to put on a show, but I imagine he would go down to the tabernacle often and worship. He would probably join in with the Levites since he was not only a king, but a priest and a prophet as well. I do not think any other king was referred to as a priest and prophet. When David joined the people in worship, they watched how the Spirit of the Lord came upon him, and in turn, he brought out his wonderful psalms of worship. David's pure worship was attractive and inviting, and I can imagine those with a similar heart watching him and joining him in worship; joining the show—the show at which God would shine forth His glory amid His worshippers.

David longed to dwell in the house of the Lord and worship Him. As he worshipped, God showed up in His beauty and glory. Then, a divine interaction took place—God and David beheld each other. They communicated with one another, and it caused a divine interaction and transformation for all the worshippers there.

David set up this array of continual worship, not because God commanded it, but because it flowed out of his love for God. Although there was worship ordained and ordered by the law, it did not command a continual 24/7 worship before the Lord. David was inspired out of his love for God in response to what God had done for him, his family, and the nation of Israel.

In 1 Chronicles 23, we read more details on how David put worship in order in the tabernacle. He appointed four thousand men to worship before the Lord with musical instruments. Later, in 1 Chronicles 25, we read that he appointed the families of Asaph, Heman, and Jeduthun to lead worship. They we responsible for proclaiming and worshipping God based on the orders of King David.

> David and the army commanders then appointed men from the families of Asaph, Heman, and Jeduthun to proclaim God's messages to the accompaniment of lyres, harps, and cymbals. Here is a list of their names and their work: From the sons of Asaph, there were Zaccur, Joseph, Nethaniah, and Asarelah. They worked under the direction of their father, Asaph, **who proclaimed God's messages by the king's orders**... All these men were under the direction of their fathers as they made music at the house of the Lord. **Their responsibilities**

> **included the playing of cymbals, harps, and lyres at the house of God. Asaph, Jeduthun, and Heman reported directly to the king. They and their families were all trained in making music before the LORD, and each of them—288 in all—was an accomplished musician. The musicians were appointed to their term of service by means of sacred lots, without regard to whether they were young or old, teacher or student.** (1 Chronicles 25:1-2, 6-8, NLT)

Each musician had an allotted time slot to worship. There were twenty-four slots. So that leads us to believe that each musician worshipped for an hour at a time, and thus, together they had continual worship before the Lord. These musicians were prophetic. As they worshipped, the Word of the Lord came forth through them, and they sang to verbalize it.

Seventy-three of the one hundred and fifty psalms are attributed to David. He was not the only psalmist who wrote the book of Psalms. There were many other psalmists in the group of men that he appointed to lead worship in the tabernacle. In most translations of the Bible, before each psalm, it mentions who the psalmist was or why the psalm was written. Here are a few from the New Living Translation:

1. For the choir director: A psalm of David
2. For the choir director: A psalm of David, to be accompanied by stringed instruments
3. For the choir director: A love song to be sung to the tune "Lilies." A psalm of the descendants of Korah (Levites – the priests)
4. A psalm of Asaph: One David appointed to lead; second most psalms written
5. A psalm of Solomon
6. A psalm of Ethan the Ezrahite
7. A prayer of Moses, the man of God
8. A song for pilgrims ascending to Jerusalem

This type of worship and prayer not only transformed the children of Israel but also had a residual effect on their nation. You may wonder how. This type of devotion was instrumental in bringing Israel and Judah together as one kingdom. It brought a continual blessing to the nation, and that prospered it. It brought justice to the people of the nation. It brought out the greatest of callings in people. If you read the Scriptures, it is not just about David being extraordinary, but you will find David boasting about his mighty men who served under Him. All those men were instrumental in expanding the great kingdom of Israel at that time.

One of the reasons I am writing so much on worship is because it is essential for our spiritual growth and communion with God. It is essential to allow us to experience God. It is essential to transform us. It is essential to help the church experience God. It is essential to enable the nation to experience revival. Worship is the doorway, pathway, and whole house to enjoying prayer.

Oh, that we would all have that desire and expression that David had. Psalms are just expressions of worship and praise to God, inspired by being in His presence and experiencing Him. Can we not all be like David? Why not? God is still the same with all the same attributes even today. In this current age, we have the new covenant and the outpouring of the Holy Spirit to live in us, not just come upon us.

Do you want to really experience God and let God become a reality to you? If so, become a worshipper of God, express your passion and desire for Him, and get ready for a lifelong journey with Him.

# Key 3:

# Prayer, His Presence, and His Word

## Passion for the Word of God

Passion for God should not end at worship. True passion for worship will lead us into worship and then directly into the presence of God so we can hear and understand His words. Passion for God, passion for worship, and passion for His Word are inseparable.

Worship will always lead to revelation. Many of the revelations that God showed me were during my personal time of prayer, worship, and meditation (reading and studying the Word of God). I cannot count the number of times God's revelatory messages rolled in and through me by the Spirit of God as I was worshipping Him. The Holy Spirt suddenly began highlighting a scripture, or He would show me a picture or a scene. He would then relate that scene to scriptures in different parts of the Bible and start putting the mystery of the Word of God into every puzzle that keeps expanding and growing. This is one of the reasons that knowing the Word and personally studying it is so important.

Proverbs 4 has one of the most outstanding instructions in the Bible. This chapter is all about a wise father (Solomon) instructing his child. Notice what Solomon, the author of Proverbs, says:

> My son, give attention to my words; **Incline your ear** to my sayings. **Do not let them depart from your sight; Keep them in the midst of your heart**. For they are life to those **who find them** And **health to all their body.** Watch over your heart with all diligence, **For from it flow the springs of life.** (Proverbs 4:20-24, NASB)

Notice the verbs that are used in this verse: attention, incline, (let them not) depart, and keep. Focus on these words and keep them in your heart as you read this chapter. The spiritual heart is the center and source of passion and emotions. It is where the spirit and soul connect. I, like Paul, say that it is the hidden man of the heart. Just as your natural heart is the key to your life on earth, your spiritual heart is the key to your spiritual life. Your natural heart pumps blood through your body, and it brings oxygen to your muscles so they can work. It brings nutrients to your body so you can stay healthy, and it cleanses the waste out of your body to maintain your body's functionality. Think about the similarity of the function of your spiritual heart—it pumps spiritual oxygen, distributes nutrients, and cleanses your soul and spirit.

"*Keep them in the midst of your heart*" means to keep the Father's words at the center of your passions. Human passion is the divine accelerant for His presence. It is expressed both in worship and in the desiring and longing for His Word. His Word starts with the Bible, but in this context, it is a personal revelation of the Bible that pumps spiritual oxygen, distributes nutrients, and has the power to cleanse us. It is not just head knowledge of the Bible, nor a theological or a historical understanding of it, nor an understanding of how the scriptures support certain doctrines, but it is the personal inbreathed revelation and understanding that we get from chewing and meditating on His words that is then inbreathed by the grace of God through the Holy Spirit.

We read earlier about the Israelites coming to Mount Horeb to meet God and the fire that was burning to the heart of heaven. The same Hebrew word for "heart" is used in both Deuteronomy and in Proverbs 4. When the passion for His Word is at the center of your heart, your attention will be fine-tuned to hear His voice that brings the Word of God alive. It is like a spiritual antenna that goes up when God begins to speak to us, and we fine-tune our spiritual frequency to hear it. We instinctively bend our ears to hear His voice, and we put His Word in front of our spiritual eyes, so we are constantly reminded of it. His Word will roll over us time and time again.

Our mind is directed to the passions of our heart, and the actions of our body follow whatever our mind is directed to. When it is our passion to keep God's Word at the center of our life, we will pay attention to it, bend our heads and ears to listen intently to it, and keep it in front of our spiritual sight. At that point, we center our life around God, rather than God around our life. He becomes the first and foremost in our thoughts and activities. That is why the first and greatest commandment is to love the Lord with all your heart, soul, mind, and strength.

When the focal point of our life becomes the Word of God, His voice becomes intimate to us. We can even recognize His voice in the midst of a noisy crowd. His voice immediately gets our attention—we listen and attend to those words, we bend our ears to hear those words, and we are drawn to the Person speaking those words. The words hit our heart and become very important to us.

When this happens, and we hear God's words, they become more than doctrines or stories to us. They become intimate revelations to us. Revelations come through intimate personal experiences, and they are the rock of stability and strength in our life. Remember what Jesus said to Peter when he made the affirmative statement that Jesus was the Christ, the Son of the living God. Jesus said, "Peter, flesh and blood did not reveal this to you, but your Father in heaven did." This revelation of who Jesus was, was the rock on which God is building each member who was and is a part of God's heavenly team. Although flesh and blood can tell you things, and Jesus was flesh and blood, it took the Father taking the Word and unraveling it in the heart and mind of Peter. Rocks are hard and very difficult to move, and that is how you will become when God's revelation lives in you. You will be moved by God and not by the weaknesses of the flesh or the fear that this world encapsulate us in.

The Sermon on the Mount in Matthew 7:13-14 reinforces what we are talking about here. First, Jesus was talking about how we have to enter through the narrow gate because the wide path and broad way leads to destruction, and many choose this path. The narrow gate, or the small or straight gate, leads to life, and few find it! It is found through the revelation of God's Word.

Just a few statements later, as a part of His Sermon on the Mount, Jesus says the following:

> **Anyone who listens to my teaching and follows it is wise, like a person who builds a house on solid rock.** Though the rain comes in torrents and the floodwaters rise and the winds beat against that house, it won't collapse because it is built on bedrock. But anyone who hears my teaching and doesn't obey it is foolish, like a person who builds a house on sand. When the rains and floods come and the winds beat against that house, it will collapse with a mighty crash. (Matthew 7:24-27)

We find the narrow gate that leads to life by listening and doing the words that Jesus spoke. He is likening this to building a foundation on a rock versus the sand. Sand will crumble during storms, but the rock of revelation will withstand the storms and anything that the gates or authority of hell can throw at it.

This revelation is life to those who find it. It denotes an effort of finding something. I know when I lose something, like my keys, I am laser focused on finding them. I open drawers and look everywhere I can to find them. We need to be like the hound dogs of heaven, sniffing out every nook and cranny until we find what we are looking for. It is a treasure hunt that never ends, because each treasure leads to another, and another, and another.

Finding the Word is finding life. Finding grace and finding life are inseparable. Finding grace is finding truth. God's Word is truth and life. Jesus said that His Word is life. In Him we find life, and His life is the light of man. Jesus said that eternal life is to know Him and to know the Father. The greatest quality of life comes from knowing Him. Knowing Him comes from communicating with Him and hearing Him.

In the next few chapters, we will talk about the sword of the Word of God coming and piercing our heart and leading us into the throne of grace to receive mercy and find grace. Then, we will learn how the Word of God brings life to those who find it. Narrow is the gate—way to life—and few find it.

> *Lord, grant us grace to hear Your Word and the courage to listen and allow Your Word to take root in our life. Help us to keep our heart constantly open to Your words so we may hide Your Word in our heart and find the way of life. Your Word is a lamp to our feet and a light to the path of eternal and abundant life.*

## Passion and Desire for the Word of God

For prayer to be productive and enjoyable, you need to experience confidence and effectiveness in prayer. Being effective in prayer is not about the time you spend at it but how much you know and understand the Person you are praying to and communicating with. Talking to someone you do not know and do not understand will not lead to the desire to communicate with them. Instead, it will lead to frustration and separation from them. Prayer becomes effective and enjoyable when you have confidence in knowing God, knowledge of who He is, and the experience of intimately communicating with Him.

John talks about this in his epistle in 1 John 5:14-15 (NASB):

> This **is the confidence which we have before Him**, that, **if we ask anything according to His will, He hears us**. And if we know that He hears us in whatever we ask, **we know that we have the requests which we have asked from Him**.

When we pray and talk to God and understand His will, our prayer becomes more interactive and relational. When you recite back to God His own words, in the essence of who He is, He responds. That response brings confidence in your relationship with Him and inspires you to know Him even more.

Knowing His will does not mean that we know how He will execute His will, nor the timing of it. Knowing His will brings faith, confidence, and patience as we wait to witness how He performs it.

One of the preeminent examples of this was Moses pleading with God to go with the Israelites to the promised land after they sinned in the wilderness by creating and worshipping the golden calf. Let us look deeper into this situation. Moses was on the mountain with God for forty days. Exodus records that he was in the presence of God for six days before God spoke to him (Exodus 24:15-18). God called Moses up the mountain, and the glory of the Lord rested on the mountain, and on the seventh day, God talked to Moses out of a cloud. For six days, Moses and God beheld each other before they began communicating.

While Moses was at the end of his time with God on the mountain, the Israelites created a golden calf and started worshipping it. They sinned and violated the first commandment that God had given them a few days before. They got anxious, insecure, and fearful, thinking that Moses and God had abandoned them because Moses had been gone for forty days, and they had not heard from God. Oh, the weakness of human beings to depart from God so quickly. The Israelites had just witnessed some of the greatest manifestations of God's power and commitment to them. They were delivered from Egypt, the Red Sea was split for them to cross over, and the Egyptian army was destroyed.

God called the Israelites into His presence to hear His voice so they would learn to revere His name. But they were fearful, so they ran away from God and told Moses to hear God for them. This is why prayer and your own communion with God is important. You cannot live on someone else's revelation or fire; you need to get your own. Much of the current church is in this state; therefore, when patience and faith are needed, the church is not able to call and rely on power and grace because they do not know the Grace Giver personally.

During the forty days that Moses was gone, the Israelites turned away from God and worshipped another god—the golden calf. They gave their gold to Aaron, and he made them a golden calf. They called it Jehovah and worshipped it with a feast. When Moses returned, he found them naked and feasting before the golden calf. Do you get a picture of how quickly they degraded themselves and fell into worshipping another god? After this incident, God judged them and said that He would still fulfill His promise and take them to the promised land, but He would not be the one leading them into it. He said that He would send His angel before them. God was going to give them the promised land because He wanted to fulfill His covenant with Abraham.

When Moses interceded for the Israelites, he would go into a tent and pray, worship, and interact with God, and God's presence would descend into the tent. Moses knew that it was God's desire to lead the Israelites into the promised land, and they were to be God's special treasure and family. Moses interceded and recalled these things before the Lord. The Lord decided to change His mind and lead them into the promised land.

I love what is recorded in Exodus 33: Moses said to the Lord, "*If you won't go with us, then don't lead us anywhere*." I would like to paraphrase this: If You will not go with us, then we are not going. The most important thing is not God giving them the promised land, but that He was going with them into the promised land. This is what distinguishes His children from the other people on the earth. Moses was telling God that the promised land was not the prize, nor was the answered prayer; God's presence with His children is the prize. What a truth for those of us who want to pray—answered prayer is not the prize; God's presence in you and working through you is the prize.

Moses prayed the essence of what we need to understand God.

> You have told me, 'I know you by name, and I look favorably on you.' If it is true that you look favorably

> on me, **let me know your ways so I may understand you more fully and continue to enjoy your favor.** (Exodus 33:13, NLT)

Moses recalled that he had received favor and grace from God. But he prayed and asked God to reveal Himself to him more, that he may know His ways, and in knowing them, he would find more favor and grace. What a prayer! He was praying to know God better. The way of God is how God sees things and how God does things; in that, you will learn the will of God for the things of life. Moses wanted to know God, His character, and His glory.

How could Moses be so bold to ask for those things? Let us remember, he had just come off a forty-day interaction with God, beholding His beauty, glory, and splendor. He sat in God's presence for forty days and learned that God, first and foremost, is a God of loving-kindness and compassion. Moses learned that He was a covenant God and that He wanted the company of His family—he knew the will of the Father.

God's decision to send an angel to bring them into the promised land was not because He wanted to separate Himself from them and be a harsh Judge. But, being a holy God, He knew that sin could not live in His presence. He knew that Israel was prone to sin, and they were a stubborn generation. It was out of the love He had for Israel more than anything else.

To reinforce the knowledge of God at the end of his prayer in Exodus 33, Moses asked God to pass by him in glory. God's glory is a result of His nature and character. Notice in Exodus 34, the conversation with God regarding reiterating Moses's prayer from the previous chapter and what he asked God:

> Then the LORD passed by in front of him and proclaimed, "The LORD, the LORD God, **compassionate and gracious, slow to anger, and abounding in lovingkindness and truth; who keeps lovingkindness for thousands, who forgives iniquity, transgression and sin; yet He will**

> **by no means leave the guilty unpunished, visiting the iniquity of fathers on the children and on the grandchildren to the third and fourth generations.**" Moses made haste to bow low toward the earth and worship. He said, "**If now I have found favor in Your sight, O Lord, I pray, let the Lord go along in our midst, even though the people are so obstinate, and pardon our iniquity and our sin, and take us as Your own possession.**"

Moses knew God and His will, and he prayed according to it through an interactive conversation in his time of worship and prayer with God.

Let us take a look at some of the New Testament writings about the knowledge of God and His Word. Peter, in his second epistle, tells us that we have been given all things that pertain to life and godly living, through an experiential knowledge from interacting with God. Jesus told us in the Gospel of John that eternal life comes through knowing the Father, the only true God, and Jesus, the Christ He sent to the world.

> By his divine power, God has given us everything we need for living a godly life. We have received all of this by coming to know him, the one who called us to himself by means of his marvelous glory and excellence. (2 Peter 1:3)

> And this is the way to have eternal life—to know you, the only true God, and Jesus Christ, the one you sent to earth. (John 17:3)

This life comes through knowing God. Eternal life is not a quantity in time but a quality of life that comes through knowing God. This is the quality of life that God has sought for us to experience and walk in, from the beginning. Much of the Christian church still believes that eternal life starts when a person dies. In death, you leave your physical, earthly body, and your spirit continues to live eternally. What quality of life will we experience in life and death? Will we be in God's presence and experience Him more and more, or will we be separated from Him in a place of everlasting darkness?

Knowing God starts and ends with feeding and meditating on God's Word. The Bible is commonly referred to as the Word of God. What does that mean? Everything recorded in the Old and New Testaments is the Word of God. But all of it is not God's Word, thought, and will. Some of it is records of the actions of different people, the thoughts of different people, and their life events. These stories are there for us to learn from so we know what is pleasing and not pleasing to God. The writer of Hebrews exhorts us to follow the same example of those who, through faith and patience, inherited the promises of God. All of Scripture can help us understand more and more about God.

> All Scripture is inspired by God and profitable for teaching, for reproof, for correction, for training in righteousness; so that the man of God may be adequate, equipped for every good work. (2 Timothy 3:16)

There is inspiration in all Scripture. Through the Scriptures, we can learn about God and how He sees right and wrong. The Scriptures prepare us for all that God wants us to do. They instruct us in righteousness—how to be in right standing with God. The question is, "How does that process work?"

Years ago, a man came up to me in our congregation. He was a faithful, serving member. He asked me, "How do I get into the Word?" "Get into the Word" was a commonly used phrase in our congregation. The man actually meant to study and read the Bible regularly and diligently. I was perplexed since he had been a faithful member of the church for years. I thought to myself, "You've been here so long, and you don't have any ongoing fellowship with God and His Word?" But sadly, I have seen this time and time again over the years. We can worship God, cry out for Him, tell Him that He is all we need and how beautiful He is, but if we do not spend time reading and meditating on His Word, our spiritual life can distill down to the doctrines that someone has taught us, the obligation to attend a church service every week, and an obligation to do some service in the churches. There is no living personal revelation.

When I first met Jesus, I started reading the New Testament repeatedly. And as I did, many times, I would stop at certain chapters, realizing that the Holy Spirit was highlighting things to me. I would meditate on it. I would ask questions like: what, where, why, and how? It felt like I was chewing on a deliciously tasty piece of meat that got more and more flavorful.

As I continued this process, I would listen to other people and preachers with passion and desire to learn from them. I read several spiritual books—hundreds of them. All this fed into the revelation that God was giving me over time.

I would memorize scriptures and take study material that was readily available in paper or digital format. As I memorized and studied, God took me through various subjects throughout His Word. Eventually, the words on the pages were written in my heart.

What do I mean by that? Let us look at what John wrote in his Gospel when describing the incarnate God dwelling in man and becoming known as Jesus, the Christ. John 1:1-4, 14 (NASB)

> **In the beginning was the Word, and the Word was with God, and the Word was God**. He was in the beginning with God. All things came into being through Him, and apart from Him nothing came into being that has come into being. In Him was life, and the life was the Light of men. The Light shines in the darkness, and the darkness did not comprehend it.…**And the Word became flesh, and dwelt among us, and we saw His glory, glory as of the only begotten from the Father, full of grace and truth.**

God and His Word are one. But, for us to understand it better, He sent His Son, Jesus, who is the Christ. He was the manifestation of the will and Word of God in flesh. Jesus said, "*I and the Father are one. He who has seen me, has seen the Father.*" He also said, "*I do whatever I see the Father do.*" All these wonderful statements present the deity of Christ, the union of Jesus with the Father, and the manifestation of the Word of God in the flesh and are recorded in John's Gospel. Jesus was the manifestation of God's will in flesh, and as we behold His Word, we behold the glory of God, and the grace and truth that brings a revelation of the Father.

I define God's grace as His willingness to use His power and ability on our behalf to bring on us that which we cannot bring on ourselves. God's grace changes us and reveals truth to us, and this is what sets us free. Just memorizing Scripture does not set us free. It is the Holy Spirit inspired truth that does that. Knowing the truth is when the Word becomes flesh inside of us.

When we read and meditate on God's Word, the Holy Spirit takes those written words and reveals to us the truth behind them. Then He writes them on our heart, and the Word becomes flesh inside of us. He becomes incorporated into our spiritual DNA, and we become like Him—we are changed from glory to glory.

We talked about passion for God, and that passion is expressed in worship. Passion for God does not end with worship. It should be followed by a deep desire to know God, and it should kindle and ignite prayer! When our times of worship and prayer lead into meditating on God's Word and fellowshipping with Him, then God will begin working in and through us. The Word becomes flesh inside of us, and the ways, the will, the purposes, the thoughts, and the judgments of the Creator Himself.

## The Word of God and the Parable of the Sower

In the Gospel of Mark, we read an amazing statement that Jesus made:

> Then Jesus said to them, "If you can't understand the meaning of this parable, **how will you understand all the other parables?** (Mark 4:13, NLT)

Here, Jesus was pointing to the importance of the parable of the sower. Jesus taught this parable in Mark 4, Matthew 13, and Luke 8, and it was the first parable recorded by all these writers. He continues with other parables. **The parable of the sower is the key to understanding all the parables.** Jesus was saying that if they could not understand this parable, they would not be able to understand any parable, or in other words, understanding the parable of the sower will give you the insight to understand all parables. It is the primary parable that Jesus went through and explained. Matthew also records that He explained the parable of the tares, but it is the only parable that Jesus explained that is recorded in Matthew, Mark, and Luke.

A parable is a story with a comparison; it is an earthly story with a heavenly spiritual meaning. The other parables in this group—the parable of the seed, mustard seed, tares, costly pearl, dragnet, and leaven—can all be understood through the truths revealed in the parable of the sower.

The disciples came to Jesus and asked Him to explain it, and Jesus went through and quoted the scriptures about having ears to hear and eyes to see—which should remind us of the previous chapter about the Word of God. Jesus tells us the seed is likened unto the Word of God. The Word is sown into the heart of man. The heart of man is like soil. Jesus classified the soil into different categories: by the roadside, rocky soil, thorny soil, and good soil.

Jesus lets us know that the soil is the heart of man. We know this because He said about the seed sown by the wayside that the devil comes immediately to steal the Word out of the heart. This is why I call the heart the "womb" of the spirit." The womb is the most intimate of all places, where the seed from the man unites with the egg from the woman and life springs forth. The womb is also the place where new life can be cared for, protected, nourished, and sheltered until the fruit of the womb is ready to come forth.

The different soil types represent different states of the inner spiritual heart. The first soil type is like the road, which is hard, and it is difficult for water to penetrate. The seeds that fall on this soil have a difficult time germinating and maintaining life. Those seeds are immediately stolen by the devil and the snares of this world. The second type of soil is rocky terrain. The seeds that fall on this soil spring up to some degree but are immediately choked because there is no deep root or commitment. So when things become harder, or criticism comes, hearts with rocky soil deem it not beneficial to follow the Lord. They make a conscious choice to do something else. When we do not take care of the garden in our heart, thorns grow; other desires become more important. Jesus describes these thorns as the cares of this world, deceitfulness of riches, and the lust for things that choke the Word in our heart. This is the time when the seeds of the world begin germinating in hearts and give growth to fleshly desires. They indulge the flesh with pleasures, powers, or riches. These things draw on us and influence us to make wrong decisions and actions, and cause us not to experience the life that God wants us to have.

The last type of soil is the good soil. Mark's Gospel says that the good soil is comparable to those who hear the Word, accept it, and produce a great harvest. Matthew adds to that description, saying, "*Those who hear the word and understand it.*" Luke describes them as those who hear the Word with an honest and good heart, cling to it, and with patience, produce a large harvest.

Once we accept something into our heart, it becomes a part of us; it becomes a part of our programming. A better way to say it is it becomes a part of our spiritual DNA. That DNA is responsible for our spiritual source code of power, strength, and motivation. Accepting the Word means to say that it is right and humbly submitting to it, allowing it to take the highest priority in our life. That is when the Word begins to direct our motivations and outward actions.

## Key 3: Prayer, His Presence, and His Word

In Jesus's time, people understood farming. They understood that if a seed was introduced into the right environment with proper care, it would yield fruit. If Jesus was incarnated in today's world, He might have talked more about computer programming and how when code is read and processed by a micro-processor, it helps execute a process and run software. Our DNA is a superb programming language that directs our body's functions as to how it should operate.

When one accepts the importance of the Word of God, then God Himself will bring revelation and personal understanding to them. That is when the words written on a page become much more than words; they become reality to the one who has experienced it.

Proverbs 4 has a wonderful commentary on the importance of keeping the Word of God at the forefront of our passions and governance of our life.

> My son, **give attention to my words; Incline your ear to my sayings**. Do not let them **depart from your sight**; Keep them **in the midst of your heart**. For they are **life to those who find them** And **health to all their body**. **Watch over your heart** with all diligence, For from it flow the springs of life. (Proverbs 4:20-23)

These statements encapsulate the importance of the Word of God and how we are to treat, revere, and pursue it. When we begin to see the Word of God as that which represents God's character and nature influencing our lives, what do we do? We give it the first and foremost of our attention.

If we give the Word our foremost attention, then we will know that we should not allow the seed to be sown on the hard roadside. We will instead prepare the soil of our heart to receive it. The Word will always be foremost in our sight and will become the governing factor for how we act and react to life. Once we give the Word our attention, we will bend our hearing toward it and make every effort to understand what God is saying to us through it. When we want to be sure that we hear exactly what is being said by someone, we usually position our head so that our ear is in the best spot to hear with clarity. It is about making the effort to hear, and recognizing the importance of what is being said.

Once we receive the Word, what do we do with it? How do we keep that seed in the best environment to geminate so the Word of God has the most optimal environment to become what it is destined and programmed to be? This is what it means to keep the Word in the center of your heart. What is being said is keep the Word at the center of where your passions and emotions are motivated; keep it in the place that triggers your heart to flutter in passion and desire, just as it would when you think about your most intimate lover.

Be like a gardener who takes care of his garden; he is passionate about planting the seeds in the best soil and in the best environment, fertilizing it, watering it, making sure it gets the proper sunshine, and keeping the weeds out so they will not choke the plant before it can bear fruit. The gardener is passionate about growing the seed because he knows the importance of producing fruit in order to live. The parable of the sower is about the importance of prioritizing hearing the Word of God, listening, and actively participating in it.

Going back to the book of beginnings, Genesis, it is no coincidence that God put Adam and Eve in a garden to begin with. The garden of Eden is likened unto our heart today. Genesis 1 gives an account of God speaking things into existence. By doing that, He put everything in divine order. But He did not speak man into existence.

> Then God said, **"Let Us make man in Our image, according to Our likeness**; and let them rule over the fish of the sea and over the birds of the sky and over the cattle and over all the earth, and over every creeping thing that creeps on the earth."

God did not speak man into existence; He made man with His own hands. As a child comes out of a woman's womb, so we came out of the womb of God. Genesis 2 elaborates more on this:

> Then the LORD God **formed man of dust from the ground and breathed into his nostrils the breath of life; and man became a living being.** The LORD God planted a garden toward the east, in Eden; and there He placed the man whom He had formed.

God took the dust of the earth and formed us just as a potter forms the clay into a pot or some other object. Then God breathed into us the breath of life, or better translated: He breathed in us the Spirit of life. God is Spirit, so He took a part of Himself and put it in us. God chooses to be incomplete without us. God completes us, and we complete Him. Man is a unique creation of God; he was not spoken into existence; he was formed by the hand of God and then breathed upon to bring life into him.

Adam and Eve were the offspring of God and placed in the garden to cultivate it and to maintain it. Some translations say, "*to tend and watch over it.*" They were placed there to guide, guard, and govern the garden. The definition of "keep" used here is that of a watchman who is to guard and protect. Adam and Eve were to protect the garden from anything that could hinder their intimacy with Him, and anything that could disrupt the order that God put things in. The very thing they were told to do, they did not do. Eve allowed the serpent to deceive her. He played on the lust of the flesh, the lust of the eyes, and the boastful pride of life. The cares of the world, deceitfulness of riches, and the lust for other things all feed this.

The serpent gave Eve a half-truth that God did not want them to eat of the tree because He knew they would become like Him, knowing good and evil. They were already like God in every way. What the serpent did not tell them was that in eating the fruit, they would become like God, knowing good and evil. They would die spiritually and separate themselves from God, and they would be under the influence of the devil to commit evil. God knows good and evil, and He always chooses good. Man, now separated from God, did not have that power like God and was under the influence of the devil until the coming of the One who would redeem them.

Eve was deceived, but Adam directly disobeyed. He was right there when all this was going on. Genesis says that Eve ate and then gave it to Adam to eat. They allowed the seeds of the words of evil to be sown into their hearts, and by that, into the garden to destroy their special fellowship and relationship with God. Notice what Eve did; she saw that the tree was good for food and could make her wise. It was a delight to her eyes. Adam and Eve already had all they needed. God gave it to them. But in their hearts, they doubted God's Word and thought they needed more than what God could offer them. Their hearts got corrupted. Immediately, they realized that they were naked, they felt shameful and guilty, and they felt a void in their hearts because they separated themselves from the very thing they were created to be. They now knew good and evil and could be influenced by the devil toward evil. They were cut off from their Source of life, and they could no longer experience the life-giving intimate fellowship with God. This fellowship was the wisdom they needed, the pleasure they were created for, and the abundant life that God provided for His family.

Adam and Eve tried to cover and fill the void inside of them, but to no avail. That void was supposed to be filled with fellowship and intimacy with God—the conduit for the life of God in this earth. God gave them the trees of the garden for food and for their pleasure. But, when God came to be with them, they hid themselves behind the trees of the garden. They substituted the pleasures of life for the pleasure of God. We still do this today, don't we? Rather than enjoying God, we try to cover ourselves with all worldly pleasures, but none satisfies. The satisfaction of life comes from being in union with the Father, Son, and Holy Spirit. It comes from taking the Word in, treasuring it, and allowing it to grow and cultivate in us so as to transform us to be and act like Him.

Our heart is like a garden. We need to watch over it with all diligence; we need to keep the bad seeds out and take the good seeds in. Paul said in 1 Corinthians 3:9 (NASB):

> For we are God's fellow workers; you are God's field, God's building.

The word "field" really means God's cultivated field. It is up to us to get the field ready and keep it free from all things that hinder the germination and growth of the seed. We labor together to make sure it grows. This is the truth behind the parable of the sower. It is simple and profound.

> *Father, help us to focus and be diligent to guard our heart. Help us to hear the Word and root out distractions and everything that causes us to lust after the cares of this world, money, and anything that can choke the Word of God out of us. Amen.*

The more we allow and understand the Word, the more we understand God. The more we understand God, the more effective, productive, real, and enjoyable prayer becomes. We will have the confidence to stand before Him and experience intimacy with Him.

## The Word: The Two-Edged Sword

There are four references to the Word of God and a sword in the New Testament. The first is in Ephesians 6, when Paul is talking about the armor of God. The word for "sword" here really means a small dagger. It is the only offensive weapon listed in Paul's prayer armor.

The other three references use a different word, which literally means a two-edged or two-mouthed sword. The second reference is in Hebrews, and the third and fourth references are in the book of Revelation (1:16; 2:12). Both references in Revelation refer to the Word as a two-edged sword that comes out of the mouth of the glorified and risen Christ, the Lamb of God. In both instances, God is speaking His Word to the church.

Early in my Christian life, I was taught that the Word of God is like a two-edged sword, and that I should speak and confess the Word over my life since it is very powerful. The words "confess" and "profess" mean the same thing. When we confess the Word over our life, we are agreeing with God and releasing faith in what He says. If the Word says that I am a son of God, I must say that I am a son of God. If the Word says I have died with Christ, I must say that I have died with Christ. If the Word says I have been created in righteousness, I must say that I am righteous. Faith comes by hearing and hearing by the Word of God. One of the most powerful things I have learned is to say and believe what God says I am.

Many times, I have preached and heard others preach the concept of confessing who I am in Christ by referencing Hebrews 4:12:

> For the word of God is **living and active and sharper than any two-edged sword** and piercing as far as the division of soul and spirit, of both joints and marrow, and able to judge the thoughts and intentions of the heart.

One day, I read the context of this scripture to better understand what it is saying. We need to read all of Hebrews 3 and 4 for context. These chapters are an exhortation for the church to not act like the children of Israel who heard the Word of God but did not unite it with faith in their hearts, and as a result, fell in the wilderness and did not attain the rest and fulfillment of the promise of God.

The Israelites turned a few-days trip into a forty-year journey. The onset of the downward spiral started at Mount Sinai. We discussed this story in the previous chapter. God called the Israelites to be a royal people and a holy nation and offered them a special place in His heart. The Israelites were a shadow of the bride of Christ. God offered them a betrothal to Himself.

When they accepted His offer, God told them that He was coming down to meet them, and He did. The meeting day was set and was much anticipated by both the children of Israel and God. God was so excited to meet His beloved that the fire burned so great. This was shared earlier in the book, but I would like to reemphasize it. Deuteronomy 4:11 says that it burned to the "heart of heaven." When I read that description, I wondered what it meant. After some meditation and study, I found that it means the center of heaven—not as a physical place, but the center of passion and emotions that make up the God of Heaven. God's heart was so excited that the passion of His love and desire for men showed forth as His fire. As stated before, the fuel to His fire is His Love. Here is a God of love, ready to meet His beloved bride, the firstborn of Israel. It is like when you first meet the one who you know is the one for you; when they walk into the room, your heart jumps for joy, and it flutters on the inside with deep emotion and love for them. That was what happened when God came to meet His beloved. But when God's heart flutters, it creates quite a commotion with fire and rumbling.

They saw God and heard His words; He spoke to them and gave them the ten commandments. Go back to Deuteronomy 4:10, which says:

> Remember the day you stood before the LORD your God at Horeb, when the LORD said to me, "Assemble the people to Me**, that I may let them hear My words so they may learn to fear Me all the days they live on the earth, and that they may teach their children**."

God wanted them to hear His words so they could learn to fear, revere, and live in awe and appreciation of who they would be in this intimate covenant relationship. They needed to hear the Word of God for themselves. Unfortunately, they became afraid and retreated back from God, fearing they would not be able to hear His Word and live. But they already did hear the Word of God and live! They withdrew back into their tents and told Moses to hear the Word for them and then tell them what he heard so they could act on it. That does not work. They needed their own revelation and experience with God. They needed to catch their own fire of God's love. In Psalm 103:7, it says that Moses knew the ways of the Lord, but the children of Israel knew His acts. Knowing His works does not cut it; you need to know and experience His Word being written on your heart for yourself.

This points to what we discussed in the previous chapter—the parable of the sower. The Word was sown into the hearts of the Israelites, but they did not take it in; they were afraid. Even in the old covenant, people could take the Word into their heart. Although it was not the new heart spoken of in the New Testament, a heart of flesh, it still could have done its work if they had allowed it. God told us that man's heart was a heart of stone back then. But God demonstrated that He could even write on a heart of stone. That is why the ten commandments were written on stone. They represented the heart of man and how God could write on it even though it was so hard.

Following this experience, Moses went into the presence of the Lord for forty days and nights. The account in Exodus is that Moses went up into the presence of the Lord, and the presence of the Lord rested upon him. After six days, God called out of the cloud and spoke to Moses about His will and desire. What a perfect example of coming into His presence to worship Him and then learning to listen to His words and have Him write them on our heart.

Moses continued with his desire to know God by asking Him for more grace to know His ways and see His glory. Knowing God's ways is to know Him and His Word, and seeing His glory is to see His nature and what makes Him up. When God passed by Moses as a fulfillment of his prayer, Moses proclaimed the Lord's lovingkindness, tender mercies, and the perfection of His judgment. Again, Moses came into His presence to worship Him and then heard His Word, which changed him.

This is exactly what Hebrews 3 and 4 are talking about. The writer says that when we hear His voice, which is His Word, His thoughts, His ways, and when they are revealed to us, we should take them in and unite them with faith so we may enter into God's rest.

Let us examine this further: The Word is sharper than any two-edged sword. In the natural realm, that sword could be so sharp that it can separate the most difficult parts of human tissue from each other so they can be recognizable. In the spiritual realm, it can do what nothing else can do—separate your spirit and your soul. Your spirit is the real you; it is what is regenerated at the new birth. Your soul is your mind, intellect, and emotions. The union of your spirit and your soul is your spiritual heart. That is where the truth of our intentions and motives lies.

When we seek God and begin to hear His Word, it will expose us and show us what is truly in our heart. The Israelites heard God's Word and did not like what they saw when God exposed them, so they ran away. We need to continually run to God and not away from Him.

Hebrews 4:12 is primarily talking about us hearing God's Word and learning to allow it to work in us. It is not us speaking God's Word. One does lead to the other, but the context and order of this is important.

There is nothing that is hidden from God's sight. The Word does expose all things, and we cannot run away from God. The Israelites thought they could run away, but that did not work. When God's Word comes forth, we hear it and interact with it. It is always better to run to God than to run away from God. Do not think that you can hide from God by running away from Him. Running to God means to say, "God, you are right. I am here just as I am, and I need your help to be transformed."

Jesus is our High Priest who can go before God for us. As our High Priest, He understands and empathizes with our weakness, which is the flesh and its influence on us that feeds our earthly desires. But as the High Priest, He also knows the power of God to overcome those weaknesses. That is why we can come boldly to the throne of grace. Boldly, meaning without shame, without guilt, and without anything that hinders us. I see this like a little child who is secure in their father's or mother's love that they crawl up into their laps at any time without hesitation. They do this because they are so secure in their parents' acceptance and love.

This is because of who we belong to and the work our High Priest has done for us. Our High Priest did not just intercede for us—He died for us, He died as us, and He took the penalty of all our sins so we can be redeemed and have the righteousness to stand boldly in His presence, confidently, openly, and plainly before God, and receive His mercy. Mercy keeps from us what we rightfully deserve. We deserve judgment, but God's mercy keeps that away from us.

We can receive mercy at any time because God is full of mercy. How do we receive this mercy? We ask for it by faith. The next step is finding grace. If mercy keeps from us what we rightfully deserve, grace brings to us that which we do not deserve. But we have to find grace. Many people go their whole life and just learn how to receive mercy, but never find grace. Those are the ones that know of God's mercy but never really have any lasting transformation.

How do we find grace? The Bible has many references to finding grace. He gives grace to the humble, contrite, and meek. Humility is a place of complete dependence on God, knowing that all truth comes from Him, and apart from Him we can do nothing. Contriteness is a place of understanding that without God, there is no good thing; it is a realization that God is all. It brings you to a place of recognition of who He is and who we are apart from Him. Meekness is humility's first cousin and best friend; I like to say that it is power under control, submitted to the will of God. The best representation of this was Jesus's interrogation by Pontius Pilate. Jesus knew that it was the will of God for Him to go to the cross. He knew who He was, and He knew the power and authority He possessed. Pilate wanted to let Him go. He knew the jealousy of the Jewish leaders and was warned in a dream through his wife that Jesus was a good Man and not what the Jews were making Him out to be. When Jesus would not defend Himself before Pilate, Pilate asked Him why. He told Jesus that he had the power to crucify Him or release Him. Jesus's reply to Pilate is a perfect example of meekness.

> So Pilate said to Him, "You do not speak to me? **Do You not know that I have authority to release You, and I have authority to crucify You?"** Jesus answered, "You would have no authority over Me, unless it had been given you from above; for this reason he who delivered Me to you has the greater sin." (John 19:10-11)

Jesus did not defend Himself. He could have had His heavenly servants come and fight for Him. But He knew that the will of God for Him was the cross. He humbled Himself under the most excruciating form of dying and sacrificed Himself for mankind.

This is the way to grace; God gives grace to the humble. Grace is typically called God's unmerited favor. As I defined before, it is God's willingness to use His ability and power on our behalf, to bring on us that which we cannot bring on ourselves. The phrase and/or concept, "God gives grace to the humble," is all over the Bible, both in the Old and New Testaments.

Let us explore some wonderful scriptures:

> The high and lofty one who lives in eternity, the Holy One, says this: **"I live in the high and holy place with those whose spirits are contrite and humble. I restore the crushed spirit of the humble and revive the courage of those with repentant hearts**." (Isaiah 57:15, NLT)
>
> "For My hand made all these things, Thus all these things came into being," declares the LORD. "But to this one I will look, **To him who is humble and contrite of spirit, and who trembles at My word."** (Isaiah 66:2)

How powerful are these scriptures! First, it says that God inhabits eternity. That in itself is amazing, and we could take a long time to wade through that subject. But, for the purpose of staying on task, we will focus on eternity being the place where God dwells with the humble and contrite. The word used for "restore" and "revive" is the same: to restore a prosperous life, be made alive, quickened spiritually, mentally, and physically. Second, the verse says that God will look at—have high regard, pay attention, and respect—the humble who have demonstrated high regard and importance for His Word.

Let us look at a couple of Jesus's statements in the book of Matthew:

> So anyone who becomes as humble as this little child is the greatest in the Kingdom of Heaven. (Matthew 18:4, NLT)

> But those who exalt themselves will be humbled, and those who humble themselves will be exalted. (Matthew 23:12, NLT)

Jesus specifically mentions how authority is gained in the kingdom of God. The kingdom of God is the dominion of God in the heart of man, and through that, authority is given to man on earth to affect the things around him. Jesus said we will be exalted by humility, which means being brought up to the highest level. There is no higher level than to live in His presence and have Him dwell with us and in us, and us in Him.

The most outstanding description of the humility of Jesus is in Philippians 2 where Paul is exhorting the Philippian church to act like Jesus, who humbled Himself as God to become a man, and He humbled Himself as a man to die for men. This released the greatest effect of God's power in the life and history of man, through the cross, bringing salvation and deliverance for all mankind for now and eternity. There was so much power released on the cross that every person can receive salvation. The moment we accept Christ, the same power that raised Jesus from the dead, which created the heavens and the earth, is released in us, and we are transfigured into the image and likeness of Jesus.

Then, there is Peter, in his wonderful letter, stating the following:

> In the same way, you who are younger must accept the authority of the elders. And all of you, **dress yourselves in humility as you relate to one another, for God opposes the proud but gives grace to the humble. So humble yourselves under the mighty power of God, and at the right time he will lift you up in honor**. Give all your worries and cares to God, for he cares about you. (1 Peter 5:5-7, NLT)

God gives grace to the humble. That is why we need to find grace in His presence by taking His Word and having high regard for it, allowing it to influence our thinking, our actions, and our life—allowing it to point out our shortcomings and not being afraid of it when it does, not running away from it but running to it, admitting the need for help, and finding the ability to be changed and transformed by God's grace.

God gives grace when grace is needed, which is when God thinks it is needed, and not necessarily when we think it is needed. Here, humility is understanding the timing and ways of God. He does things perfectly, in His own time, not in the way we think or the time we think. Here is when faith in God and patience work together to bring us to the place of unconditional surrender to the will and Word of God.

This is why we need to find grace. We find grace as we stay in His presence, hear His Word, wait on Him, and seek Him first under all circumstances. This process of listening and hearing God gives us the grace to receive truth—the truth which then proceeds to free us and brings us to the destiny of God's calling. It enables the image of God to manifest in our lives.

Let us all pray the prayer of Moses when he was interceding for the children of Israel:

> *Lord, give us more grace and favor to know Your ways, to know Your thoughts, and to know Your judgments. Have Your glory pass before us, and proclaim Your name to us. Have mercy on us, and bestow on us the grace to receive the truth. Give us grace to not run from Your Word and Your presence, but to run to Your Word and Your presence. Amen.*

## The Word Trains Us to Discern Good and Evil

Learning about God is to recognize Him and His ways; it is to see how God sees and judges right from wrong with full transparency of the truth—how God examines what is good and evil.

This is such an important subject. In the beginning, Adam and Eve failed to understand this and were deceived, hence, they disobeyed God. There were two trees in the center of the garden: the Tree of Life, which would have fed them with all they needed to live an abundant life, full of the presence of God, His goodness, kindness, justice, righteousness, and mercy. The second was the tree which would feed them with knowledge of not just good, but evil: the Tree of Knowledge of Good and Evil.

It is important to define what is good and what is evil. We may think it is easy, but it is not. We can do good things with evil motives, and they never produce good results. Goodness is doing, acting, and living in such a way that whatever you do is not just for your benefit but has a distinct benefit to help others. Jesus said in the Gospel of Mark that God alone is good, and everything He does is for our benefit, even when it is at His expense (Mark 10:18). The ultimate example of that was Jesus's sacrifice on the cross, where He demonstrated His love for us while we were yet separate from God and going our own way. He fulfilled the old covenant and paid the penalty for our sins at the everlasting court of justice.

The court of heaven is where the Father is the Judge, and the prosecutor is the devil—the accuser of the brethren. Our defense attorney is the Great Advocate: Jesus, the Christ. The devil accuses us of sin and rebellion and points out all our rebellious acts against God: every sin, every iniquity of passive indifference before God, and the active transgressions against Him.

Our Advocate calls His Witness, the Holy Spirit, and asks the Holy Spirit for evidence that can provide a defense for all of the accusations. The Holy Spirit points to the shed blood of Jesus on the cross. The blood speaks as payment for the penalty of our sins; it speaks mercy and forgiveness. Then it speaks to our complete redemption to restore us back to the position of a beloved child of God. Jesus's shed blood and broken body are all we need. He is our substitute. He died *for* us and *as* us. Once we identify with Him and receive Him, God considers us and treats us the same as Jesus, the Christ.

The devil, represented as the serpent, did the complete opposite. He used his ability and cunningness to twist the truth and manipulate Adam and Eve to do something that was not in their best interest. It was in the devil's best interest though, because he separated them from God, took their authority, ruled over them, and influenced them for evil.

God can see the heart and motives of man. If there is one thing Jesus always went after, it is the truth in the heart of man. He did this with the religious leaders and the apostles while He was on the earth, and He does it with us today.

Let us rehearse Jesus's interaction with Peter after Peter confessed his faith in Jesus the Messiah—the One for whom the Jews were waiting. Soon after Peter's confession, Jesus told Peter that God had revealed to Him that Jesus was the Christ. Jesus would build His church, and with that revelation, authority would be released in Peter. He would have the keys to the kingdom of heaven and would be a ruler in the kingdom with the authority of binding and loosing. This is the kind of authority that comes with leadership, and it was a direct reference to those in authority in the natural world who can bind and loose people. The religious leaders at Jesus's time had the power to take control of people's lives. Jesus later on addressed how this authority comes out as a servant's authority and how it can be used for good.

In Matthew's Gospel, right after this incident with Peter, Jesus told the disciples the end game and culmination of His ministry on earth; it was not to be made a ruler on earth, but to go to the cross at the hands of the religious leaders and die. Peter, perplexed at hearing this, took Jesus aside and rebuked Him. I am sure it looked good, "Listen Jesus, I am your protector. I cannot let this happen to you." Immediately, Peter's motives were revealed. They were corrupted by his desire for power. Jesus gave Peter the largest, MEGA rebuke recorded in the New Testament. He spoke to Peter and said, "*Get behind me SATAN*" (Matthew 16:23). He was essentially saying, "Peter, your selfish interests are getting in the way of God's plans, and you are allowing Satan to work through you. You are selfish and self-centered."

This was right after Jesus gave Peter His greatest commendation for professing that Jesus was the Christ, the Son of the living God. It sometimes seems that after we have our greatest victories, we have our greatest tests; and often, we suffer great defeats. Pride is an evil, slippery slope that finds its way into our lives very easily.

Right after the discourse here, there are three other discourses in the Gospels that are recorded on the subject of who is the greatest in the kingdom. In the first discourse, Jesus took a little child, put him in the midst of His disciples, and told them that they need to become like a little child. I am paraphrasing here. He said that if they do not become like a little child, they cannot even get into the kingdom, let alone be a leader in it. They needed to display the humility, simplicity, and the faith that a child has in his parents. The second time this argument happened, James and John came with their mother to ask Jesus if they could sit at His right and left hand in the kingdom. These were the two highest positions of authority in a kingdom, next to the king. Jesus let them know that this was only for the Father to decide, and He told them that leadership in His kingdom is not like leadership in earthly kingdoms—in His kingdom, leaders must become servants. And finally, at the last supper, the disciples started to argue about who would be the one to betray Jesus after He said that one of them would. The same argument cropped up again as to who was the greatest. Jesus then got up from the table, washed their feet, and demonstrated kingdom leadership. I write on this subject extensively in my book, *Kingdom Master Builders*.

The disciples were having trouble distinguishing good and evil. They did not realize that their motives were evil. They were more concerned about their position in the kingdom than about doing the will of God the way God does it. Their senses were not exercised to discern this yet. "Exercise" here means a very vigorous workout. Our vigorous spiritual workouts come from the things we face in life, how we stand in faith during those times, and how we apply what God has shown us. The result is our ability to stand on God's Word and trust Him in the midst of trial, tribulation, pain, and suffering.

Eventually, Jesus was arrested, taken to Pilate to be judged, and condemned to death by crucifixion at the bequest of the Jewish religious leaders. What Jesus predicted was finally happening, but the disciples still did not understand what was going on. When Jesus was crucified, the world that they knew and had been a part of for three-and-a-half years, crumbled. They went from being on top of the world, walking and being an intimate part of the Messiah's ministry, having positions in Jesus's ministry, to all of a sudden, collapsing like a house of cards.

They were bewildered and tried to make sense of what happened. Although Jesus told them about these things many times, it never sunk in. They were fearful, so they were hiding. They quit the ministry and went back to the fishing business. The pain, suffering, and disappointment must have rolled over them like waves of a sea.

Three days later, they heard from Mary Magdalene that Jesus had risen, just as He had said. Measured hope started to arise in their hearts. Jesus appeared to them and talked to them about the kingdom and what was going to happen. I think Peter must have been the most discouraged because he was the one who boasted that he would never betray or deny Jesus, and he eventually did.

This whole scenario tested their faith and exposed what was really in their hearts. It got them to a place where they could clearly see their heart and discern the evil motives from the good motives. When Jesus arose, He explained to them what had happened; He admonished them for their unbelief and explained furthermore about the kingdom. He may not have said anything different from before, but somehow, they heard it differently and, in their hearing, it changed them. With the combination of the Word sown in their hearts, their faith to weather the storm, and the grace and mercy of God, they came out on the other end with matured faith and understanding. They were beginning to exercise their senses, and they were able to start discerning the truth of what Jesus said. Through that, they were able to identify the evil motives that rested in their heart and be transformed by God's grace and work in them.

As the disciples heard about what was going to happen to Jesus and then witnessed it, they began experiencing the truth of what He said.

This is the same process we go through that allows us to know and understand God and walk with Him.

This is why prayer and communion with God are so essential to our Christian growth. We learn to hear His voice and listen to His Word that is preached. We meditate, pray, and commune with Him. But the truth of the matter is that true transformation happens only when we take what we have gotten from the Lord, live out our life in faith in the best and worst of times, and stand in faith. It is like going through a vigorous exercise we never enjoy until we feel and see the results in our body.

The writer of Hebrews puts it this way:

> For though by this time you ought to be teachers, you have need again for someone to teach you the elementary principles of the oracles of God, and you have come to need milk and not solid food. For everyone who partakes only of milk is not accustomed to the word of righteousness, for he is an infant. **But solid food is for the mature, who because of practice have their senses trained to discern good and evil.** (Hebrews 5:12-14)

The writer was admonishing the people to grow up in the things of God. If there is one thing we need in the body of Christ, it is to discern the difference between good and evil. The written Word, spoken by the mouthpiece of God—the Holy Spirit—combined with our faith and love for God, works these in us as we go and live our faith and apply it to our daily life. These key things get worked out in communion and prayer before the Lord.

I want to reiterate how important it is to discern between good and evil. Adam and Eve failed at this. According to Paul, in 2 Corinthians, this is the one thing that we will be judged for as believers—our deeds done in our body, whether they were good or evil. Yes, if we believe in Christ and the work of the cross, we will be with Him, but the rewards and blessings God wants to give us as believers are based on what we have done in the flesh (2 Corinthians 5:10). Our works will be judged as to whether they were good or evil. It is not the magnitude of our works that is judged, but our motives; did we do because God wanted us to do, and did we do it because we truly love God?

> *God, help us to discern the difference between good and evil, both in our lives and in those around us. Grant us grace to receive the truth and be transformed by it so we can experience You and be Your instruments through which others can see the truth of who You are. Amen.*

## The Word of God and Intimate Prayer

True intimacy flows from our heart—the center of our passions and emotions. It is the joining place of the spirit and the soul. This is why the first commandment is the most important. Jesus said that all the words and the prophets' sayings can be distilled to this one statement: "*And you must love the LORD your God with all your heart, all your soul, and all your strength, and all your mind*" (Luke 10:27, NLT). Whatever is first and foremost a passion in our heart is where we will direct our soul, thinking, and mental energy. Our soul drives our mind and intellect. The passions of our heart direct our thoughts and intellect. Our mind will focus on whatever is rooted in our heart, and that will fuel our actions.

If it is in our heart to be a great athlete, our mind will dwell on it and direct our body to be in constant motion, practicing and performing the respective tasks. If it is in our heart to be an artist, our passion combined with our mind will direct our body to develop the skills needed to become the best artist we can be. We can make countless analogies like this, but the idea is the same.

Jeremiah 17:9 tells us the heart is deceitful and wicked. Outside of the context of what is being said does not give us the whole picture of the spiritual representation of the heart. Jerimiah and Ezekiel both say that in the new covenant, God will create in us a new heart and give us a new spirit. The New Testament says that we can move mountains when we believe with our heart, and salvation comes from confessing with our mouth and believing with our heart. If the heart was only wicked, faith and salvation could never be possible. Our heart can become wicked and deceitful when we trust in men and in our flesh. We are deceived by our self-centeredness, and evil seeds grow in our heart. The heart is the womb of the spirit. It is where the Sower sows the Word. Other things can be sown in there too, and if we are not careful, they can grow up and choke the Word.

In the Old Testament, the ten commandments were written on stone tablets. This is a representation of the spiritual state of man. Man was spiritually dead and was separated from God. Just as God was able to write the ten commandments on tablets of stone, He can write on man's stony heart. Talking of the new covenant, Ezekiel 36:36 (NLT) says:

> And I will give you **a new heart, and I will put a new spirit in you.** I will take out your stony, stubborn heart and give you a tender, responsive heart. **And I will put my Spirit in you so that you will follow my decrees** and be careful to obey my regulations.

When we receive the work of Christ, we are born again; our spirit is born again, and we become a new creature. Our spirit is re-created in the image and likeness of Christ, we have a new heart, and we have God's Spirit within us. We have a heart of flesh. It is much easier to write on flesh than on stone!

When we are intimate with someone, we open our heart to them and share some of our most personal thoughts. Because of this, a special bond and communion occurs. A human being is created from the most intimate of acts. Through that passionate act, a seed and an egg are united, and flesh is created. Just as a baby can be born and flesh comes into being through an intimate act of communion and union, so can the seed of the Word of God germinate in our heart and become flesh in us through an intimate act of face-to-face communion. In natural terms, it is the groom who can experience the glory of the bride. The same can be said for the Word becoming flesh; Jesus being the Word, became flesh, and we could behold the glory of God in Him, and that attracted us to Him. When we turn our attention to Him, we experience His glory and grace, and truth is imparted to us. In the intimacy of this experience, the Word germinates in our heart and is formed in us.

The Word becomes flesh inside us by a spiritual act of intimacy. The Word, which is the seed, is planted in the womb of our spirit. When the passions of our heart are focused on beholding God and giving our attention to Him, the resulting intimacy becomes a union with God, and the Word becomes flesh in us. Transformation happens.

There are so many references in Psalms and Proverbs about the Word being written in our heart, or treasuring the Word of God in our heart. Psalm 119:11 says that we treasure the Word in our heart so we will not sin against Him. Proverbs 3 talks about writing mercy and truth on the tablet of our heart

> My son, do not forget my law, But let your heart keep my commands; For length of days and long life and peace they will add to you. Let not mercy and truth forsake you; Bind them around your neck, write them on the tablet of your heart, and so find favor and high esteem in the sight of God and man. (Proverbs 3:1-4, NKJV)

When we listen to someone talking, we tend to make eye contact with them so we can concentrate on what they are saying. We carefully rehearse what is being said and repeat it in our mind over and over again until we memorize it. Saying it over and over is a form of meditation. We keep it at the forefront of our mind and experience it as a governing force in our life. We let the words penetrate into our internal makeup and our inmost being. We enjoy the change that has occurred in us, making sure that nothing can take that away from us. This is how I studied for my final exams in college. I did this for hours until what I was being tested on was written in the forefront of my being.

Jesus is always knocking on the door of our heart. He wants to touch us and have access to the most intimate places of our lives. When

Jesus is talking in the book of Revelation about standing at the door and knocking, wanting to come in, He is not talking to the unbeliever, but to the believer. He is speaking to us and trying to get our attention through His Word. Let us look at the context in Revelation 3:20-21 (NASB):

> Behold, I stand at the door and knock; if anyone hears My voice and opens the door, I will come **in to him and will dine with him, and he with Me**. He who overcomes, I will grant to him to sit down with Me on My throne, as I also overcame and sat down with My Father on His throne.

This verse is a statement of intimacy and fellowship. Jesus says that he who overcomes will be granted to sit down with Him on our Father's throne. Paul writes that we are already seated with Him in heavenly places. This is our position in Christ. This experience of our position in Christ comes with an intimate relationship.

This reminds us of what Jesus was saying to the disciples in the upper room as recorded in John 13-17. He was talking about abiding in Him, or remaining in Him.

> Jesus answered and said to him, "If anyone **loves** Me, he will keep My word; and My Father will **love** him, and We will come to him and make Our abode with him. (John 14:23, NASB)

The emphasis in this verse is not just on obedience, it is on loving Him. It literally says, "*If you keep loving me, you will keep my word, and I will make my dwelling and abode in you.*" This is a statement of intimacy. The more we love Jesus, the more we will want to obey Him and keep His Word. This results from God dwelling in us and having His Word take root in our heart. This is the place where germination of the seed happens, and the Word becomes flesh inside of us. It is transformative and life-changing.

**Key 3: Prayer, His Presence, and His Word**

When we think about passionately seeking God, we need to picture it as an intimate dinner with our most beloved, where we are dining and communicating with one another. This is a place where influence happens—not just God influencing us, but we influence God as well. Effective prayer is not always about the amount of time you spend in prayer; it is about the intimate relationship and the words we share. Think of Moses's intimate time of prayer with God, and him reciting God's Word back to God about God's original intent to go with the children of Israel into the promised land. Israel sinned, rejected God, and went after another love and worshipped it. But in the intimate time pf prayer, Moses was able to influence God and remind Him of His previous words and get Him to change His mind.

Effective supplication, intercession, and answered prayer are born out of an intimate prayer life that is rooted in the Word of God and through the Word becoming flesh in us. Reminding God about our prior conversations, and the words He revealed to us, leads to an effective prayer. Jesus wants this and hungers after this. Pointing to the Word of God and telling God that His Word promises healing, salvation, deliverance makes prayer, supplication, and intercession effective.

That is why God made so many powerful statements about answered prayer. Answered prayer is born out of faith, and faith comes by hearing and hearing by the Word of God. Hearing comes out of an intimate and fulfilling prayer life. Jesus said that we can move mountains through faith. He said that we can ask anything in His name, and the Father will do it. He said that we can use His name and pray for the sick to be healed, and they will be healed. The Word of God and intimate prayer cannot be separated. They are in union, and they bring true spiritual growth and an effective and powerful prayer life.

# Key 4:
# Identity, Faith, and Your Position Before God

## Vision, Purpose, and Leadership

In the previous sections, we expounded on the desire and hunger for prayer, and the importance of worship and the Word of God. Each of those should lead you to a revelation of who God is and your position before Him.

I want to start this subject from the book of Genesis, take it through the old covenant, and into the Gospels, which are really transitional writings that lead into the new covenant and the restoration of our position before God. We will end in the book of Revelation.

We all ask the questions, "Who are we?" "Why are we here?" and "What is our purpose?" Understanding the answer to these questions will undoubtedly change how we communicate with God.

Years ago, while contemplating Proverbs 27:18, God gave me a revelation of vision, purpose, and leadership.

> Where there is no vision (divine revelation), the people are unrestrained (naked, without restraint). But happy is he who keeps the law.

This verse directly applies to identity and the questions we asked. Identity, in this context, is the condition of being oneself. This scripture in Proverbs means we will have no direction, leadership, or purpose if we do not understand who we are. The more we understand who we are, the more secure we will be in our identity. The more secure we are in our identity, the more effective we will be in our prayer and faith living. The ending effect is that you are the "oneself" God designed you to be.

In Genesis 1, we read that God created everything. But when it came to man, God said:

> Then God said, "**Let Us make man in Our image, according to Our likeness**; and let them **rule over the fish of the sea and over** the birds of the sky and over the cattle and over all the earth, and over every creeping thing that creeps on the earth." **God created man in His own image, in the image of God He created him; male and female He created them.** (Genesis 1:26-27, NASB)

The difference we see is that man was created in the image and likeness of God Himself, or better yet, the Trinity—notice how God said let "US" make man? Man was put in leadership over all other creation. God created man as His offspring—externally and internally: externally in form and internally as a triune being. God is Father, Son, and Holy Spirit. Man is spirt, soul, and body.

In Genesis 2, we read more details on how God created man:

> Then the LORD **God formed man out of dust from the ground and breathed into his nostrils the breath of life; and man became a living being**. (Genesis 2:7, NASB)

Notice what God said, and how the creation of man was different from every other creation. This is the only creation where God formed something. Every chemical in man's body can be found in the earth. God did something different with man; using His own hands, He formed man's body and made man in His image and likeness. Like the care an expert potter takes in making every curve of a pot, so God shaped us. Then He did something even more stunning—He breathed into us the breath of life, or the spirit of life. In John 4, Jesus told us that God is Spirit. So that means God took some of His very essence and put it in us. As a child is birthed physically from a woman's womb, man is spiritually birthed from God. We are the offspring of the magnificent Creator.

God took His very essence and put it in us. I like to say that God chose to be incomplete without us. Why else would God have gone through what He did to bring us back to Himself? He sent Jesus, God incarnate, to die for His creation. I remember when my oldest son was born; he fell asleep on my chest as I was holding him. I had the distinct feeling that he was a part of me, bone of my bone, flesh of my flesh. It is hard to describe the depth of emotional connectiveness that I experienced. Why would God be any different? We are spirit of His Spirit.

This is why man and God have such a great longing for each other. Even in the most fallen and deprived state, man longs for God. Man was created to fellowship in the garden. God and man had face-to-face interactions and intimate communication. God put man in the garden for pleasure, and the pleasure of the garden was secondary to the pleasure of being in face-to-face communion and interaction with God. God would show up just to be with man. Man was the highest form and the best of the best of God's creation.

Man was like God in every way. In Psalm 8, the psalmist says that God made man a little lower than Himself, but above everything else that He created. He gave man dominion over the garden of Eden and asked man to cultivate it. They were the lords of the earth and set there to protect the gift God had given them. He wanted man to guard the garden from the evil one—the devil—who fell from the highest position before the throne of God in heaven because he tried to exalt himself above God. God made man greater than all that He had created and gave man the highest position in all of creation.

The devil came with a lie and a half-truth in Genesis 3:4-5:

> The serpent said to the woman, "You surely will not die! For God knows that in the day you eat from it your eyes will be opened, and you will be like God, knowing good and evil."

The lie was that man would not die, and the half-truth was that their eyes would be opened, and they could be like God, knowing good and evil. Man and woman were already the offspring of God; they were His children. The only difference I can see is that God knew both good and evil but had the ability to always choose good. It was true that man could become like God knowing good and evil, but the devil did not inform man that the consequence of their disobedience would result in separation from God.

When death entered man, it was a cataclysmic event. The spiritual DNA of man was corrupted and mutated by sin and death. Paul writes extensively about this in Romans 5. Here is a sample from that chapter:

> Therefore, just as through one man sin entered into the world, and death through sin, and so death spread to all men, because all sinned. (Romans 5:12)

Man and woman were separated from God. They were fearful, shameful, and afraid of God. They covered themselves because they lost their natural covering—the glory of God. They covered themselves with fig leaves. They lost their position and calling and gave it over to the devil.

But from that point on, God put a plan in place to redeem man and woman and bring them back to Him. God took away their effort to cover their sins—the fig leaves—knowing it would never bring redemption to them. God covered man and woman with the skins of animals. God provided man and woman a covering and promised to bring them back to their glory and their position before Him.

**Key 4: Identity, Faith, and Your Position Before God**

In Roman 5:15, 17, Paul writes about the power of redemption through Jesus's death on the cross and His resurrection:

> But the free gift is not like the transgression. For if by the transgression of the one the many died, **much more did the grace of God and the gift by the grace of the one Man, Jesus Christ, abound to the many**. For if by the transgression of the one, death reigned through the one, **much more those who receive the abundance of grace and of the gift of righteousness will reign in life through the One, Jesus Christ**.

The point here is to understand that we are created to be God's offspring—in spite of all the massive detours we have taken. God has restored us to our position before Him, and we have been restored to right standing with Him. Therefore, we have rightful access to Him without shame or guilt.

Getting back to the subject of vision, purpose, and leadership, once we understand our position before God, it becomes a guiding force for our lives. The greater the vision or revelation we have of who we are, who God is, and who He created us to be, the clearer we will see our purpose. Purpose is the reason someone or something exists. We exist because God wanted a family. We exist because we are the offspring of God. We exist because God loves us and wants us to experience Him, and He wants to experience us. We exist to guide, guard, and govern the earth. We exist to expand God's influence and kingdom on earth. We exist to glorify God and reflect His nature.

Man is not an accidental evolution. Man exists because God wanted us. God is the force and power that set everything in motion. He released the light of His presence on the earth and inside of us. The release of His life was the force that put everything together from a state of chaos to the highest level of divine order. The greater the vision and revelation of this, the more we walk in our purpose, and the more we will lead and influence the world system around us for the dominion of God.

This leads us into His presence with a sense of belonging and purpose. We realize that each of us has a part to play in this magnificent plan of God. We co-labor with Him, and in our prayer life, we experience the revelation, our vision grows, and the understanding of our purpose becomes more real. This instills in us an assurance that will lead us and others around us into God's presence.

## The Old Covenant and Our Identity

God had a plan from the beginning of creation, and after man's fall, He wanted to restore man back to his position. To do that, He first needed a man to walk in covenant with Him so He could have entry to redeem man and impart to him the life of God. That man was Abram. Reading Genesis 12 through 25, we see God interact with Abram.

In Genesis, God appears to Abram and makes him an offer. He tells Abram what he needs to do to accept the offer. I am not going to unpack the whole life of Abram and its importance, but I want to point out a couple of things. God wanted to bless Abram and make him a blessing to the world. God said that He would make Abram a blessing, and that blessing would be through one of Abram's descendants. Little did he know that descendant would be Jesus. Through Jesus—the promised One—God brought forgiveness, redemption, and restoration to man, and He brought him back to his original position and identity with God.

In Genesis 15, God initiated the old covenant with Abram. When a covenant was cut (an animal was sacrificed), it was the legal contract of the day. An animal would be sliced in pieces, and men would walk between those pieces. We read in a previous chapter that as Abram was walking through the pieces (covenant), he saw two beings of light passing through the covenant ritual, representing God the Father and God the Son (Jesus).

After Sarah finally conceived at ninety-nine years of age, Isaac was born. He was the heir and the line through whom Jesus would come. He was the promise fulfilled of the line of Abraham. When Isaac was about twelve years old, God asked Abraham to offer him as a covenant sacrifice. So Abraham obeyed God and took Isaac to be sacrificed. Now, Isaac knew what was needed to perform sacrifices to Jehovah, since he had more than likely participated in sacrifices with his father many times. But this time, he realized that the sacrifice itself was not there. Isaac asked Abraham about the sacrifice, and Abraham told him that God would provide. When they reached the altar, Abraham put Isaac on the altar and was about to sacrifice him. As he lifted his arm to sacrifice his son, God saw Abraham's obedience and his willingness to offer Isaac, his beloved son of promise. He stopped Abraham and showed him a ram stuck in the thicket. He provided a sacrifice for Abraham, just as He provided His Son, Jesus, as the ultimate sacrifice for us.

Abraham was the man God needed. Later on, we read that the Israelites, who are the descendants of Abraham, were delivered from Egypt by God because of His promise to Abraham. Notice God's heart toward man again. After the Israelites were delivered from Egypt, God brought them to Mount Sinai so they could worship Him and He could be their God, and they could be His beloved firstborn.

In Exodus 19:3-8 (NLT), we see God revealing more of His plan and what He wanted for Israel.

> Then Moses climbed the mountain to appear before God. The LORD called to him from the mountain and said, "Give these instructions to the family of Jacob; announce it to the descendants of Israel: 'You have seen what I did to the Egyptians. **You know how I carried you on eagles' wings and brought you to myself. Now if you will obey me and keep my covenant, you will be my own special treasure from among all the peoples on earth; for all the earth belongs to me. And you will be my kingdom of priests, my holy nation.' This is the message you must give to the people of Israel."** So Moses returned from the mountain and called together the elders of the people and told them everything the LORD had commanded him. **And all the**

> **people responded together, "We will do everything the LORD has commanded." So Moses brought the people's answer back to the LORD.**

Some translations say that the Israelites are God's special possession, a treasure special to Him, and if anyone recognizes this special relationship, it could be a treasure unto them as well. This treasure could be in the present and in the future. In the present, by blessing God's special treasure, anyone could be blessed. In the future, knowing that the One coming through this lineage would bring forgiveness, redemption, and eternal life.

God was going to make them a kingdom of priests and a holy nation. Anyone could come to God as a priest and minister and experience Him. Although there was a special place for the king, priest, and prophet in Israel, everyone had access to the presence of God.

God came down and met Israel, and the elders of Israel came up and dined with Him. When we think of the Israelites in the wilderness, we cannot but think of God delivering them from Egypt. However, I tend to think more of how God manifested Himself to them and was present among them in all His glory.

In Exodus 33:7, we read that Moses set up a special tent outside the camp where ANYONE could come and seek and meet the Lord.

> Now Moses used to take the tent and pitch it outside the camp, a good distance from the camp, and he called it the tent of meeting. **And everyone who sought the LORD would go out to the tent of meeting which was outside the camp**.

When Moses entered the tent, the glory of God descended on it, and Moses experienced face-to-face communion with God. But the tent was not limited to Moses to come in and out to fellowship with God. Anyone among the Israelites could enter the tent and come before the Lord, worship, fellowship, and interact with Him. Although the Scriptures do not say this, I wonder if the cloud fell on other people as they came to worship God with a pure heart. I would think so.

In Exodus, we read about the intimate prayers and conversations Moses had with God. We read of Moses's bold intercession for the children of Israel. We read about God passing before Moses and proclaiming His glory. We also read Moses's prayer to know God, when he recalled how he received favor and grace from God, and how God revealed His ways to him so he might have more favor and grace. God enjoyed this interaction with Moses and was happy to grant him his request.

This was another step in God's plan to redeem man. But I want to point out that God's desire was to give man status and stand with him and fellowship with him. He wanted man to worship Him, and through worship, He wanted to reveal Himself to man so man could experience the most wonderful being, who calls him His treasure. Man had status; this became his identity that to this day sticks with the Jewish people—God's chosen and beloved. Today, this is not limited to the Jewish people; anyone can be the chosen and beloved of God.

Next, God made another covenant with man, that another deliverer like Moses would come. God knew the current covenant could only take man so far; it could not restore the position of man back to the fullness he was created for.

In the old covenant, there were prescribed ways by which man could come to God. A temple made by man represented the path to God. There were prescribed ways of worship and sacrifices made from the blood of lambs and goats. Then, there was the Day of Atonement, where the high priest would go in with a perfect lamb, offer it, and spread its blood on the mercy seat that rested in the holy of holies—the place where the presence of God dwelt. This sacrifice was offered for forgiveness of sins and was a type and representation of the One coming from God who would redeem man.

The writer of the book of Hebrews describes the new and old living way. He talks about Christ being the new living way into the presence of God.

> So Christ has now become the High Priest over all the good things that have come. He has entered that greater, more perfect Tabernacle in heaven, which was not made by human hands and is not part of this created world. With his own blood—not the blood of goats and calves—he entered the Most Holy Place once for all time and secured our redemption forever…For Christ did not enter into a holy place made with human hands, which was only a copy of the true one in heaven. He entered into heaven itself to appear now before God on our behalf. And he did not enter heaven to offer himself again and again, like the high priest here on earth who enters the Most Holy Place year after year with the blood of an animal. (Hebrews 9:11-14, 24-25, NLT)

## Identity: Our Position—In Jesus's Words

In the Old Testament, we see numerous promises of a spiritual upgrade coming—a new covenant that would allow man to experience God and come closer to the identity he was created for.

The prophet Ezekiel said that God was going to give man a new heart and put a new spirit within him. Man's heart would no longer be like stone but would be a heart of flesh—a tender, responsive heart—a heart that God can easily write His words and impressions on. Ezekiel also says that God would put His Spirit within man; that means God would dwell in man.

Since the fall of man, God did not dwell within man. Man died spiritually and separated himself from God. Now God changed this by sending Jesus in human flesh. Jesus came as a Man, began His ministry, and pointed man to God. John the Baptist beautifully declared, "*Behold, the Lamb of God who takes away the sin of the world.*" (John 1:29)

Jesus talked about being born again. He said that we have to be born of water and the Spirit to enter the kingdom of heaven. Jesus became a sacrifice; He became the unblemished sacrificial Lamb and took away the sins of the world. He brought to us forgiveness and redemption and took away our sins. He satisfied the high court of heaven. Paul writes in the book of Romans that all of us have sinned and fallen short of God's glory. Sinful nature was passed down to us, and we needed someone to change this. We needed a powerful event to happen to break the unity of sin and death within man. This event was God becoming a Man and offering Himself as a sacrifice for us. This powerful event changed all of history.

I liken this event to a spiritual atomic blast. An atomic blast splits an atom and releases a tremendous amount of energy. This energy can be used constructively or destructively. This energy destroys everything within its radius. It also releases radiation into the atmosphere, which can destroy human tissue and inhibit its ability to protect the immune system.

Similarly, the cross of Christ releases an "adamic blast." It split the old Adam and his sinful nature from the new Adam (Jesus, the Christ). This is the most powerful event in all of human history. It birthed a new creation. Its blast radius has reached throughout all eternity and is still going. When someone calls on the name of Jesus, the God who said, "*Let there be light*" and created the heavens and the earth, again says, "*Let there be light.*" That blast reaches inside the person, and they are born again in the image and likeness of God in their spirit. The light of the glory of God in the face of Jesus blasts through the old man, destroys sin and death, and creates new life.

In the New Testament, there are so many references to the new being that happens at the new birth. We read in the Gospel of John that Jesus said that as many as received Him, He gave them the right to become a child of God (John1:12). We are taken by God into His family. We are a favored child in the household of God. We get to live in the state of eternal life, which is the abundant life that Jesus talked about.

In John 8, Jesus said that a servant cannot remain in the master's house; they can work there, but at the end of the day, it is only the family that remains in the master's house. We were servants under the old covenant, but Jesus set us free, and now we are sons who belong in the Master's house.

In John 15, Jesus tells us that we are no longer slaves (servants). A slave or servant is not aware of the secrets and details of the master of the house. We not only have the right to remain in the Master's house, but we are His friends as well. God called Abraham His friend, but now, we all are God's friends through faith in Jesus and the power that God released into us through that faith.

In John 17, we read Jesus's prayer for His disciples and future disciples, and those who believed in Him through them. We see the intimacy and position they had. Jesus said that He has given us His glory that we may be one with Him as He is one with the Father.

These statements by Jesus speak to the identity we have, our position in Him, and our calling. God gives us a revelation and understanding of our identity and calling, which awakens boldness in prayer before Him that we may walk in our position, calling, and purpose.

## The New Covenant and Our Identity

Most of the New Testament was written by the apostle Paul. Paul was not with Jesus during His earthly ministry and did not experience all the things Jesus's disciples experienced at the cross and at the resurrection. Yet, Paul had a greater understanding and revelation of Jesus's life. He understood in the spiritual realm the power of the cross and what happened at Jesus's death, burial, and resurrection. Many of his powerful writings—Romans, Galatians, Ephesians, Philippians, Colossians, and 1 and 2 Corinthians—are full of revelation about Jesus's substitution for us on the cross. And if we choose to receive His redemption for man, Jesus becomes our substitute, and we can experience identification with Him.

When we accept this and identify with Jesus, God considers us like Jesus and treats us the same as Him. Then, the power of resurrection releases into us a new birth. First, we become a new creation breathing God's Spirit and life. Jesus, like Adam, had God's breath in Him, which is the breath of life, and He became a living soul. Similarly, we have a new inbreathing, and a new creation happened.

Paul explains this in 2 Corinthians 5:17:

> Therefore if anyone is in Christ, he is a new creature; the old things passed away; behold, new things have come.
>
> This means that anyone who belongs to Christ has become a new person. The old life is gone; a new life has begun! (NLT)

We are new-creation beings. Man is a spirit, he has a soul, and he lives in a body. The spirit is the real you; it is the essence and character that makes you who you are. The soul is the color of your spirit; it is your mind, intellect, and emotions. The body is your covering. When we receive Jesus as our Lord and Savior, we become born of the Spirit of God. We came into this world and were born of water, and then when we receive Jesus, we are born of the Spirt.

Let me explain in detail what happens when we accept Jesus as our substitute for sin: He pays our debt, He forgives our sins, and He gives us a new life. When we ask Jesus to come dwell in us, God says, "Let there be light in your spirit." The light of the knowledge of the glory of God in the face of Christ releases the adamic blast of the resurrection through the cross (2 Corinthians 4:6). Jesus, our substitute, was crucified, dead, and buried. He descended into the lower parts of the earth—hell. Then the glory of God entered hell and breathed life back into Him, and raised Him from the dead. Then He ascended into heaven and was seated again at the right hand of the Father. He is our substitute. Jesus started in heaven at the right hand of the Father and then shed His glory to become a Man. Jesus counted it not the prize to be held more than anything else to be with the Father, but the prize was pleasing the Father by shedding His glory to bring man back to Him. He shed glory as a Man and decided to do the will of the Father and go to the cross. He did that to redeem man.

Jesus was crucified, and we were crucified (Galatians 2:20; Romans 6:6). Jesus died, and we died with him (Romans 5:8). Jesus was buried, and we were buried with Him (Romans 6:4; Colossians 2:12). Jesus was made alive, and we were made alive (Ephesians 2:5; Colossians 2:13). Jesus was raised from the dead, and we were raised from the dead (Colossians 3:1, 2:12; Romans 6:4). Jesus is seated in heavenly places, and we are seated in heavenly places (Ephesians 1:20, 2:6).

When we receive this by faith and faith alone, as new creations in Christ, we begin to experience God and learn that we are the righteousness of God in Christ. We are right and in one accord with God. In being in one accord with God, we have peace with God. Peace results from the prosperity of our new harmonious relationship with God through the work of the cross.

Righteousness is a state of being right with God, meaning, there is no hinderance in our relationship with Him. Paul put it so wonderfully in 2 Corinthians 5:21:

> He made Him who knew no sin to be sin on our behalf, so that we might become the righteousness of God in Him.
>
> For God made Christ, who never sinned, to be the offering for our sin, so that we could be made right with God through Christ. (NLT)

With this comes other positions and standings before God. First, we understand that we are His children, and as a child, we have the rights of inheritance (Ephesians 2:11, 14; Galatians 4:6). God is our inheritance, and we are His inheritance. We receive the benefits of being an heir. An heir receives the inheritance once the benefactor dies. The problem with that is you receive the benefits because the person passes away, and your relationship with the person ends. In God's kingdom, we get both—we get the inheritance and the relationship because Jesus died and was raised from the dead, never to die again. Only God could make such a thing happen!

On the converse, we are God's inheritance.

> I pray that the eyes of your heart may be enlightened, **so that you will know what is the hope of His calling, what are the riches of the glory of His inheritance in the saints**. (Ephesians 1:18)

For God to receive His inheritance, we need to die. But, just as Jesus was raised from the dead, we too are raised from the dead. God receives His inheritance and continues to have a living relationship with us.

This work that Jesus did brings us into fellowship and intimacy with God.

> For God made the only one who did not know sin to become sin for us, so that we who did not know righteousness might become the righteousness of God through our union with him. (TPT)

We are all part of the royal family in the kingdom of God. We understand that God wanted to make the Israelites a holy nation, a royal priesthood, and a special treasure to Himself. But what the old covenant could not do—because it was only a fleshly representative of what God Himself had to do— was accomplished by the new covenant. He destroyed and condemned sin in the flesh so that all the requirements of redemption might be fulfilled. That is why in Revelation 5, we see the exalted Lamb, and the angels describing Jesus as follows:

> And they sang a new song, saying, "Worthy are You to take the book and to break its seals; for You were slain, and purchased for God with Your blood men from every tribe and tongue and people and nation. **You have made them to be a kingdom and priests to our God; and they will reign upon the earth**." (Revelation 5:9-10)

When you read Paul's writings, you will find many wonderful statements of who we are and what we have been made into through the work of the cross. We are God's workmanship created in Christ. Let me describe this. Just as God was contemplating the earth, and the Holy Spirit was viewing how the earth was formless and void, God said, "*Let there be light!*" These words took what was formless and void and put it in the perfect creative order of God. The same God who said, "*Let there be light*," shines in our heart when we receive the work of the cross by faith. He speaks light into our spirit, and we are recreated in divine order. We are God's special project. He created a new work in us and made us a new creation. He created us in His own image and likeness again, so He can dwell in us and fellowship with us, and we can dwell in Him and fellowship with Him.

Not only are we the children of God, but there are several references throughout the Bible on other relational positions we have before God.

Imagine how this could affect how we communicate and interact with the living God. We are in the King's chamber having conversation and communion with Him. This brings us to a whole new place of communication and interaction with God. Paul in his letter to the Romans says that Jesus was the firstborn among many brethren.

> For God knew his people in advance, and he chose them to become like his Son, so that his Son would be the firstborn among many brothers and sisters. (Romans 8:29, NLT)

Since Jesus was the firstborn from the dead, He is our big Brother, and we are His siblings. Christ, the Anointed One, refers to His deity. Jesus was raised from the dead by the glory of the Father and the power of the Holy Spirit. When we are raised from the dead, our spirt is raised and created in the image of God and inbreathed with His Spirit again. The divine dwells in man again. We are children—the offspring of God. We have been made the temple and the dwelling place of God; our bodies are the temple of the Holy Spirit.

Lastly, the church as a whole is commonly referred to as the bride of Christ. Jesus is making His bride ready by washing her with the water of His Word. He sealed His church with the Holy Spirit and gave Him to us as a deposit. This means the born-again experience and the outpouring of the Holy Spirit is just the beginning. I like to say that it was as if God put a ring on our finger and marked us for Himself. One day, as we read in the book of Revelation, there will be a marriage supper of the Lamb (Revelation 19:7).

The relationship between God and us is similar to a human family relationship. God is our Father, we are His children, Jesus is our big Brother, and we are the bride of Christ. We could write volumes discussing our identity in Christ. The Bible is simply a story of a Father and His family.

The point here is to understand that we have a standing and right to be in God's presence and commune with Him. This is the foundation for continued, bold, enjoyable, and powerful prayer times with the Father, Son, and Holy Spirt. Take it in. Confess that you are a child of God! Say that Jesus is your big Brother! Say that you are a part of the bride of Christ and one day will enjoy the marriage supper of the Lamb! Keep saying it. Say that the Holy Spirit is your Helper—a Friend that sticks closer than a brother! Say that you are the beloved of God! Say that you are His workmanship and perfectly created masterpiece. Say that you are the temple and the dwelling place of God, and you are created to dwell with Him and He with you!

## Receive It All By Faith

From time to time, we may feel that we are not that important to God because of our shortcomings and faults. Despite them, God's confession about you does not change. How can we walk in this confidence? How can we experience this? By faith alone!

We receive all of this by faith. But how does this happen? It is amazingly simple: by hearing these things over and over and over again. The more we hear it, the more we understand God's plan and love for man.

We see His lovingkindness and compassion toward us, which leads us to His grace. Grace is not just unmerited favor. God manifests His unmerited favor to us by His willingness to use His power and ability on our behalf even though we do not deserve it.

Faith is a response to the grace of God. When we see and understand all that God has done for us, how He feels about us, and what He has called us to, then our faith in Him increases. Paul states in Romans 5:1-2:

> Therefore, having been **justified by faith**, we have peace with God through our Lord Jesus Christ, through whom also we have obtained our **introduction by faith into this grace in which we stand;** and we exult in hope of the glory of God. (NASB)

Paul says it again in Romans 4:16:

> **For this reason it is by faith, in order that it may be in accordance with grace**, so that the promise will be guaranteed to all the descendants, not only to those who are of the Law, but also to those who are of the faith of Abraham, who is the father of us all.

Grace comes before faith. We are brought into the kingdom and given an identity with God by grace through faith. They are both gifts from God, so in the end we understand that it is He who has done the work, and we just have to believe and act on it.

This faith brings us into right standing with God. Right standing is righteousness, and this is what brings us to a place of faith in God. I cannot say it any better than Paul does in Romans 1:17:

> For in it the righteousness of God is revealed from faith to faith; as it is written, "BUT THE RIGHTEOUS man SHALL LIVE BY FAITH."

## Key 4: Identity, Faith, and Your Position Before God

There were two things that got Jesus's attention: faith and unbelief (lack of faith). He marveled at both of them. Jesus admired the centurion's faith as he came to ask for healing for his servant (Matthew 8:5-13). He told Jesus, "*Just say the word and my servant will be healed.*" (Matthew 8:8)

> Now when Jesus heard this, He marveled and said to those who were following, "Truly I say to you, I have not found such great faith with anyone in Israel." (Matthew 8:10)

He also admired the Canaanite woman's faith who would not take no for an answer but kept coming to Him until her daughter was healed (Matthew 15:21-28). Great was her faith!

> Then Jesus said to her, "O woman, your faith is great; it shall be done for you as you wish." And her daughter was healed at once. (Matthew 15:28)

Jesus enjoyed the faith of the woman with the issue of blood (Mark 5:25-34). She was out of compliance with the Jewish law by being out in public while she was bleeding. In spite of it all, she kept pushing through the crowd, weak and ashamed, but relentlessly pursuing her healing. She was desperate for a healing touch from God. There were hundreds of people pressing around Jesus, but she got His attention by touching the hem of His robe. This touch is the touch of deep love and faith. It caused the power of God to flow from Him and heal her. Jesus knew what had happened, but He stopped and asked, "Who reached out to me in passionate (my interpretation) faith?" Jesus stopped because her faith touched His heart. He saw her, and when He did, she realized that she could go nowhere, and she told Him her story, not knowing how He would react. But Jesus, forgetting about the crowd and fixing His eyes on this woman with love, compassion, and excitement, said, "*Daughter, your faith has made you well*" (Mark 5:34). Jesus called her, "daughter," which is a term of endearment for a covenant child. Jesus's response was exciting and endearing to the woman.

Jesus introduced the subject of faith with the parable of the mustard seed. The mustard seed is exceedingly small in size, but it grows into a great bush. Faith is remarkably similar. In Mark 11:22-24, Jesus talked about having this kind of faith in God. This kind of faith can speak to mountains and make them move. In this context, Jesus was imparting radical authority and power to the church, which must be received by faith. These things had not been heard of or understood before.

Jesus came to His hometown and instructed the people there, but they did not believe. Therefore, Jesus could do no mighty miracles or release God's power over them. He was disappointed because of the hardness of their heart and their unbelief.

After Jesus's resurrection, His disciples did not believe the testimony of Him being raised from the dead. Now, that is something! Jesus had told them several times about what was going to happen to Him and that He would be raised from the dead. He was the guy who did mightier miracles than anyone who had ever lived. He gave them plenty of reasons to believe. But they struggled, and He reprimanded them for their unbelief when He appeared to them after His resurrection.

In John chapters 13–17, we read about what Jesus said and did during the last supper. Jesus, aware of His impending death on the cross and the coming of the new covenant, told His disciples many important things. However, they did not understand them. Many of Jesus's statements were about prayer and ways to approach God the Father, and the Son. These statements were radically different from what the Jews had experienced in their practice of Judaism. These are prayer statements. Let us take a look at them:

> Truly, truly, I say to you, he who believes in Me, the works that I do, he will do also; and greater(more) works than these he will do; because I go to the Father. **Whatever you ask in My name, that will I do, so that the Father may be glorified in the Son. If you ask Me anything in My name, I will do it.** (John 14:12-14)

> You did not choose Me but I chose you, and appointed you that you would go and bear fruit, and that your fruit would remain, **so that whatever you ask of the Father in My name He may give to you.** (John 15:16)

> In that day you will not question Me about anything. Truly, truly, I say to you, **if you ask the Father for anything in My name, He will give it to you. Until now you have asked for nothing in My name; ask and you will receive, so that your joy may be made full.** (John 16:23-24)

These statements have had a profound effect on the Christian church. This is where the authority of using the name of Jesus was set in motion. This is why, to this day, we end our prayers in Jesus's name. It is the name above everything. It is the only name that has authority over everything in heaven, on the earth, and under the earth. This is the name through which we have the power to cast out demons and lay hands on the sick. This was bestowed upon Jesus because of the great sacrificial work He did on the cross.

Once Jesus was raised from the dead, these things began to happen. In Acts 3, we see Peter practicing this when he said to the beggar, "*Silver and gold I do not have, but what I do have I give you: In the "NAME" of Jesus Christ of Nazareth, rise up and walk*" (Acts 3:6, NKJV). That is exactly what happened! The power of God was released through faith in Jesus's name—the beggar's body was made whole, and he arose and walked. This is an exact fulfillment of what Jesus told His disciples a few weeks before His death. The resurrection was the evil one's worst nightmare because, instead of having just one person anointed by the Holy Spirit—as with the Son of God—all who received Jesus's finished work on the cross received the same anointing. They were doing greater works in number because there were now many of them.

Once the beggar was healed, Peter had a great crowd for his second big sermon recorded in Acts. He said that on the basis of faith in Jesus's name, the beggar was healed. The healing and the sermon created a stir among the people and produced another great harvest in the kingdom of God. This upset the religious leaders. They arrested Peter and John and asked them by what power they did this miracle. Peter boldly said that the miracle was done by faith in the name of Jesus—the Jesus whom they crucified. Talk about throwing cutting, powerful words at them! The religious leaders were stunned. They put Peter and John out and discussed the matter. They realized that they had a real problem. They also realized that Peter and John were with Jesus, and guess what? They were acting just like Jesus! Acts records that the religious leaders observed the disciples' boldness and understood that they had been with Jesus.

Realizing that they could do nothing, and that a miracle had taken place, the religious leaders tried to intimidate them and get the disciples to stop speaking in the name of Jesus. But Peter knew that was where the power was—access to the Father and access to an intimate prayer life for them and for others.

The question for us is: How does this enrich our prayer life? It is the ingredient that feeds the heart of man with the seed of the Word of God that grows our faith. Growing our faith will grow our prayer life. It will grow into intimacy and confidence with God. It will grow into a place of ongoing fellowship and joy in the Father's presence. It will grow into a powerful conduit for the kingdom to bring healing, deliverance, and an inward transformation that will outwardly affect others.

We receive this revelation by faith in Jesus's name, power, and boldness.

## Hearing His Word, and Faith

Prayer and faith go hand in hand; like Jesus and the Holy Spirit, they are the same in purpose, and they work together. Prayer leads to communication with God; intimate communication with God leads to hearing God; and hearing God leads to faith. One cannot separate an intimate prayer life from a life of growing in faith.

I want to reiterate and take us back to an account I mentioned on previous pages because I want to emphasize it as it relates to the chapter title. God called the Israelites out of Egypt and brought them to Mount Sinai. During this Exodus, we read about some of the greatest miracles performed on earth. Because Egypt did not want to let the Israelites go, God brought terrible plagues upon the Egyptians. God delivered the Israelites with Egypt's wealth; it became the payment for Israel's services to Egypt. He kept the Israelites in the wilderness, and their clothes and shoes did not wear out. He split the Red Sea and allowed them to walk through it. He destroyed the greatest army known at that time.

All of these great miracles were performed so the Israelites could go to the wilderness to worship God, and God's covenant promise to Abraham could be fulfilled. As we discussed earlier, worship was not just for God, but also a basis for the Israelites to start a relationship with God so He could begin revealing Himself to them.

I want to summarize what happened in Exodus 19 and 20, which was later recalled by Moses in Deuteronomy 4 and 5. These chapters are descriptions of the same event. Exodus is a recount of what happened when Israel accepted God's invitation to be His own special treasure—a holy nation and a nation of priests to God. God called the nation of Israel to meet with Him. He came down from Mount Sinai to speak with them so they could hear His voice. The Deuteronomy narrative was through the eyes of Moses and was written about forty years after the encounter at Mount Sinai. It was Moses's writing to Israel, exhorting them to follow the Lord, because he knew that his time on earth was short, and his death was near. Also, it was Moses's last exhortation to the children of Israel after experiencing God's presence and guidance for forty years in the wilderness. I like to say that Exodus is more a letter of the law, while Deuteronomy is the spirit of the law and is likened unto Romans in its theological importance to the old covenant.

Israel accepted God's invitation of betrothal, and God told them to prepare themselves for their meeting with Him. After three days, the children of Israel came to the foot of Mount Sinai, and God came down to visit them there.

> Remember the day you stood before the Lord your God at Horeb, when the Lord said to me, "Assemble the people to Me, that I may let them hear My words so they may learn to fear Me all the days they live on the earth, and that they may teach their children." You came near and stood at the foot of the mountain, and the mountain burned with fire to the **very heart of the heavens**: darkness, cloud and thick gloom. (Deuteronomy 4:10-11)

As God came down to meet them, fire burned to the very heart of the heavens. The mountain shook, and there was thunder and lightning. Was the mountain shaking because God was mad, or did He want to scare them? Remember the situation; God had given them a special offer—I call it an offer of betrothal. Jeremiah the prophet references this in Jeremiah 2:2:

> Thus says the Lord, "I remember concerning you the devotion of your youth, the **love** of your betrothals, your following after Me in the wilderness, through a land not sown."

God was coming down to meet His bride—His beloved. Since the fuel to God's fire is His love, and God was so excited to meet His bride, the shaking, thunder, and lightning happened. When a holy God interacts with a world full of sin, there is bound to be a reaction. God's love and desire were burning so great that it seemed like the fire was burning from heaven to earth.

Think about a time in your life when a beloved was presented to you—perhaps your wedding day. If you are married, think about how you felt when you saw your spouse walking down the aisle or standing at the altar; what was happening in your heart, and what emotions engulfed you? Was there an intense excitement, a rush of emotions, and love flowing all over and through you? Or recall the first time you met your spouse or someone you love; there may have been other people around, but every ounce of your emotion and attention was focused on that person you love. Your heart was fluttering, your legs were weak, and you may have had a hard time putting words together!

Now, relate that feeling to the incident at Mount Sinai. The Israelites came to the mountain to worship God and accept His offer of betrothal. It was time to seal the relationship. They were going to be God's people, and God was going to be their God. The Israelites were going to worship God, and God was going to reveal Himself to them.

God wanted to meet the Israelites so they could hear Him speak the words of the covenant. They needed to personally hear those words so they could make a decision to follow Him. Upon hearing God's words, a godly fear and reverence gripped them and caused faith and trust to rise up in their hearts. God wanted them to hear His voice so they could learn to fear His name. We cannot truly fear, revere, or trust God until we personally learn how to hear God. The fear of God that is not an overflow of hearing God is just a religious fear that will never produce a relationship with Him. God wanted the Israelites to build their faith and trust in Him through their personal interaction with Him.

The Israelites' response tells us everything. They were scared and said that they could not stand and hear God's voice, else they would die. That was not true, though, because they had just heard God's voice and did not die. Why did they say that then? In the presence of a holy God, they felt exposed and naked, and their sinful tendencies and desires were exposed. They were in a vulnerable position, and they did not have the faith or knowledge that, even amidst their weakness, God was not going to reject them. God wanted them to see His true nature. He wanted faith to well up in their hearts, but they rejected His voice. They erred in their hearts not knowing the living God. They told Moses to hear from God what He wanted them to do. But they did the opposite of everything Moses told them to do. They were like a bride running away from the groom and into the arms of another lover. They built a golden calf and went back to worshipping the Egyptian god during the forty days Moses spent with God on the mountain.

Running away from God and not hearing Him for themselves did not work out for them, and it will not work out for us either. We can witness the miracles of God, learn doctrines and scriptures, but unless we learn to experience God for ourselves, our faith will never grow, influence, or change us. The psalmist rightly says in Psalm 103 that Moses knew the ways of God, but the children of Israel knew His acts. Remember Moses's prayer when he was interceding for Israel after their great sin of idol worship of the golden calf. He went to intercede for the children of Israel and said, "*Now therefore, I pray You, if I have found favor in Your sight, let me know Your ways that I may know You, so that I may find favor in Your sight.*" (Exodus 33:13)

> Take care, brethren, that there not be in **any one of you an evil, unbelieving heart that falls away from the living God**. (Hebrews 3:12)
>
> Therefore, let us fear if, while a promise remains of entering His rest, any one of you may seem to have come short of it. For indeed we have had good news preached to us, **just as they also; but the word they heard did not profit them, because it was not united by faith in those who heard**. (Hebrews 4:1-2)

We established that faith comes by hearing and hearing by the Word of God. We need to choose to come into God's presence and hear His voice. The more we hear His voice and understand His Word, the more faith grows inside of us.

The writer of Hebrews exhorts us to not fall short like the children of Israel did when they heard the Word of God. He goes on to describe the most accurate way the Word of God works in us when we choose to hear it in faith, believe it, and act on it.

There is something about intimate prayer and meditating on God's Word that facilitates the growth of our faith. We can hear people preach the Word of God, discuss the Word with others, read books, watch videos or podcasts, but the knowledge gained needs to be enhanced by one's own prayer and meditation on the Word of God. Otherwise, we become faithless believers, having a form of godliness; we become religious believers who may go to church or religious events and participate in various outreaches but internally have no personal experience with God. God wants us to come into His presence and learn to hear His voice so we may learn to trust, revere, and walk with Him. We need our own personal story and testimony about how God has spoken to us, worked with us, and seen us through various trials and tribulations in life.

## Faith to Faith

All of what we talked about in this section leads to faith in God. Faith is a powerful substance; it releases power from the most powerful event in human history: the cross. It is a living substance that molds our lives. And without faith, it is impossible to please God.

> Now faith is the assurance of things hoped for, the conviction of things not seen. (Hebrews 11:1)
>
> And **without faith it is impossible** to please Him, for he who comes **to God must believe that He is and that He is a rewarder of those who seek Him**. (Hebrews 11:6)
>
> And without faith living within us **it would be impossible to please God**. For we come to God in faith knowing that **he is real and that he rewards the faith of those passionately seek him**. (Hebrews 11:6, TPT)

We are powerless to please God in any way than to live, walk, and have our being in faith. Faith, and faith alone, brings us into His presence. Faith is the result of believing in the gift of God that has been given to us because of who we are and not because of what we have done. There is nothing man could do to earn this.

Why so? Because faith is relational. Faith works through love; it is energized by love. Our faith is a response to the grace of God, which shows God's willingness to help us and work on our behalf, even though we do not deserve it. Faith pleases God. It speaks to a relational union with God, knowledge of Him, learning about Him, and communing with Him. Pleasing God has to be by faith because any other way is by the work of man, who is spiritually dead and cannot bring life. Faith destroys the old man and brings life to the new man.

We have to personally believe who He *is* (in present tense) to us. Let me illustrate this by recalling what happened when Moses first appeared before God. Moses saw God manifest Himself as fire in a bush. The bush was burning, but the bush was not consumed the way fire commonly consumes matter. God manifested Himself in the form of fire. God had a plan for Moses and chose to use Him. When Moses asked God, "*Who shall I say sends me?*" God said, "*The 'I am, that I am.' The 'I Am' is sending you.*" The 'I Am' is our self-existent almighty God. In this context, God appears too large but also notably personal.

Most people have some faith in a creator. They may call their creator many things, but it all refers to a nebulous being somewhere, who is magnificent and unreachable, and with whom there is no real understanding or personal experience. God is the 'I AM.' But the 'I AM' becomes the 'He IS,' when we receive Him as our personal God and believe His words, and we realize that He wants a personal relationship with us and personally works on our behalf.

I think back to when I realized this. The gospel of the kingdom had been spoken to me, and the words of Jesus highlighted to me that God loved me and had a plan for me, and He manifested His Son in this world to reconcile me to Him. I heard that Jesus came that I might have life and have it more abundantly. Hence, I could know God and experience Him, and that is where eternal life started for me.

The more I contemplated this, the more an unseen force was influencing me, moving me, and revealing God to me. I began conversing with God and asked Him if this unseen force was real or just a fantasy in my head? I came to a point where His Word was like a seed sprouting in my heart. I recalled hearing that if we confess with our mouth and believe in our heart that God raised Jesus from the dead, we could receive His plan. That is exactly what I did. I expressed faith in God with my words and asked Him to come into my heart and be my Lord and Savior. He became my 'HE IS,' and I knew at that point that God stepped out of the eternal realm and into my heart; He started to dwell in me, and I in Him. I received Him by faith as a result of the grace of God shown to me, and not because of anything that I could do.

He is a rewarder of those who continually and diligently seek Him. The first reward we get is to experience His presence. We establish a relationship with Him. We start to experience the abundant life He mentioned. We experience eternal life—the quality of life that God lives.

Seeking God starts and ends with prayer. I am yet to meet someone who has a deep relationship with God without a consistent, intimate prayer life. Also, I have never met anyone who has strong faith in God without an intimate, consistent prayer life. Men of faith and prayer consistently take time out of their everyday mundane to get alone with God and commune with Him. They do not do this out of obligation, but out of enjoyment and necessity, knowing that the life they need is in Him, the wisdom they need is in Him, and everything that leads to life is in Him.

I love listening to people with an intimate prayer life and strong faith, pray. The things that consistently intrigue me are the intimate statements that men say while seeking God. I hear men praying to know more of God.

In prayer, God reveals Himself to us. He takes the Word of God and makes it real. His reward starts with His presence. There is no greater reward than living in God's ongoing presence. In His presence, there is fullness of joy, beauty, and splendor. Show me a person who continuously walks in God's presence, and I will show you a person who is blessed in many ways: spiritually, physically, and emotionally. That does not mean that we will not go through trials and tribulations. It means your faith in God will see you through your trials and tribulations, and you will be comforted by Him in ways you could not foresee or understand. This process will transform us and make us into someone we could not even fathom.

His presence brings purpose. That purpose will drive us because we understand who we are and what He has made us to be. It strengthens us. It brings out the creativeness of the Creator within us. It brings out our gifts and calling. It is like clay in the hands of a potter; molded and shaped into who God created us to be.

The more we walk in this life of faith through prayer, the more we will see the unwavering and perfect righteousness of God in the affairs of our life and in the lives of men around us. The righteousness of God is revealed to us by faith upon faith. The process of becoming what God intended us to be is the result of an intimate prayer life with God.

Understanding identity, faith, and our position before God is key to an enjoyable, productive, and intimate prayer life. We should ask and pray that God would impart a reality of our identity to us, thereby empowering our faith and drawing us more and more into an intimate, ongoing, and communicative prayer life.

> *Father, help us to see these truths, and expand our faith by speaking Your words into us. Draw us like a magnet into Your presence that we may grow and walk from one level of faith and understanding to the next, and the next, and the next! Amen.*

## Faith, Prayer, and Intimacy With God

In the last few chapters, we read about the importance of faith, and that our faith in God will never go beyond our prayer life and our intimate communion with Jesus. With this context, I want to re-highlight Mary of Bethany. Mary had been in the secret place, where she communed with the Lord, understood what He was experiencing, and learned that He was going to the cross.

Note how her intimacy with God birthed her strong faith in God. Mary is mentioned three times in the New Testament, and every single time she is mentioned, she is at the feet of Jesus; she was in a constant state of worship and communion with Him.

The first instance is recorded in Luke 10. Jesus and His disciples were at Lazarus's house, and Martha was in the kitchen preparing food for at least fifteen people. Anyone who has prepared a meal for that many people knows that it is not a small feat. Now, Mary was not helping Martha; she was so taken with Jesus that she spent her time sitting at His feet and listening to Him, just as the other disciples did.

Martha, as the Scriptures say, was fussing far too much about serving her guests. As I was studying what the word "cumbered" means, I came across some interesting word pictures. One picture had a face of a person who expressed anxiety. The face was twisted and implied mental distraction. So in Martha's case, her anxiousness of serving the crowd, and the resentment that was building against her sister because she was not helping, were manifesting through her facial expressions.

So here's the scene: Mary is at the feet of Jesus, taking in every word that He was saying, staring deeply into His eyes. She was so taken with Him that she was oblivious to everything around her. She had her Savior and Lover of her soul in front of her, and she was not going to let anything interrupt her devotion to Him.

We know the story. Martha was in the kitchen, concerning herself with feeding and taking care of her guests. I can imagine her working very hard and muttering, "Where is my sister? I need her help!" She peered into the other room and saw her sister just sitting there. This went on and on until Martha could not take it any longer. The Message translation says that she went in and interrupted them. A better description of what happened based on the words used would be "stepping up to" or "bursting into." It was an explosive act. Martha could not hold her emotions any longer, and she verbally blasted Jesus and her sister.

Martha was admirable in her desire to take care of Jesus and the rest of her guests, but we can disguise our service for God as a substitute for intimacy and a desire to know Him. Many people in the church today substitute their service to church, attendance in church, or service to a pastor for a relationship with God. Substituting service for relationship is a work of the flesh; it cannot become a substitute for the cross or a substitute for a relationship with God. Service without prayer, intimacy, and relationship leads to another form of religion.

I love Jesus's reaction to Martha's frustration. He does not condemn Martha for her actions but commends Mary for hers. He basically said, "Martha, you are getting worked up over nothing. But Mary has chosen the *one thing* that is important to God." God saw a person whose heart longed to know Him and love Him; a person who did not care about the traditions of men or what other people thought about her devotion to Him.

The apostle Paul writes on this subject in his dissertation in **Philippians 3:8-9, 12-15 (NLT):**

> Yes, **everything else is worthless when compared with the infinite value of knowing Christ Jesus my Lord. For his sake** I have discarded everything else, counting it all as garbage, so that I could gain Christ and become one with him. I no longer count on my own righteousness through obeying the law; rather, I become righteous through faith in Christ. For God's way of making us right with himself depends on faith…I don't mean to say that I have already achieved these things or that I have already reached perfection. But I press on to possess that perfection for which Christ Jesus first possessed me. No, dear brothers and sisters, I have not achieved it, but I focus on this one thing: **Forgetting the past and looking forward to what lies ahead, I press on to reach the end of the race and receive the heavenly prize for which God, through Christ Jesus, is calling us**. Let all who are spiritually mature agree on these things.

Paul's *one thing* was to know the living Savior. That was the fuel to his fire; that is what kept him going through all the trials and tribulations he endured.

The Lord specifically revealed to me that the reason for Paul's long-term success was this mentality—God and then ministry. Some people interpret this portion of Scripture to say that Paul was pushing his goal of finishing his earthy ministry, but that is not really what Paul is talking about here. Paul's spiritual secret for success in ministry was that he first loved God and *then* the people.

It is very important that we keep first things first—God first, knowing and loving Him, and *then* loving our brothers. As a matter of fact, you really can't do the second part well unless the first part is in place, because people can drive you NUTS!

Mary being at Jesus's feet signifies a position of worship, intimacy, and communion. Her position expressed her desire and need for Him. She worshipped God, and Jesus responded to her.

The second time Mary was at Jesus's feet, she anointed Him with a flask of highly expensive perfume. This event is recorded in Mark 14:1-9, Matthew 26:6-13, and John 12:1-8.

> She has done what she could and has anointed my body for burial ahead of time. I tell you the truth, wherever the Good News is preached throughout the world, this woman's deed will be remembered and discussed. (Mark 14:8-9, NLT)

Again, in this story, Mary does something that was not popular or commonly understood by man, but was pleasing to God. Mary brought a very costly bottle of perfume that was worth a full year's wages. Imagine taking a full year's wages and offering it to the Lord. That is what she did. The question is why? Well, Jesus said that she did it for His burial. He knew that His time was short, and so did Mary. She knew because she had heard what Jesus said. What an act of worship! Wait a minute; you mean the apostles did not know that it was Jesus's time or understand Jesus when He talked about dying on the cross? Jesus told them numerous times that He was going to be handed over to the chief priests and scribes, and that He was going to die and rise on the third day.

Worship is the funnel through which God reveals Himself and His ways to us. Mary's intimacy with Jesus produced a relationship with

Him. She knew in the spirit and through conversations with Jesus that His time was short. The disciples did not understand that though. When you have this one-thing relationship with God, you will hear things that others do not hear—even if they are part of the same conversations as you. The disciples even rebuked Mary for the things Jesus commended her for doing. In fact, Jesus commended her more than anyone else in the New Testament, with the exception of John the Baptist.

With this relational history between Jesus, Mary, Martha, and Lazarus, let us recount the story again of Jesus raising Lazarus from the dead in John 11:1-44. I know this has been repeated before in earlier pages, but it is so compelling, I want to reiterate it.

Jesus heard that His beloved friend Lazarus was sick, and yet, He waited two days before going to his house. He eventually got there and learned that Lazarus had already died and had been in the grave for four days. From this we can infer that Lazarus died before Jesus got the message of his death. We could infer many reasons why Jesus waited, but the key point is that He only does what He sees His Father doing. Jesus knew that Lazarus died, because He told His disciples that he died and his sickness would not end in death, but that the glory of God would be manifested. The glory of God was manifested when Jesus raised Lazarus from the dead.

When Martha got word that Jesus was coming, she left the house and went to meet Him. She got right to the point when she saw Him and said, "*If only you had been here, my brother would not have died.*" Jesus told her that her brother would rise again. Martha, not knowing exactly what Jesus meant, said, "*He will rise…at the last day.*" Jesus tried to get her to understand that He is not only the resurrection on the last day, but He is also life, and that He could raise Lazarus to life again in this life. But clearly, Martha did not understand what Jesus was saying, although she believed that Jesus was the Messiah and the Son of the living God. To me, it sounds like she did not understand what Jesus said and was trying to sound spiritual.

As Jesus was waiting at the outskirts of the village, Martha went back to Mary and told her that Jesus was calling for her. Mary immediately got up and went to Jesus. **As soon as she saw Him, she fell at His feet, as a mark of worship, honor, and respect.** We discussed earlier that worship captures God's attention. We read in the New Testament about people worshipping God. The leper and the Canaanite woman received healing when they worshipped God. Worship brings us into the presence of God.

After Mary fell at Jesus's feet and worshipped Him, she said the same thing that Martha said: "*If only you had been here, my brother would not have died.*" Jesus saw Mary weeping. Mary—the one who attended to him, the one who sat at His feet and communed with Him, the one who learned and touched His heart, the one who was persecuted for Him. She was in much grief. Her grief touched His heart. He was troubled, and hence, He groaned in the spirit. He went to Lazarus's tomb and wept. Why did He weep? He wept because His beloved Mary wept.

Jesus is the High Priest who understands our weaknesses and is touched by them. He is also the One who sits on the throne of grace, and the One to whom we can go in time of need to find grace and receive mercy. Mary moved the heart of God, but Martha did not. It is intimacy that produces faith. Intimacy and worship open our ears to hear God, not just listen to words about Him that have no transformational power. Once, when I was preaching on this subject, someone said to me that Mary did not show any faith in her words because she did not directly ask Jesus to heal Lazarus. Sometimes we can live in such a box that we do not see the forest through the trees. It is true that she did not say anything specifically identifiable. But we all know that those who are intimate with each other can speak and communicate in both actions and words. Many times, because of the closeness between two people, they know exactly what the other is saying by just looking into their eyes or by their body language. Mary and Jesus had that kind of intimacy, and her worship ignited it.

I know that God is a God of faith and emotion. Our passion and love for God will result in our faith in God, and that will move Him. He is moved by His bride. If we forget or overlook this fact, we can become very mechanical rather than enjoy a loving, intimate relationship with

God. We are not led by our emotions, but when they are driven by love, passion, and faith in God, they act as a catalyst for our faith exploding in power. That is why Paul wrote in Galatians 5:6 that faith works (is energized) through love.

If you compare the words that Mary and Martha told Jesus, they are exactly the same but worlds apart in terms of underlying motivation and relational equity. Martha went to Jesus as soon as she heard that He was coming, and said, "*Lord, if you had been here, my brother would not have died.*" When Mary came to Jesus, she bowed down and worshipped Him, and then said, "*Lord, if only you had been here, my brother would not have died.*" Jesus said to Martha, "*Lazarus will rise again.*" Martha's response was religious. She repeated what she had heard Jesus say many times before. So Jesus had a discourse with her to try to get her to believe in Him and what He was about to do. Jesus asked her if she believed, and Martha gave Him another religious response that He was the Son of the living God. She did not simply answer the question.

That is what religion does to us; we hear a doctrine or some thought, and when we are confronted with a situation where true faith in God is needed, we regurgitate Christian doctrine that has no spiritual substance behind it in our personal life. It sounds good and looks good, but underneath, in our understanding, it is empty. If we doubt and are having a hard time believing, we should just admit it and ask Jesus to help our unbelief. We know that Martha did not believe Jesus, because when Jesus asked for the stone to be rolled away from Lazarus's tomb, Martha said, "*Lord, the smell will be terrible.*" Mary, on the other hand, fell and worshipped Him. When Jesus asked for the stone to be rolled away, Mary made no other comment but followed Jesus and watched what He did.

Jesus, while at Lazarus's tomb, prayed, "*Father, you always hear me, but I said it out loud for the sake of all these people standing here, so that they will believe you sent me.*" What is Jesus referring to here? He is referring to having told His disciples that Lazarus just sleeps, because he was speaking in faith, knowing the plan of God and that the glory of God would be shown forth.

This was a powerful miracle. Lazarus was already embalmed and wrapped in grave clothes. I cannot imagine how he would have hopped out of the tomb. The power of God quickened him and made him alive. It was surely the power of the Holy Spirit manifesting through three gifts: the working of miracles, the gift of faith, and the gift of healing. This is the most spectacular healing recorded in the Bible, based on the situation. Jesus did this miracle at least partially moved by Mary of Bethany's deep faith, passion, intimacy, and love for Him.

# Key 5:

# Baptism in the Holy Spirit and Speaking in other Tongues

## The New Testament Explanation of Tongues

First, I want to explain the value and benefits of praying in tongues and how it tremendously helped my overall prayer life and interaction with God. Since this book is called *Prayer, His Presence, and Intimacy With God*, I want to emphasize how praying in tongues has allowed me to progress in all of these areas. I want to lay out the New Testament's explanation of how we can receive this gift, its various manifestations, and how it works within our lives, both personally and corporately.

The only spiritual gift or manifestation of the Spirit that was not present in the Old Testament times, but was present in the New Testament times, is the manifestation of tongues. Since it was a part of the new covenant, which was instituted by Jesus's work on the cross, which allowed the Holy Spirit to dwell in us, there has to be a lot of importance to it. Since the day of Pentecost, the account in the book of Acts, and the rest of church history, this subject has stirred a lot of debate. It really was brought into prominence in the early twentieth century with the outpouring at the Azusa Street Revival, which God re-emphasized as the

Pentecostal message. It spread like no other time in church history. This resulted in numerous Pentecostal denominations, like the Assemblies of God, Foursquare, as well as many other independent Pentecostal associations. This subject has resulted in a lot more debate on the baptism of the Holy Spirit and the gift of tongues.

In my early Christian years, I was exposed to the baptism of the Holy Spirit as seen in the book of Acts. I remember being at a large outdoor camp meeting called "Jesus 78" in Mount Union, Pennsylvania. There were thousands of people camping and attending meetings, worshipping and praising God, and listening to preachers. This was all very new to me because, just the week before, I received Christ as my Lord and Savior and had the assurance that He came into my heart. Seeing all these people worshipping God happily, enjoying and excited about God, was all very new to me. It made a profound impact on my desire to search out and know this God.

One night, a minister was talking about the baptism of the Holy Spirit and the power that comes with it. We read that Jesus told His disciples to wait in Jerusalem until the Holy Spirit comes upon them, and then they will receive power. We also read in the Gospel of John that Jesus breathed on His disciples, and they received the Holy Spirit. All of this may sound confusing and contradictory, but no; it is the fulfillment of exactly what Jesus talked about. In John 4, we read that the Holy Spirit will spring up as wells of everlasting life in us. And in John 7, we read that the Holy Spirit will flow out of us like rivers of living water. These scriptures refer to the Holy Spirit coming upon us and living within us. I refer to this as the Spirit within us and the Spirit upon us.

So getting back to the camp meeting narrative, the minister who was preaching about the baptism of the Holy Spirit made a call for all those who wanted to receive it. I wanted it too, so I answered the call by going toward the minister. There were other people who came forward as well—over a hundred people. We were all ushered into a tent at the side of the main meeting. There, someone explained more on the subject and prayed over us to receive the Holy Spirit, just as they did in the book of Acts. They encouraged us to raise our hands and ask for it and receive it. Little did I know, years later, I would be one of those people who would explain the baptism of the Holy Spirit to people wanting to receive it in similar settings.

I did what I was told, and God did what He said He would do. I asked God to fill me with the Holy Spirit and give me the manifestation of other tongues. I felt a presence come over me. Then, an utterance had to flow out of me. In the Gospels, Jesus said that the Father knows how to give the Holy Spirit to those who ask Him. I opened my mouth and asked Him, and words gushed out of my mouth in a language I knew not. I was baptized in the Holy Spirit, and I began speaking in other tongues.

I was as green as green could be pertaining to the things of God. I received Jesus a few weeks before as my Lord and Savior; I asked Him to come into my life and forgive me of my sins. I knew that He came into my life, and I was different than I used to be. A few days later, after the Jesus 78 meeting ended and I came home, my brother asked if I spoke in tongues when I got baptized in the Holy Spirit. I said, "I think so." He said, "What do you mean you think so?" As I said, this God stuff was all new to me. He told me to speak in tongues so he could hear it. I started to speak in tongues, and he said, "You got it!" I never doubted it from that day onward. Paul said, "*I will pray with the spirit, and I will also pray with my understanding*" (1 Corinthians 14:15, NKJV). So I made the decision to speak in tongues.

The Holy Spirit comes within us when we receive Christ. We are born again, we receive eternal life, and the Spirit springs up within us and brings the knowledge of God to us. Our spirt is made alive, and God comes and dwells in us and reveals Himself to us.

The Holy Spirit comes upon us to flow out through us as rivers of living water. This gives us power to bring the kingdom of God to others. This is what happened on the day of Pentecost; the disciples were transformed from meek and frightened people to powerful members of the kingdom of God. That same day, Peter stood up and preached boldly in the city where Jesus was crucified and where he had denied Him. This is what we refer to as the baptism of the Holy Spirit with the evidence of speaking in tongues.

There are five instances of tongues in the book of Acts; three of them have direct evidence of the believers speaking in tongues, and in the other two, the believers spoke in tongues, though it was not noted at that point. We will discuss all five instances in this chapter.

In Acts 2, we read that Peter stood up after the Holy Spirit was poured out, and as he spoke to the crowds, they were deeply moved by his words. They asked Peter what they needed to do to be saved, and three thousand men plus women and children were added to the kingdom that day. Then, the wonderful healing of the crippled man at the Gate Beautiful happened, followed by another large harvest. We see other great miracles and movements of power following: people healed by the shadows of the apostles, supernatural rescue of the apostles, Philip preaching in Samaria with great power resulting in miracles and more outpouring of the Spirit, Saul converted by a vision, Peter raising the dead, and then the outpouring of the Spirit among the gentiles. The disciples received power and preached the gospel in Jerusalem, Judea, Samaria, and to the gentiles, just as Jesus told them. The message of the gospel and the power of the Holy Spirit upset everything in the world at that time.

I want to outline from the New Testament the different manifestations of speaking and praying in tongues and the purpose of each. The manifestation of tongues is a personal prayer language for believers to edify and build themselves up spiritually. Then, there is a manifestation of tongues with an interpretation that is for the edification of the church when we assemble together. Although both are related, they are distinct types of manifestations of the Holy Spirit. One needs to be baptized in the Holy Spirit to receive their personal prayer language of tongues and to speak to the church for its edification through the interpretation of tongues. Another manifestation of tongues is a sign for unbelievers, as we read in 1 Corinthians 14:22.

Let us start with Paul's explanation to the Corinthian church. The nine gifts of the Spirit mentioned in 1 Corinthians 12 are for edification or building up. The word "edification" is used throughout the New Testament but quite significantly in this chapter. Edification is the process of promoting growth in spiritual wisdom and understanding. It denotes growing to full spiritual maturity—to experience and become what Jesus purposed for us through the work of the cross.

Spiritual gifts are used to build people up and not to puff them up through manifestation. It is amazing how fast we can become prideful when God manifests a supernatural power through us. Chapter 13 emphasizes that love is more important than the supernatural manifestation of gifts. We are nothing in our spiritual growth unless love is our motivation to flow in our gifting to bring edification to others. It is meant to promote our spirituality. In chapter 14, Paul explains the gifts and how they are to be used when people assemble together to worship God.

> To another various kinds of tongues, and to another the interpretation of tongues. But one and the same Spirit works all these things, distributing to each one individually just as He wills. (1 Corinthians 12:10-11)

From the above scriptures, we learn that there are various kinds of tongues. The Greek word for "tongues" is *genos*, which can be interpreted in numerous ways. It can denote people of the same country, different nations, or people speaking diverse languages. There are various languages known and unknown to men. Paul refers to speaking in tongues as a language of men and angels. When the gift of tongues is manifested in an individual, the language uttered is not known or understood by the person speaking it. It is an utterance divinely inspired by the Holy Spirit. Just as there are diverse languages, there are also diverse manifestations of tongues.

We read in the book of Acts and in Paul's letter to the Corinthians about how the gift of tongues should operate in the church. Praying in tongues is a prayer language given to a believer to edify and build them up, and it is a sign of the supernatural power of God to an unbeliever.

Tongues can be manifested in a congregation and then interpretated; this is equivalent to prophecy. The apostle Paul discusses these manifestations in 1 Corinthians chapters 12-14.

Let us endeavor to dive deeper into the subject and into the Scriptures to understand this most important part of one's prayer life.

## Baptism In the Holy Spirit and Speaking In Tongues

The manifestation of tongues began on the day of Pentecost when the disciples were baptized with the Holy Spirit. This was foretold by John the Baptist when he said that there is One coming who will baptize people with more than just water. This One came and baptized people with the Holy Spirit and fire. Luke writes that Jesus told His disciples to wait in Jerusalem until they were clothed with power from on high.

> Gathering them together, He commanded them not to leave Jerusalem, but to wait for what the Father had promised, "Which," He said, "you heard of from Me; for John baptized with water, **but you will be baptized with the Holy Spirit not many days from now.**...But you **will receive power when the Holy Spirit has come upon you; and you shall be My witnesses both in Jerusalem, and in all Judea and Samaria, and even to the remotest part of the earth."** (Acts 1:4, 8)

The disciples were going to be baptized with the Holy Spirit, and power would come upon them. Then they would be Jesus's witnesses in Jerusalem, Judea, Samaria, and the rest of the world. As I said, there are five instances in the book of Acts where the Holy Spirit was poured out on people. The sequence of these instances falls in line with what Jesus said: first in Jerusalem, Judea, Samaria, and then to the gentiles and to the rest of the world.

Let us recount each instance as it pertains to speaking in tongues. In Acts 2, we read that the disciples were filled with the Holy Spirit and began to speak in other languages they did not know. Since Jesus told them to wait in Jerusalem until they were baptized in the Holy Spirit, we can relate this instance to the baptism of the Holy Spirit with the evidence of speaking in tongues. When the Holy Spirit came, the book of Acts recounts that it sounded like a violent, rushing, mighty wind. Have you ever heard a violent rushing, mighty wind? It makes a lot of noise and is noticed by all who are in the area. When it got to where the 120 disciples were gathered, it appeared as a large flame of fire, which distributed itself upon all who were there. I like to say that it distributed itself because it was not an ordinary flame; it was a manifestation of God Himself distributing the flame of His presence to all who were gathered there. It must have been like a big fireball coming down from heaven with a blasting sound because of the force and power it had. The reason I describe it this way is because when you look in the Old Testament at the manifestation of God's presence on Mount Sinai, God appeared as fire. The Bible says that God is a consuming fire. When the children of Israel came to present themselves to God at Mount Sinai, God descended in the form of fire. The whole mountain trembled greatly. We see two things there: fire and a loud shaking of the mountain. Between those two effects of God's holy presence, it must have been quite a spectacle!

Once again, God was excited to meet His beloved treasure, His peculiar people, His royal priesthood, and interact with them. I think the commotion on the day of Pentecost was not just from speaking in tongues, but from the noise prior to it. It must have been like a fire tornado from an extremely hot forest fire. The heat is so great that it creates these loud sounds and looks like a tornado. The rushing mighty wind of God's fiery presence was coming to distribute Himself on everyone who was in that upper room. If a natural fire can create such a loud sound, how much more the presence of a holy God coming to distribute Himself on His people would be? It would be loud and disruptive. I would like to conject that God was announcing His dwelling in man. This was a fulfillment of a promise made many years before.

Everyone around town must have heard it, and out of curiosity, they came to see where it had come from, which eventually led to where the disciples were gathered. The disciples must have spilled out of the upper room into the streets, speaking in languages that were not their native tongues but were understood by foreigners visiting Jerusalem.

What manifestation of tongues did the disciples have? Was it their personal prayer language or tongues and interpretation for the church? The answer is obvious. The disciples were praying in a personal prayer language they knew not. It was also a sign to the unbeliever because unbelievers (those visiting Jerusalem at that time were Jews, but not believers in Jesus as the Christ as of yet) recognized the language of the tongues that the believers in the upper room were speaking, and they could understand what was said as if it was their native tongue. It is said that they were speaking of the mighty deeds of God. According to the book of Acts, there were at least twelve different ethnicities with different dialects in Jerusalem at that time.

> And they were amazed and astonished, saying, "Are not all these who are speaking Galileans? And how is it that we hear, each of us in his own native language? Parthians and Medes and Elamites and residents of Mesopotamia, Judea and Cappadocia, Pontus and Asia, Phrygia and Pamphylia, Egypt and the parts of Libya belonging to Cyrene, and visitors from Rome, both Jews and proselytes, Cretans, and Arabians—we hear them telling in our own tongues the mighty works of God. (Acts 2:7-11, ESV)

Now if there were 120 people in the upper room, most of them Galileans, and they all spoke in different tongues, it must have been quite a commotion and interesting to watch! With all that noise, it would have been hard to distinguish what was being said. These people were in Jerusalem at the time to celebrate the feast of Pentecost (Leviticus 23:15-21), which was fifty days after the Passover, which also was when Jesus died. When this feast occurred, the Jews from the surrounding areas would flock to Jerusalem to worship and participate in the feast, as instructed in the Old Testament. What a perfect time for the day of

Pentecost to happen and God to announce His presence coming upon all men who wanted it.

Here come the disciples from the upper room after being blasted by the Holy Spirit, all speaking in different dialects inspired by the Holy Spirit. They came out in the streets in their new state of being, a new creation in Christ, filled with the Holy Spirit. They were the new temple created with the hands of God, and God had come to live in them and flow out of them.

It was a commotion to all the people who heard them speaking in their native dialect about the mighty deeds of God. One group was speaking an inspired utterance they knew not, and the other group heard them speak of the mighty deeds of God. Talk about an attention getter. What mighty deeds were they talking about? My educated guess—the salvation that was brought by Jesus at the resurrection.

The upper room incident was the first manifestation of tongues in the New Testament. All the 120 disciples who were gathered there that day were baptized in the Holy Spirit with the evidence of speaking in tongues. As a result of that, they also received power from heaven. I would say that this is the law of the first occurrence of tongues in the Bible, meaning, when a dispensation of God at work happens, He sets a precedent for how to understand it in the future.

The transition from the old covenant to the new covenant had happened. The book of Acts is a demonstration of how things are to proceed. It is said that Acts is a transitional book. I say the transition had already happened, and in Acts, they were setting precedents. The transitional books are the Gospels. Jesus came to fulfill the old covenant and teach us about the Father, and that is exactly what He did, finishing with the cross and the resurrection. That is why Jesus said on the cross, "*It is finished.*" The old covenant was fulfilled, and the sacrifice was done on the cross. The New Testament started when Jesus rose from the dead and defeated sin. He ascended to the heavenly mercy seat and poured out His blood, which sealed the new covenant. All those who by faith receive what Jesus did are members of the kingdom of God and are partakers of the new covenant blessings.

The second instance of the outpouring of the Holy Spirit happened in Acts 8. Philip, one of the apostles, was preaching in Samaria about Jesus, the Christ. We know from John 4 that Jesus Himself ministered in Samaria. He tilled the soil there and prepared it for the time after His resurrection. Philip was getting the Samaritans' attention because he was casting evil spirits out of people and healing the sick. He preached through the power and manifestation of the Holy Spirit. People were repenting, receiving Jesus as the Christ, being forgiven of their sins, and being baptized in water.

When the apostles heard that the Samaritans accepted the Word of God, they sent Peter and John to join Philip so they could pray for them that they might receive the Holy Spirit because it had not fallen on them. What do we mean by "fallen on them?" Fallen on them means to rush and press upon or to fall in one's embrace. The only other example we see before this is the day of Pentecost.

When Peter and John arrived, they laid hands on the new believers and prayed for them to receive the Holy Spirit. Now, it does not specifically say that the new believers spoke in tongues when hands were laid on them by Peter and John, but it is apparent that is what happened. How can we deduce that? There was a man named Simon in Samaria, who was a sorcerer. He practiced various magical arts claiming to be a holy person, and the Samaritans had high regard for him. But when Philip came with the power of God, people stopped fearing Simon and started looking to the one holy and true God.

We read in Acts 8 that even Simon believed in Jesus, the Christ, after he witnessed the miracles performed by Philip. When Simon saw that the Holy Spirit came upon the Samaritans through the laying on of hands by the disciples, he wanted that power too. He offered the disciples money to receive the ability to do that.

> Now when Simon **saw that the Spirit was bestowed through the laying on of the apostles' hands**, he offered them money, saying, "Give this authority to me as well, so that everyone on whom I lay my hands may

> receive the Holy Spirit." But Peter said to him, "May your silver perish with you, because you thought you could obtain the gift of God with money! You have **no part or portion in this matter**, for your heart is not right before God." (Acts 8:18-21)

The question is, how did he know that the Holy Spirit came on them? I have prayed for hundreds of people to receive the Holy Spirit, but to this day, I have not seen the Holy Spirit's shape with my natural eyes. I will tell you what I have seen though: I have sensed an unseen presence come upon people, and I have seen their reaction to that presence. That reaction is because of the Holy Spirit moving in them, and by faith, they open their mouth and speak in tongues.

Simon must have seen and heard the disciples speaking in tongues. As I just stated, I have prayed for many people to be baptized in the Holy Spirit, but I have never seen the Holy Spirit with my eyes. I have only seen the manifestation come on people and have heard them speak in tongues. Based on all the other instances in the book of Acts, that could be the only deduction.

Peter responded to Simon and said that his heart was not right. Why? Because Simon wanted power rather than a relationship with the Power Giver. He wanted to use this power to influence and control the Samaritans the same way he did as a sorcerer. Peter, through the power of God, exposed his evil motives and showed the Samaritans and Simon that there is a greater true power.

Peter said that Simon should not have any part in this "matter." The word "matter" here is the Greek word *logos*, which means "words." Peter was saying that Simon will have no part in these words (tongues) being spoken.

The apostles knew that the gift of the Holy Spirit was poured out on people because they heard them speaking in tongues. Even though this instance does not directly say that when they were baptized in the Holy Spirit, they spoke in tongues, again, it can be easily deduced that is what happened based on the discussion with Simon and what was commonly accepted among the first-century church, as recorded in the book of Acts.

The next instance of someone being filled with the Holy Spirit is in Acts 9. Jesus appeared to Paul on the road to Damascus, and Paul had his magnificent conversion experience. He was told to go and wait in the city until God told him what to do. Also, Paul was blinded during his encounter with Jesus, so he could do nothing but wait. He was in a place of complete dependence on God. A man with such power and vigor was reduced to nothing so God could do something in and through him. Paul tarried for three days and ate nothing. During that time, he had numerous personal encounters with God. One of them could have been the vision of Ananias coming to see him and laying hands on him. Acts records that God spoke to Ananias and told him that Paul was in the city praying, and that he should see him and pray for him to receive his sight.

Ananias had heard about Paul and what he was doing to his fellow brethren, and he questioned the Lord regarding this. God assured him and told him of Paul's calling. Ananias was one of those who dwelt in the secret place in prayer with God. He was a man of prayer who dwelt with God, knew His voice, and believed with faith despite his thoughts and the thoughts of others.

Ananias obeyed God and ministered to Paul. He laid hands on Paul and, immediately, Paul received his sight and was filled with the Holy Spirit. Again, how do you know when someone is filled with the Holy Spirit? Do they speak in tongues? In this instance, we do not read that Paul spoke or prayed in tongues. But when Paul was writing his letter to the Corinthians, he wrote that he spoke in tongues more than any of them and that he prayed in the Spirit to edify himself. We also read in the later chapters of the book of Acts that Paul was telling believers they would receive the Holy Spirit if they believed. Also, Paul laid hands on believers, and they were filled with the Holy Spirit and spoke in tongues. We will dive more into this later. Since the common belief at the time was that when people were filled with the Holy Spirit, they spoke in tongues, it is safe to assume that this was the first time Paul spoke in tongues.

### Key 5: Baptism in the Holy Spirit and Speaking in other Tongues

Now let us go to my second favorite account in the book of Acts of those who received the Holy Spirit and spoke in tongues. It is second after the day of Pentecost. It is the story of Cornelius, the centurion. The manifestation of the Holy Spirit, in this instance, signified a change in direction for the church. The Holy Spirit was being poured out to all nations. Remember, Jesus said that the Word of God and the outpouring of the Holy Spirit would start in Jerusalem, Judea, Samaria, and then the rest of the world. The first three already were set in motion as recorded in the first nine chapters of the book of Acts.

Peter was traveling around the regions outside of Jerusalem, performing mighty miracles and preaching the gospel. He raised a woman from the dead while in Joppa and stayed there and ministered to the people of that city. In the meantime, there was a centurion who lived In Caesarea, another port city, which was mostly inhabited by the gentiles.

The description of Cornelius's character is exemplary. First, being a Roman centurion meant he was a man of much authority. He had the choice to use his authority for good or evil. We read that Cornelius was a God-fearing man of prayer and generosity. He was so outstanding that his prayers and generosity came up as a memorial before God. Cornelius was the only human we read about whose passion for God filled the atmosphere around him and ascended to the nostrils of God.

> About the ninth hour of the day he clearly saw in a vision an angel of God who had just come in and said to him, "Cornelius!" And fixing his gaze on him and being much alarmed, he said, "What is it, Lord?" And he said to him, "**Your prayers and alms have ascended as a memorial before God**." (Acts 10:3-4)

This reminds me of the scene described by John in Revelation 8, when the prayers of the saints ascended to the nostrils of God, and God responded. The word "memorial" is the same word Jesus used to describe how heaven viewed Mary's sacrificial offering when she anointed Jesus for His burial. Mary had this one-thing communion with Jesus, and

Jesus said He would not take it away from her. Let me describe that one-thing heart's desire. It is like when that one person you love walks into a crowded room; you take notice of them, and all the chatter and activities in the room disappear because of the desire you have for that one person. I also described it earlier as "Simeon's secret place."

Cornelius was pursuing the secret place. His life was an expression of passion and desire that created a memorial before the Lord. I think the memorial was a constant burning flame of passion and desire that sat before the Lord and was fueled by their dual passions for each other.

God was supernaturally responding to Cornelius's prayer and sovereignly decided to use him in a major event in church history. The angel told Cornelius to call for Peter but did not tell him what was going to happen or why.

In the meantime, God was preparing Peter. Until this point, "The Way" was limited to the Jews and the Samaritans. As per the book of Acts, "The Way" referred to the message of the gospel about Jesus being the Messiah and the One who was sent to bring deliverance to Israel. The Jews were still adhering to their traditions and laws about associating and mingling with the gentile nations of the world. I like to refer to this as the second major shift in church history. The first was the day of Pentecost with the outpouring of the Holy Spirit and the welcoming of all nations into the kingdom of God.

Paul states this so perfectly in Ephesians 3:1-7 (NLT):

> When I think of all this, I, Paul, a prisoner of Christ Jesus for the benefit of you Gentiles… assuming, by the way, that you know God gave me the special responsibility of extending his grace to you Gentiles. As I briefly wrote earlier, God himself revealed his mysterious plan to me. As you read what I have written, you will understand my insight into this plan regarding Christ. God did not reveal it to previous generations, but now by his Spirit he has revealed it to his holy apostles and prophets. **And this is God's plan: Both Gentiles and Jews who believe**

> **the Good News share equally in the riches inherited by God's children. Both are part of the same body, and both enjoy the promise of blessings because they belong to Christ Jesus. By God's grace and mighty power, I have been given the privilege of serving him by spreading this Good News.**

Peter had a vision signifying that the old Jewish laws and segregation were no more, and if God made all nations free and clean, then they are free and clean indeed. Then the Holy Spirit told Peter that three men had come to see him and that he should go with them. Talk about a divine setup!

Peter left the next day with the three men to meet Cornelius and his family. Cornelius sensed that something important was happening, and so did Peter. As soon as Peter arrived, Cornelius began to worship him. Peter stopped him and told him that he was just a man and a servant of God. As they talked, Peter realized that their meeting was supernaturally set up. Peter asked Cornelius why he had sent for him, and Cornelius narrated the vision he had to Peter in front of all who were there.

Peter then began to preach, and as he did, he realized that God does not show favoritism, and the work Jesus did on the cross was to bring all men together and save them. Peter relayed the gospel to Cornelius's family. He told them how Jesus was anointed of God and how He healed people and delivered them by casting out demons. He told them how Jesus was put to death on the cross and that God the Father raised Him from the dead on the third day. He told them that Jesus commissioned us to go preach the good news of the gospel, and all who believe would be forgiven of their sins.

In the midst of the sermon, an amazing thing happened: the Holy Spirit fell on "all" who were listening to the message. The Jewish believers were amazed! How did they know that the Holy Spirit fell on them and that they were baptized by the Holy Spirit? They heard them SPEAKING IN TONGUES and praising God just as it happened on the day of Pentecost. The manifestation of the baptism of the Holy Spirit was speaking in other tongues. This is the second most important event in the book of Acts, after the day of Pentecost.

> Even as Peter was saying these things, **the Holy Spirit fell upon all who were listening to the message.** The Jewish believers who came with Peter were amazed that the gift of the Holy Spirit had been poured out on the Gentiles, too. **For they heard them speaking in other tongues and praising God**. (Acts 10:44-46, NLT)

This created problems among the Jewish believers in Jerusalem. So Peter went back and explained to them the two visions and told them that what had happened to them on the day of Pentecost, happened to the gentile believers as well.

> "As I began to speak," **Peter continued, "the Holy Spirit fell on them, just as he fell on us at the beginning. Then I thought of the Lord's words when he said, 'John baptized with water, but you will be baptized with the Holy Spirit**.' And since God gave these Gentiles the same gift he gave us when we believed in the Lord Jesus Christ, who was I to stand in God's way?" When the others heard this, they stopped objecting and began praising God. They said, "We can see that God has also given the Gentiles the privilege of repenting of their sins and receiving eternal life." (Acts 11:15-18, NLT)

Again, we see that speaking in tongues is a manifestation of the baptism of the Holy Spirit that has now been poured out on everyone.

The last recorded instance of the baptism of the Holy Spirit is in Acts 19. Paul was on his third missionary journey at that time. This instance is significant because it shows the transition of the second great move of the church and the Holy Spirit. The first move was for the Jews and their related parties, and the second move was for the nations. This does not mean that the first move ended. It just means that it expanded by the sovereignty and will of God.

Paul went to Ephesus and found those who believed in Jesus as the Christ and accepted Him by repentance. Now based on the text, it seems clear that they had a good understanding of what Jesus had done on the cross or that He was the Christ. Being filled with the Holy Spirt and speaking in other tongues was not really important to them. One can accept Jesus and be saved and live just like any Christian believer. But Paul said that there is more for those who want more: it is the baptism of the Holy Spirit.

Paul asked the Ephesians the following:

> "Did you receive the Holy Spirit when you believed?" he asked them. "No," they replied, "we haven't even heard that there is a Holy Spirit." "Then what baptism did you experience?" he asked. And they replied, "The baptism of John." Paul said, "John's baptism called for repentance from sin. But John himself told the people to believe in the one who would come later, meaning Jesus." As soon as they heard this, they were baptized in the name of the Lord Jesus. **Then when Paul laid his hands on them, the Holy Spirit came on them, and they spoke in other tongues** and prophesied. (Acts 19:2-6, NLT)

Again, we see that the manifestation of the baptism of the Holy Spirit was evidenced by speaking in tongues.

In summary, the instances in the book of Acts were to show us the pattern of what God was doing at the onset of the church age. The book of Acts is a thirty-year account of selected events after the resurrection of Christ and the establishment of the Christian faith as a fulfillment of the Judaic law. Just as John said in his Gospel, if all the things Jesus did in His three-year ministry could be recorded, they would be too many to be written.

From the day of Pentecost, Jesus has been multiplied in His disciples. That is when the disciples realized and experienced what Jesus said about Him going away. He was going away so another Comforter could come and not just be with them, but be in them so they could do more work than He did.

Each instance recorded in the Scriptures is important in the establishment of doctrine and precedent. God was pouring out His Spirit on all flesh and baptizing them with the Holy Spirit, and the evidence for this was the gift of tongues. When Peter stood up on the day of Pentecost, he quoted the prophet Joel. (Acts 2:17-18, NLT):

> 'In the last days,' God says, 'I will pour out my Spirit upon all people. Your sons and daughters will prophesy. Your young men will see visions, and your old men will dream dreams. In those days I will pour out my Spirit even on my servants—men and women alike—and they will prophesy.

In 1 Corinthians 14:21, Paul quotes Isaiah 28:11. It was foretold that He would speak to His people with strange languages and through the lips of foreigners.

The outpouring of the Holy Spirit with the manifestation of speaking in tongues is for all who ask and believe—until the end of the church age.

## Is Baptism In the Holy Spirit and Speaking In Tongues for All?

I have heard this question since my early Christian days, and I am still answering it for people almost four decades later. **The answer is YES! All those who want it, who believe and ask for it, will receive it by faith.**

One of the reasons this question comes up is 1 Corinthians 12:30, which says that all do not speak in tongues. Some people quote this scripture and say that not all receive this gift. They do not understand the difference between praying in tongues and speaking in tongues in the church, which must be followed by an interpretation. They also do not understand that Paul was talking to people within a church or corporate gathering.

He also stated in his discourse to the Corinthians that he desired they all speak in tongues (1 Corinthians 14:5). Why would Paul desire anything for the church that was not the will of God? He spoke in tongues more than all of them (1 Corinthians 14:18), meaning, he spent a lot of time edifying and building himself up by speaking in tongues. He also told them not to forbid speaking in tongues (1 Corinthians 14:39). All these scriptures need to be read in the full context of 1 Corinthians 12-14 to get a complete understanding of the conversation and subject.

The issue is that some people quote 1 Corinthians 12:30 out of context from its complete subject encapsulated in 1 Corinthians 12-14. Then, they do not read or study it before they talk themselves out of seeking and receiving the baptism of the Holy Spirit with the evidence of speaking in tongues. Paul wrote these chapters to teach the church the different gifts of the Spirit and how they are to operate when the body of Christ assembles. The purpose of these gifts is to build up the body. Motivated by love, the gifts flow through the body to help and edify other members of the body. The gifts and callings people have do not determine their importance in the body—every part of the body is important. By this, Paul was trying to establish some reasonable order in the assembly as believers got together and worshipped, and the gifts of the Spirit began to manifest. Paul also distinguished between speaking in tongues as personal prayer and communication with God, and speaking in tongues as inspired utterance to the church.

Before we address the context of what Paul was taking about, I want to go back to the book of Acts and highlight what happened to the people when the Holy Spirit was poured out on them. These instances set the precedent for establishing a pattern and understanding of how these manifestations happen.

> **And everyone present was filled with the Holy Spirit and began speaking in other languages**, as the Holy Spirit gave them this ability. (Acts 2:4, NLT)

> Then Peter and John laid their hands upon these believers, **and they received the Holy Spirit.** (Acts 8:17, NLT)

> Even as Peter was saying these things, **the Holy Spirit fell upon all who were listening to the message**. The Jewish believers who came with Peter were amazed that the gift of the Holy Spirit had been poured out on the Gentiles, too. **For they heard them speaking in other tongues and praising God.** (Acts 10:44-46)

> Then when Paul laid his hands on them, the Holy Spirit came on them, **and they spoke in other tongues and prophesied. There were about twelve men in all.** (Acts 19:6-7)

None of these instances indicate that some received the Holy Spirit while others did not. Based on this understanding, the baptism of the Holy Spirit was verified by the receiver speaking in tongues. The question is can we receive the baptism of the Holy Spirit without speaking in tongues? My answer based on the book of Acts is no. I will caveat that by saying that I have seen people filled with the Holy Spirit, and I know that if they would just open their mouth in faith, they could speak in tongues. Sometimes their natural mind gets in the way, or they are too timid and will not open their mouth. Sometimes it is on the tip of their tongue, but they start to speak and get scared, or try to figure it out themselves, or fall into unbelief, and then they stop speaking in tongues. The book of Acts says that THEY SPOKE in tongues as the Spirt gave them utterance (Acts 2:4). The Spirit is always willing to give utterance, but we need to open our mouth in faith. God is not going to come down and move your lips for you!

Let us revisit Paul's question and discuss it in context with the body of Christ. All of his statements about tongues are directed to an assembly of believers, commonly referred to these days as a church service.

> All of you **together are Christ's body, and each of you is a part of it. Here are some of the parts God has appointed for the church:** first are apostles, second are prophets, third are teachers, then those who do miracles, those who have the gift of healing, those who can help others, those who have the gift of leadership, those who speak in unknown languages. Are we all apostles? Are we all prophets? Are we all teachers? Do we all have the power to do miracles? Do we all have the gift of healing? Do we all have the ability to speak in unknown languages? Do we all have the ability to interpret unknown languages? Of course not! So you should earnestly desire the most helpful gifts. But now let me show you a way of life that is best of all. (1 Corinthians 12:27-32, NLT)

Based on the context here, Paul is saying that when we come together corporately, not everyone is called to the above functions or offices. Not everyone in the church is called to the fivefold ministry: apostle, prophet, evangelist, pastor, teacher. Nor does everyone operate in the gifts of the Spirit in the same way. God distributes gifts to each of us as He sees fit. If someone has a tongue for the church, they should speak, and another should bring its interpretation. This is equivalent to prophecy. Prophecy in the church age is usually foretelling a message for edification, exhortation, and comfort. This is a gift that manifests among the members of the church, but it needs to be separated from those who are called to the fivefold ministry as a prophet. Their gifts bring forth revelation with words of wisdom and other manifestations of the Holy Spirit.

In 1 Corinthians 14, Paul gives some guidance and outlines how the Holy Spirit and His gifts should manifest in an assembly. He did this because the Corinthians, in their zeal and immaturity, had a lot of people speaking in tongues in their assembly, and it was chaotic. He says that the fivefold ministry is called to lead the congregation and work with God to bring order to the assembly. As God leads, one may speak in tongues as a message to the congregation; this is utterance inspired by the Holy Spirit and is different from praying in tongues. Once the interpretation of a tongue is given, it brings edification to the church because the people receive an exhortation from God that they can understand. Paul's concern was that all the people in the congregation should be edified by the Word of God when they come together.

In 1 Corinthians 14:13-16, Paul distinguishes between speaking in tongues in the congregation and praying in tongues privately:

> Therefore let one who **speaks in a tongue pray that he may interpret**. For **if I pray in a tongue, my spirit prays, but my mind is unfruitful.** What is the outcome then? I will pray with the spirit, and I will pray with the mind also; I will sing with the spirit, and I will sing with the mind also. Otherwise if you bless in the spirit only, how will the one who fills the place of the ungifted say the "Amen" at your giving of thanks, since he does not know what you are saying?

The assembly, or church, is edified when they can understand what is being said. This can happen through preaching, revelation, speaking a psalm, prophecy, and tongues with interpretation. If everyone in the congregation, including the minister, is speaking in tongues and unable to understand each other, then how can they help build up one another in the body, or someone who is outside the body—who is not familiar with Christ or has not received Christ as their personal Savior—or someone who has not seen such manifestations. They could see it as a sign of something supernatural, which may get their attention; but after a while, if that is all they are doing, as Paul said, they may think everyone is mad. That also does not mean that during a time of worship, we can all speak in tongues. Those times are for us to worship and speak to God. But once the service or assembly is guided by the leadership to a time of edification of the church, we should not all be shouting out in other tongues except by inspiration that should have an interpretation. Even this is subject to the leader and the guidance of the person leading the service.

Paul's focus was to bring order to the assembly. If we were to assemble and have a common service, there may be a time for singing in worship. During that time, people could pray in tongues to edify themselves. By doing so, they are building themselves up spiritually and enhancing their time of worship. Anyone in the congregation can do this. Then, there may be a time in the service when someone delivers a message and everyone focuses on the messenger. This can be a revelation, a prophecy, a tongue followed by an interpretation, a song, or a teaching. It could also be a combination of all those things. These are all done to build up the congregation so they can grow in their relationship with God. During that time, if a person, or multiple people, blurt something out in tongues, it does not do anything to edify or build up the church. That is why Paul needed to bring order to the Corinthian assembly. They were so excited about the Holy Spirit that they could not discern the common gift of praying in tongues that one can do anytime they want. As Paul stated, I will pray with my spirit, and I will pray in my understanding. He made the conscious decision. That is different than the Holy Spirit coming upon you to give a tongue to be interpreted. That happens to you periodically.

Since corporate ministry time is focused on edifying the church, Paul said that two or three people can be allowed to speak in tongues, assuming the tongue is divinely inspired utterance, followed by its interpretation. The reason he said this is so people do not just blurt out together all at once in their prayer language of tongues. He wanted people to understand the difference between the manifestations and use them intentionally in appropriate situations.

How can we discern the difference between the manifestation of speaking in tongues for the church and personally praying in tongues? A manifestation of speaking in tongues to the church will be an inspired utterance. The deliverer of the tongue will feel an unusual unction to speak forth. Paul writes that he prays with his spirit and with his understanding. Once you are filled with the Holy Spirit, you can pray in tongues at any time by the act of your will. There is generally no inspired unction to pray in tongues, just a desire to do so. This builds you up. When you are speaking in tongues to the church, the anointing of the Holy Spirit will come upon you, and it will dissipate when done. You may feel pressure build inside of you, or as if a fountain were to burst forth. Now, these actions are still subject to your will and to the leadership and timing in the assembly. But the one delivering the tongue, interpretation, or prophecy is well aware of the anointing upon them. The Holy Spirit flows through them to others like rivers of living water.

Paul encouraged the church to be zealous for spiritual gifts; he told them to hunger after them. These gifts in the church are to help build the body, not for self-exaltation as someone special that God is working through. We are all special. What is most special is what God is actually doing through a weak, imperfect vessel to help others in the body. This is why Paul said that when he comes to a corporate assembly, he would rather speak a few words with his understanding than a thousand in tongues. Praying in tongues is not the least of the gifts. It is just the least important when you come together as a congregation to minister truth to edify and build each other up.

These last two chapters are written to explain and reveal that tongues are for today. It is an outward manifestation of the baptism of the Holy Spirit and something to be desired by all believers. So many instances have been written in the Bible to help believers understand the various manifestations of the gift of tongues as it pertains personally and corporately. Next, let us take a look at the benefits of praying in tongues—how it brings enhancement to our prayer life, and how it helps our communication with God and leads us to greater intimacy with Him.

## The Benefits of Praying in Tongues

The first benefit of praying in tongues is that you edify and build yourself up spiritually. It is like an exercise for your spirit man. If you were to exercise physically, what would it do to your body? If you exercise aerobically by extensive running, biking, or swimming, your muscles build up and you develop endurance and strength. I have consistently worked out and exercised physically most of my life. One of the things I do is road biking. When I first started, I only biked a few miles. As time went by, I began to bike more miles and kept training until my muscles and respiratory endurance could withstand a "century." A century, as bikers call it, is a 100-mile bike ride, which I have done about four times now. The same could be said for weightlifting. I can quickly tell after a few weeks of consistent lifting that my muscles are stronger than they were before.

Think of praying in tongues as exercising and strengthening your spirit man's influence over your mind and body.

> For one who speaks in a **tongue does not speak to men but to God; for no one understands**, but in his **spirit he speaks mysteries**. One **who speaks in a tongue edifies himself**; For **if I pray in a tongue, my spirit prays, but my mind is unfruitful**. What is the outcome then? **I will pray with the spirit, and I will pray with the mind also; I will sing with the spirit and I will sing with the mind also**. (1 Corinthians 14:2, 4, 14-15)

Here, Paul specifically says that when he speaks in tongues, he edifies himself. The word "edify" commonly means to build or erect a house or restore a building; spiritually, it means to facilitate or promote Christian growth, strength, or grace in us. Early in my Christian life, I noticed that when I prayed in tongues, my spiritual life was enhanced. Practically, it allowed me to be more in tune with the Holy Spirit and more perceptive in my understanding of Scripture. It also gave me greater inner spiritual strength to resist sin and temptation, and greater sensitivity to the other gifts of the Holy Spirit to work though me as the Lord sees fit.

Jude encourages us to pray in the Holy Spirit, which means to pray in tongues. This does not mean that when we pray in our natural language we are not praying with the help of the Holy Spirit.

> But you, beloved, **building yourselves up on your most holy faith, praying in the Holy Spirit**. (Jude 20)

"Building yourself up" means building upon the current foundation by praying in the Holy Spirit. Another analogy is a battery charger attached to a charging station to make sure it has enough life to perform its tasks. Well, how long and how often should we do this? My answer is, as much as you want and need to do it. Paul said that he prayed in tongues more than all the Corinthians. One of the main reasons Paul was able to accomplish the things he did was because he continually prayed in tongues.

Although I was baptized in the Holy Spirit and prayed in tongues periodically early in my Christian walk, it was about five years before I developed a better understanding of this and endeavored to pray hours at a time in tongues. I learned to do this as a part of my personal prayer time. I remember one specific instance when I spent the better part of a day just praying in tongues and then went to a meeting that night. I was sitting there just talking to people, and I felt the power of God flowing out of every word I said. It felt like an electrode was shooting bolts of electricity off of me. After that, it felt like my battery was fully charged, and I had the juice to use when I needed it!

Many years into my Christian walk, I specifically remember being prompted to pray in tongues more than I used to. I was battling strong anxiety issues I had never experienced before. Sometimes life has a way of wearing you down; between work, ministry, and family, there was always a lot on my plate. My plate was running over—not with good things though. I was overburdened, anxious, and fearful, and I could not seem to get out of it. It was frustrating because I was having trouble executing things in life that I had done very well for years. One day, I was sitting in my car, at a place I would go to pray every morning. While I was contemplating my situation, I was prompted by the Holy Spirit to pray in tongues. From that day on, I began to consistently pray in tongues each morning. This practice slowly strengthened me and helped me to hear God and work though the issues with which I was dealing. It helped me learn, make some adjustments, and understand the ways of

God more. It brought a combination of spiritual strength and revelation, which in turn brought heartfelt repentance and humility before God. This humility allowed me to receive grace to change and be transformed by God. It put me on a path of spiritual growth and victory. Thank God for the gift of praying in tongues!

This was a result of building myself up in the Holy Spirit, and how this happened is exactly how Paul describes it in Romans 8:26-28:

> In the same way the Spirit also helps our weakness; for **we do not know how to pray as we should, but the Spirit Himself intercedes for us with groanings too deep for words**; and He who searches the hearts knows what the mind of the Spirit is, because He intercedes for the saints according to the will of God.

The Holy Spirit helps us in our weakness. Our weakness is our flesh, and God understands it and empathizes with us. That is part of Jesus's identification with us as man in flesh. Jesus came to identify with us in the flesh so we could learn to identify with Him in the strength of the Spirit.

When dealing with my weaknesses, I knew what the Scriptures say about anxiety and fear. I quoted them, repented, worshipped, and prayed with my natural words to express the divine understanding I had. But I was falling short. I needed extra help and spiritual power to overcome my weaknesses. When I did not know how to express myself, or what to pray with my natural words, the Holy Spirit, through tongues, began interceding for me. The word "intercede" means "to take hold of together with against." The Holy Spirit works with our spirit and helps us stand against our weaknesses that so easily entangle us. Paul does not explicitly say that groaning is praying in tongues, and he does not say it is not either.

I can only share what I have experienced with God. There would be times when praying in tongues was like a deep guttural utterance coming forth from me. I could sense the Holy Spirit doing something in me because He knew the will of God for me, and He knew what I was going through. The Holy Spirit intercedes, petitions, and converses on our behalf according to the will of the Father. He was working on my behalf too. He was building me up, strengthening me, revealing God to me, and guiding me to work through the difficulties and issues in my life. If I did not pray in tongues as much as I did, it would have been much more difficult to experience the victory I eventually had. This process is not just for difficulties; it is for all aspects of spiritual growth and understanding that God will work through us. He wills and works His good pleasure through us.

This manifestation is not just limited to praying for yourself. It can be an inspired prayer or intercession for others. God may bring to your mind a situation or a person, and you may pray in tongues because you may not know how to pray for them. As you pray in tongues, sometimes you will gain understanding of what and how you are praying, and then you can pray that in your natural language. This could also fall under the category of "interpretation." Paul says that if you speak in tongues, you may interpret. He never said that interpretation is just for an assembly.

This brings up two questions: Is praying in tongues intercession? And, should intercession always be in tongues? Like Paul, I will pray with my understanding, and I will pray with my spirit. The object of praying in tongues is to gain understanding, and with that understanding, pray in our natural language, quoting the Word—the will of God. Praying in tongues can sometimes be intercession for others, and sometimes intercession for yourself. I do not recommend limiting your prayer and intercession time just to tongues, but do not forget the benefits of tongues that can help you with intercession.

I like to think of Paul's statement in Ephesians 6:18, at the end of his explanation and exhortation about putting on the armor of God. Paul says, "*With all prayer and petition, pray at all times in the Spirit.*" As we pray in the Spirit, sometimes through revelation or interpretation, God will show us in our natural language what we just prayed. The more we can grow spiritually as individual parts of the body, the more we can strengthen the other parts around us. We can work in unity as a whole body and grow into the fullness of the body of Christ.

There is nothing unbiblical about spending time alone to pray with our understanding and in other tongues to build ourselves up. If we think about this logically, the more we build ourselves up, the more we will be able to build up others in the assembly by taking some of what has been imparted to us and imparting it to them.

This leads into another particularly important benefit that comes from speaking in tongues: more revelation and understanding of God. This understanding will always be backed up by Scripture. Paul states that when he speaks in tongues, he speaks mysteries—hidden or secret things. Secrets are governed by God and are not well understood by unspiritual people. They can only be known and understood through divine revelation. In the New Testament, God made known these divine revelations by His Spirit. The Holy Spirit is given to us to reveal truth. It is His job to reveal the Father and Son to us.

Paul explained this to the Corinthians in 1 Corinthians 2:6-10:

> Yet we do speak wisdom among those who are mature; a wisdom, however, not of this age nor of the rulers of this age, who are passing away; **but we speak God's wisdom in a mystery, the hidden wisdom which God predestined before the ages to our glory**; the wisdom which none of the rulers of this age has understood; for if they had understood it they would not have crucified the Lord of glory; but just as it is written, "THINGS WHICH EYE HAS NOT SEEN AND EAR HAS NOT HEARD, AND which HAVE NOT ENTERED THE HEART OF MAN, ALL THAT GOD HAS PREPARED FOR THOSE WHO LOVE HIM." **For to us God revealed them through the Spirit; for the Spirit searches all things, even the depths of God.**

The Holy Spirit reveals to us the mysteries of God. Praying in tongues is not the only way through which He does this, but it is one of the ways He uses. God has always desired to reveal Himself to man, but it was difficult for man to understand Him. However, with the new covenant initiated, God redeemed man and dwells in him, so man has a conduit to understand the various aspects of God.

I have personally put this to the test. I cannot count the times I have prayed in tongues and revelation came to me. By revelation, I mean an understanding of the Scriptures. Sometimes I see a picture or a scene in my spirit, and from there, the Lord highlights some scriptures to me, and I start to see them in a new light. Then I begin to study those scriptures and meditate on them. I discuss them with God, and it becomes an ongoing conversation with Him as He builds that truth inside of me. Most often, it starts small, but over time, it builds into a revelation I can find in many places in the Word of God.

I specifically remember a time when I went into my prayer closet—which was actually a closet—and I began praying in tongues. All of sudden, a mystery was revealed to me about how God's power creates in the heavenly realm and manifests in the natural realm—a spiritual law of physics. In the earthly realm, there are several laws of physics. One of them is the second law of thermodynamics. According to this law, in this world, everything goes from a state of order to disorder; it is called decay or entropy. Spiritually, we understand that this happens because of sin. Sin causes spiritual death, and spiritual death causes physical death. Spiritual death affects all of creation. God spoke to man about this after man's fall in Genesis 3. Everything in this world will eventually decay. Everything goes from a state of order to disorder.

In heaven, and in God's spiritual realm, it is the exact opposite though. Everything goes from a state of non-order/disorder to order. There is constant life through the power of God's Word. God's Word operates according to a principle of heavenly physics.

As I was trying to understand this mystery, God highlighted some scriptures to me. Starting in Genesis 1, when the earth was formless and void, the Spirit of God was hovering over the face of the waters. Then, God said, "*Let there be light.*" He took what was formless and void and put it into divine order with His words. His words are carried by divine light and glory. The world is no longer formless and void (Genesis 1). The book of Hebrews says that God holds all things together by the word of his power (Hebrew 1:3). Paul tells us that the same God who spoke light into existence has shone light in our hearts to give us the light of His glory in the face of Christ (2 Corinthians 4:6). When we receive Jesus, God shines His light in our heart, recreates our spirit, and puts it in divine order.

Revelation unravels mysteries and brings the knowledge of God. The knowledge of God releases eternal life into our heart (John 17:3). Jesus said that eternal life starts with the knowledge of God the Father and God the Son. Eternal life is the quality of life in heaven that Jesus gave us access to while we are on earth. When we leave this body after our natural death, we will go to a place where we can receive and walk without hinderances and influences of the flesh, the devil, and the world.

Jesus also said that revelation comes from the Father, and when revelation comes, it is like a rock. It builds a solid foundation of truth inside of you that allows you to stand against all evil and contrary forces in the world. I have come to the conclusion that I need all the help I can get to be strong and live the Christian life that God has called me to live. So I am going to use every tool at my disposal, and tongues is one of them.

I am sure that one of the reasons for Paul's great understanding of the mysteries of what happened from the cross to the throne is that he prayed in tongues so much. I also think that his praying in tongues strengthened him and sustained him through the most challenging times in his life. He outlined what he went through in 2 Corinthians 11, and you can read it all through the book of Acts as well. He wrote two-thirds of the New Testament. The revelation of the identification, the substitutionary work that Christ did for us, and the union that happened in our identification can be expounded as:

Jesus was crucified; we are crucified
Jesus died; we died
Jesus was buried; we were buried

> Jesus was made alive, or quickened; we were made alive, or quickened
>
> Jesus was raised from the dead; we were raised from the dead
>
> Jesus is seated in heavenly places; we are seated in heavenly places

The core of many of Paul's epistles came to Paul through revelation. A revelation is an explanation of a divine puzzle in which God puts all the pieces together. This is exactly what Paul said in Galatians 1:11-12:

> For I would have you know, brethren, that the gospel which was preached by me is not according to man. **For I neither received it from man, nor was I taught it, but I received it through a revelation of Jesus Christ.**

As I waded into a deeper prayer life, God began to give me pieces of many spiritual puzzles. As I meditated on them, I found another piece and then another piece. Frankly, as long as you are on this earth, God will keep adding pieces. That is what happened to Paul. When we put together the references in the Scriptures, we see that Paul spent three years in Arabia after his conversion. I am making an educated guess here, but I believe that during that time, Paul was in the presence of God, and God must have downloaded many things to him. Also, Paul must have spent a lot of time praying in tongues. These revelations kept increasing as he walked with God. Paul quoted scriptures from the Old Testament to emphasize his revelation, but the Holy Spirit must have painted a picture and showed him those references in the Old Testament.

I can tell you from my experience with God, that is exactly what happened with me. He would give me a revelation and lead me to specific scriptures. I would meditate on it and pray with my understanding, and then pray in tongues, and continue meditating on it more. The more revelation, followed by more scriptures, the more my understanding and knowledge of God increased.

### Key 5: Baptism in the Holy Spirit and Speaking in other Tongues

There is one more benefit of speaking in tongues: by doing this, we build ourselves up and become more sensitive to the manifestations of the other gifts of the Holy Spirit. We can hear and discern the voice of God, and the prompting of the Holy Spirit, more clearly. These promptings are categorized by Paul as gifts in 1 Corinthians 12 (NKJV):

- Word of wisdom: revelation of God's will and purpose relating to the future
- Word of knowledge: revelation of something, usually about the past or present
- Discerning of spirits: supernatural ability to see into the spiritual realm and identify spirits (not just evil spirits)
- Supernatural faith: a powerful knowing or belief that something will happen
- Gifts of healing: manifestation of God's power to heal people
- Working of miracles: manifestation of God's power to do the impossible or unfathomable
- Prophecy: divine utterance to foretell a message from God for edification, exhortation, and comfort
- Interpretation of tongues: the same as prophecy but manifested through tongues first and then followed by its interpretation
- Different kinds of tongues: inspired utterance in a language one does not know

The Bible has plenty of narratives and examples of these gifts in action, but we are just going to focus on the gift of tongues here. The more I pray in tongues, the more I sense what gift God wants to manifest through me to edify and benefit the church. This builds my faith so I will step out and do what He prompts me to do. It is great to sense the gift, but it takes greater faith to step out and do what we are prompted to do in spite of the risk of failure or making a mistake.

The reason we went through this subject in much detail is to understand the importance of the baptism of the Holy Spirit and the resulting manifestation, which is speaking in tongues. This book is about prayer, God's presence, and intimacy with Him. Speaking in tongues is a key tool that has helped me pray more intimately and effectively, and it helped me to experience the presence of God more definitively.

I hope and pray that you will come to the place where you too can say like Paul, "*I pray in tongues more than you all!*"

# Key 6:

# Just Do It! Practical Application for an Intimate Prayer Life

## Introduction to the Lord's Prayer

There is a special and important ingredient for experiencing God. A lot of people have the best intentions for it, but they never set aside time or prioritize it. If you are like me, you like structure to accomplish a task. In the following chapters, I want to talk about a few well-known scriptures on prayer and give you a model prayer and plan to follow through to experience an intimate prayer life. The first is the Lord's Prayer, and the second is Solomon's prayer and God's answer when the first great Temple was dedicated to the Lord. Both of these prayers have similar elements and are in line with the keys we discussed in the previous chapters.

When Jesus started His earthly ministry, there were notable differences in His communication and explanation of God when compared to the religious leaders of the time. These differences were noticed by all who heard Jesus. He referred to God as "Father." He made His relationship with the Father sound personal and intimate, not one that was caught up in just tradition, ceremony, and repetition. This relationship produced an excitement and manifestation of God that the people in the religious system did not experience or understand.

We see this first mentioned when Jesus preached the Sermon on the Mount, as He described heart attitudes and actions that are pleasing and not pleasing to God. The Sermon on the Mount was like Jesus taking a machete to a thick forest, where the branches of the forest were getting in the way so the people could not see and know where they were going. Jesus was cutting up the religious thoughts of the day and separated the forest from the trees. He explained the true character and nature of the God they served, making it plain and simple for those who wanted to hear. The Bible says that He instructed the people with authority, unlike the religious leaders of the time. It took authority, freedom, and confidence to explain the nature of the Father. Not only did Jesus speak this way, but His words were confirmed with miracles and manifestations of the power of God.

Right after the Sermon on the Mount, Jesus came down the mountain and encountered a leper. The leper asked Jesus to heal him if it was the will of God. Jesus answered by first touching the unclean leper and then telling him that it was the will of God to heal him. The leper was miraculously healed. Also, we read about Jesus healing the centurion's servant and multitudes of other people. He even cast out demons with His words. Jesus did not just talk about having authority and the understanding of God; He demonstrated these through His words and actions.

Jesus referred to God as "the Father" over two hundred times in the Gospels—mostly in the Gospel of John. John's Gospel has some unique perspectives. For example:

> So the Jewish leaders began harassing Jesus for breaking the Sabbath rules. But Jesus replied, "**My Father is always working, and so am** I." So the Jewish leaders tried all the harder to find a way to kill him. For he not only broke the Sabbath, **he called God his Father, thereby making himself equal with God.** (John 5:16-18, NLT)

The Jews knew that Jesus, by saying that God was His Father, was making Himself equal to God.

The Father and I are one. (John 10:30, NLT)

We can conclude from these that Jesus was different. He claimed to be God incarnate and knew the Father and the will of the Father. Jesus said that He only did the things He saw the Father do, meaning, He had an intimate relationship with the Father, so He knew the ways of the Father—how He would act and react to things in life. He was full of grace and truth that only came from the Father. He poured that grace and truth upon us so—through Him—we can behold the glory of the Father.

During Jesus's ministry years, He had a practice of going away alone to spend time in personal communion and fellowship with the Father. One account is recorded in Mark 1:35-37:

> **In the early morning, while it was still dark, Jesus got up, left the house, and went away to a secluded place, and was praying there**. Simon and his companions searched for Him; They found Him, and said to Him, "Everyone is looking for You."

Why did Jesus do this? I can think of a number of reasons. The first that comes to mind is because He enjoyed and loved fellowshipping with the Father. As a Man, He needed to depend on the Father and express that to the Father, and the Father poured the Holy Spirit on Him without measure.

In Luke 6, we read that Jesus spent the whole night in prayer before He chose His twelve apostles. One would have to conclude that these two events are connected; Jesus was learning the will of the Father regarding those to choose.

In Luke 11:1, we read that Jesus went away from the disciples to a certain place, and when He came back, they asked Him to teach them to pray:

> It happened that while Jesus was praying in a certain place, after He had finished, one of His disciples said to Him, **"Lord, teach us to pray just as John also taught his disciples."**

At this point, Jesus went through a second iteration of the Lord's Prayer. The first was recorded in Matthew 5-7 as part of the Sermon on the Mount.

The substance of both the recorded prayers in Matthew and Luke are close, but I want to focus more on what is recorded in Matthew 6:5-13:

> When you pray, you are not to be like the hypocrites; for they love to stand and pray in the synagogues and on the street corners so that they may be seen by men. Truly I say to you, they have their reward in full. But you, when you pray, go into your inner room, close your door, and pray to your Father who is in secret, and your Father who sees what is done in secret will reward you.
>
> And when you are praying, do not use meaningless repetition as the Gentiles do, for they suppose that they will be heard for their many words. So do not be like them; for your Father knows what you need before you ask Him.
>
> **Pray, then, in this way:** 'Our Father who is in heaven, Hallowed be Your name. Your kingdom come. Your will be done, On earth as it is in heaven. Give us this day our daily bread. And forgive us our debts, as we also have forgiven our debtors. And do not lead us into temptation, but deliver us from evil.' [For Yours is the kingdom and the power and the glory forever. Amen.]

Jesus was instructing His disciples on how to pray and not be like the hypocrites or the religious leaders of the day. He pointed out a couple of things: first, He told them not to pray so as to be heard and be seen by men and appear pious and religious; second, He told them not to pray in meaningless repetition. By meaningless repetition, He meant just saying the same thing over and over again—a repetition that has no passion, substance, or knowledge of God. Remember, prayer is communication with God, and part of that communication is communion. If I were to talk to someone all the time and just repeat the same words over and over, it would not be much of a relationship.

Why is it that the most repeated verbatim prayer Christians pray across all denominations is the one that comes right after Jesus said not to repeat a prayer in meaningless repetition? I have been a part of many Christian services over the years where we would repeat this prayer when we gather as an assembly. I am not saying that this repetition is meaningless, but there is more substance to the prayer and more meaning to the prayer than mere repetition. When the disciples came and asked Jesus to teach them to pray, He repeated what He said previously in the Sermon on the Mount. I think that Jesus, in this prayer, was explaining how He communicated with the Father, and He gave us a blueprint for prayer, communion, and fellowship with God.

I received this revelation one day when a friend of mine wanted to do a class on the Lord's Prayer, for the men in our church. We were going to lead it together; he was going to oversee the class, and I was going to teach the substance of it. We had a group of about fifteen men. It was a time of great blessing to see the men get together and hunger for prayer, because when it comes to prayer, the ladies typically outpace the men by quite a distance. My experience is that when a prayer meeting is called in the church, the attendance is at least two to one in the ladies' favor.

As I meditated on the Lord's Prayer, I realized that what I have learned about prayer is similar to what is encapsulated in the Lord's Prayer. I then concluded that the Lord's Prayer is not a prayer of repetition, but a blueprint of how we can approach, commune, and communicate with God. I then started consciously using that blueprint in my own life.

Most people who have met the Lord Jesus have been told that they should pray and be intentional about it. But soon, they lose the desire to pray as a result of inconsistent action. Many times, after five minutes into prayer, they are lost, distracted, bored, and have no plan for how to proceed. I want these folks to use this blueprint to help establish their prayer life. I think the rest will take care of itself. We need to make the decision to just do it.

## The Lord's Prayer: Part 1

The Lord's Prayer starts as follows in Matthew 6:9:

> Pray, then, in this way: Our Father who is in heaven, Hallowed be Your name.

Jesus taught His disciples to pray just as He prayed. He began by acknowledging God as the Father who resides in the majesty of heaven. He told them to acknowledge God—Jehovah—as their Father, just as He did. That in itself points to an intimacy and connection with God that the disciples may have never realized God wanted to experience with them.

Jesus then acknowledged the holiness of God. He said, "Hallowed be Your name." To hallow means to regard as holy. Holiness is a subject that most of us do not understand. But I have endeavored to explain it a few times before in this writing.

Holy is His name. Within His name is a description of Himself. God has many names. In the Old Testament, He reveals Himself as the Most High—El Elyon. There is no one higher in rank or majesty. El Shaddai: God Almighty. Elohim: my Creator. He is referred to as Jehovah or Yahweh, the self-existing almighty God—the Great I Am. There are many descriptions of God in the Old Testament connected with "Jehovah." They are His covenant names, and some of them are as follows:

- Jehovah Rophe: the Lord our Healer
- Jehovah Jireh: the Lord our Provider

- Jehovah Nissi: the Lord our Banner
- Jehovah Shammah: the Lord who is there
- Jehovah Tsidkenu: the Lord our Righteousness
- Jehovah M'kaddesh: the Lord our Sanctifier
- Jehovah Raah: the Lord our Shepherd (Friend)
- Jehovah Shalom: the Lord our Peace

There are similar names that describe the character and nature of God manifested through Jesus in the New Testament, all of which are brought out in the unique Gospel of John:

- Jesus said, "I am the Bread of Life."
- Jesus said, "I am the Light of the World."
- Jesus said, "I am the Way, the Truth, and the Life."
- Jesus said, "I am the Door of the sheep."
- Jesus said, "I am the Good Shepherd."
- Jesus said, "I am the Resurrection and the Life."
- Jesus said, "I am the True Vine."

I am not going to go through all the names of God in the Bible; that would be a book of its own! But I want to give some insight into how they lead us to understand the nature and character of God and how that, in turn, moves us to worship Him.

Jesus told His disciples that when they pray, they should start by worshipping God the Father. This goes back to why I spent so much time explaining why worship is especially important for an intimate, ongoing prayer life. God seeks after those who worship Him in spirit and truth. Worship is like self-fulfilling prophecy; the more you do it, the more you want to do it, and the more you enjoy it. The more you enjoy it, the more you are filled with a desire to do it more often.

God wants us to worship Him so He can reveal Himself and His secrets to us. The more He does that, the more we behold something new about His nature and being. This then inspires us to worship Him. With this knowledge comes eternal life; not quantity of life, but the quality of life that Jesus brought. Eternal life is knowing the only true Father, and the Son whom He sent. God uses the medium of the Holy Spirit within us to accomplish this.

The desire and need for prayer does start with our will, but as we move our will to pray and seek God's face, He feeds us with desire for Him and draws us unto Him. We realize that, as He does this, we desire more of Him.

Worshipping God will feed your passion for Him because we are created to worship and fellowship with Him. It will infuse the atmosphere around you with a divine accelerant. God will respond and light your passion on fire with His love. Then, you will begin to experience and enjoy a lifetime of fellowship with Him.

Let us go back to some practical application of what Jesus said in the Lord's Prayer. When you set yourself apart to pray, start with worship. It can be as simple as taking some of the names of God and acknowledging who He is, and specifically, who He is to you. You can say you worship Him for being your Shepherd, your Peace, your Healer, and your Savior—that is who He is. You worship God for who He is, and you praise Him for what He has done. Sometimes it can be just singing a song of worship from your heart, or singing along with a song to which you are listening. This can intertwine with thanksgiving and praise. Thank and praise God for what He has done. The more you endeavor to do this on your own, the more you will feed your heart's sincere desire—that which you were created for—and you will be on your way to experiencing God's presence in prayer. This leads to intimacy with the Creator.

I hope you now understand the importance of what Jesus said. When you pray, start with worship; this is the first step of the blueprint for how to fellowship with God.

## The Lord's Prayer: Part 2

> Your kingdom come. Your will be done, On earth as it is in heaven. (Matthew 6:10)

The above statement is a continuation on the subject of worship because worship is more than just words. It is submission and yielding to the will of God in the life we live—our spirit, soul, and body. Let me connect the dots for you.

Jesus is making a statement and a declaration that the kingdom of God has come on earth as it is in heaven. Let us dissect that statement. The kingdom of God was a subject particularly important to Jesus! From the very beginning of His ministry, Jesus constantly talked about the kingdom of God and the kingdom of heaven. In the Gospel of Mark, we read that Jesus began His preaching by proclaiming:

> The time is fulfilled, and the kingdom of God is at hand; repent and believe in the gospel. (Mark 1:15)

John the Baptist told people to repent because the kingdom of heaven is at hand. In Matthew 4, we see that Jesus started to preach the same thing. In the book of Matthew, there are 114 references to Jesus talking about the kingdom of heaven. Between all four Gospels, there are 188 references to the kingdom of God, most of which are in Mark and Luke. In Acts 1, we read that after Jesus rose from the dead and appeared to His disciples, He talked to them for forty days about things concerning the kingdom of God. So it should not take a lot of spiritual perception to realize that the message of the kingdom was of vital importance to what Jesus was expounding to the people. After being taught by Jesus about the kingdom during His ministry on earth and after His resurrection, the disciples still did not understand that the kingdom was primarily a spiritual kingdom. They continued to ask Jesus whether He was going to restore the kingdom to Israel, still thinking that He was going to set up His earthly kingdom at that time, just like any other king would do.

Jesus gave them insight to this in Luke 17:20-21:

> Now having been questioned by the Pharisees as to when the kingdom of God was coming, He answered them and said, "The kingdom of God is not coming with signs to be

> observed; nor will they say, 'Look, here it is!' or, **'There it is!' For behold, the kingdom of God is in your midst (within you).**"

The word "kingdom" refers to dominion and encompasses the influence of the dominion or will of God within the hearts and minds of men. This is why Jesus said in the Lord's prayer, when He prayed for God's kingdom: "*Your kingdom come. Your will be done, on earth as it is in heaven.*" In heaven, the kingdom of God exists because His perfect will is affecting the hearts of all creatures there, and as a result, His dominion rules all of heaven. It is a dominion that enables each person to be willing to follow Him by their own free will because of the perfection, beauty, and holiness of the King.

Since God formed man from the dust of the ground, Jesus prayed that the will of God needs to be done in our lives. This is a prayer of submission to God. Worship shows reverence for God, and in our worship, we acknowledge there is Someone greater than us who needs to be worshipped and obeyed. Humility is where we entirely submit to God. Prayer is the place where we acknowledge and express that verbally, and by the commitment of our lives to the will of God, we worship God with our actions.

This is the exact subject that Paul addresses in Romans 12:1-2:

> Therefore I urge you, brethren, by the mercies of God, **to present your bodies a living and holy sacrifice, acceptable to God, which is your spiritual service of worship.** And do not be conformed to this world, but be transformed by the renewing of your mind, so that you may prove what the will of God is, that which is good and acceptable and perfect.

Paul was urging the Romans to present their bodies as a living sacrifice to God. In the Old Testament, the people sacrificed animals. But in the New Testament, Paul tells the people to present their earthly bodies as that sacrifice. The problem with living sacrifices is that we still have the choice to crawl off the altar and take over the lordship of our lives. Paul says that this process of being a living sacrifice is our spiritual service of worship. True worship is not just words from our mouth but our acts of submission to God and His will. Whatever we present our bodies to and submit to is what we worship. We can worship many things. We can worship money, power, and sex. We can submit our mental and physical energy to any of these. Whatever is most important to us receives our worship.

In the Old Testament, we read that people used fire to burn the sacrifice. Our spiritual sacrifice is a result of the passion we have for God that produces the divine accelerant in the spiritual atmosphere. But now, the fire is God Himself. He baptizes us with the Holy Spirit and fire. We are a sacrifice that keeps burning with the presence of God, and the only thing that is consumed is that which hinders us from walking with Him. We bring the sacrifice, and God brings the fire.

The result of this is that we are not conformed to the world in our thinking, character, and actions. These ways are the desires of the flesh—the desire for power and being consumed by pride. But we are transformed, metamorphosized, changed to reflect the new man that was created at the new birth. Our thinking and thought patterns change. Then we prove what the will of God is, because His will is being done on earth. The earth—our bodies—are now influenced by the renewed mind that is fueled with the power of God that changes us.

Many times, when I am teaching, I ask people what our greatest spiritual weapon is. I get the typical answers: prayer, the Word of God, the Holy Spirit, the gospel, etc. But I am yet to find what I am looking for. All of the above are wonderful and powerful spiritual weapons, but none of them will work through us without us being a submitted vessel. Our greatest weapon on this earth is our body. Just as the devil has his greatest effect on this earth through a person who yields to him, God has His greatest influence on the world through yielded vessels.

Paul says it so concisely in Romans 6:12-13:

> Therefore do not let sin reign in your mortal body so that you obey its lusts, and do not go on **presenting the members of your body to sin as instruments of unrighteousness; but present yourselves to God as those alive from the dead, and your members as instruments of righteousness to God.**

Our body is an instrument—or weapon—of righteousness for God. The word "instrument" is better translated as "arms used in warfare." That is why warfare and worship go together!

This concept can be seen in Jesus's life. He was always about doing the will of the Father. Remember, He only did what He saw the Father do. Jesus's great spiritual battle was fought in the garden of Gethsemane. He knew it was the will of the Father for Him to go to the cross and be the sacrificial Lamb, but the weight and pain of the situation was wearing on Him. We read His prayer to the Father in Matthew, Mark, and Luke. Here is Matthew's version:

> He went on a little farther and bowed with his face to the ground, praying, "My Father! If it is possible, let this cup of suffering be taken away from me. **Yet I want your will to be done, not mine."** (Matthew 26:39, NLT)

How do we apply this to our personal prayer life? This kind of prayer is a prayer of commitment to the Lord—it is a prayer of submission. Part of our prayer time can consist of declaring our desire to serve Him, to yield our life to Him, to submit to Him, and communicate our dependence on Him. We can meditate on scriptures like Romans 12:1-2 and Romans 6:12-13, and recite them back to the Lord. We can meditate on the lives of people in the Bible who struggled and overcame in this area.

## The Lord's Prayer: Part 3

> Give us this day our daily bread. (Matthew 6:11)

These are a few words from the Lord's Prayer that are full of spiritual meaning. Yes, we can pray for natural food so we will not go hungry. But this has so much more meaning than that. Jesus said in John 6 that He is the Bread of Life, and whoever comes to Him will never hunger or thirst. Jesus is the Word of God. The beginning of the Gospel of John says:

> In the beginning was the Word, and the Word was with God, and the Word was God…And the Word became flesh and dwelt among us, and we beheld His glory, the glory as of the only begotten of the Father, full of grace and truth. (John 1:1, 14, NKJV)

Jesus also said that man shall not live by bread alone, but by every Word that proceeds from the mouth of God. This part of the Lord's Prayer is a prayer to hear, learn, and understand the Word of God. But more specifically, "Lord, where are You leading me, and what are You teaching me in this time and season?"

There are many things that we can do to learn the Word of God. We can memorize scriptures, read the Bible every year, read spiritual books and commentaries, and listen to sermons. All of these can edify and build us up. But the prayer, "*Give us this day our daily bread,*" is much more significant. It is what God is making alive by working in us and through us in this time of our life. I like to say that the written Word—the Word that is in our mind—gets spiritually digested and becomes spiritual substance in us and changes us. We get our own personal revelation of the Word. It becomes our rock. Just like when Jesus told Peter that it was not flesh and blood that revealed to Him that Jesus was the Messiah—the Son of the living God—it was His Father in heaven. It is the Father and the Son through the Person of the Holy Spirit who reveal spiritual truths.

A couple of confessions here: In forty plus years of my spiritual walk, I have never read the Bible in its entirety in a year, although I have read the entire Bible during those years. Over the last twenty years, I rarely read a whole book in the Bible. Many times, I intend to do this, and I start reading a book in the Bible, but it does not take long before I run into a verse that gets my attention and have to stop and meditate on it. I get immersed on the subject of the verse, and then reading the whole book comes to an abrupt halt. I usually get some leading from the Holy Spirit on a subject, and then I tear myself away from where I was and follow Him wherever He leads me.

Once, a friend of mine walked up to me and described how the Lord leads her. She said it is like something you would see in older movies or TV shows when newspaper delivery boys were more prevalent. They would drive by on their bikes and throw the newspaper on the person's lawn or front doorstep. But in her case, the newspaper would hit her on the head and fall to the ground. That would get her attention, and she would see the front-page headline in bold letters emphasizing the story. But to understand the story, she would need to open the paper and read the details and fine print on the interior pages.

That is exactly what the Holy Spirit does to me! He gets my attention on a subject, and then it is up to me to open the whole book (Bible) and read all the fine print about it. Many times, this process for me can take several years. One such incident happened to me many years ago. I spent a lot of time studying the subject of divine healing. I memorized every scripture I could find that talked about divine healing. I read over twenty books on divine healing. I read about the lives of the greatest healing evangelists. I read the accounts in the Gospels, the book of Acts, and other writings in the New Testament. I consistently prayed for the sick and saw many peopled healed by God's divine power. Then, one day, when I was in prayer, the Lord told me that He wanted me to study a certain subject. I was excited and thought God was going to guide me into a new subject I knew nothing about and give me some deep revelation. He said, "I want you to study divine healing." My first thought was, "What do you think I have been doing over the past couple of years!" Then He said to me, "I want you to study the way I did it." He wanted me to study the way Jesus ministered to the sick, especially the personal interactions He had and the subsequent healings recorded in the Gospels.

Do you know what my first thought was? *This should not take too long; I have read these accounts hundreds of times.* Although I never said it outright, I felt like I knew the subject well. Oh, how small our knowledge and thinking are when compared to God! I started with the first account in Matthew 8, where Jesus healed the leper. It took me months to move on from the first four verses! One might think I was slow or cannot read well, but I was so taken with the story that I realized how much of the miracle I had missed and its importance in New Testament theology. I was undone for weeks as I would think about it. I learned so much from it that it changed me. There is much more to every subject we think we know, because God's knowledge and understanding are infinite and holy. These studies eventually turned into my first book, *Understanding Divine Healing Through the Ministry of Jesus*.

This fits what I wrote about passion and the Word of God and the explanation of Proverbs 4:20-23.

> The word is life to those who find it.

Jesus encouraged us to seek, and He promised us that we will find. We do not find anything without looking for it. The Holy Spirit is here to lead us into all truth. It is such a simple and profound statement: Give us this day our daily bread.

Asking God for our daily bread is asking Him for spiritual sustenance every day. When Jesus quoted to the devil Deuteronomy 8:3—that man shall not live by bread alone, but by every Word that proceeds from the mouth of God—He was in a state of intense hunger at the end of His forty-day fast. The Word of God is our sustenance. It is what brings us daily life and spiritual nourishment.

We are expressing our desire and dependence to make the Word of God come alive to us. We are opening our heart to God for Him to discern the true intents of our heart. We speak His Word so we can have our thoughts changed and transformed to line up with His thoughts. We are asking for grace to receive the truth. Jesus was full of grace and truth, and we partake of the fullness of His grace and truth. We cannot understand God's Word just because that is what we want. We can understand His Word only because He opens our eyes when we have an open heart. The Word brings us to the very throne of grace so we can receive mercy and find grace. This is us taking, eating, and digesting the Word of God and absorbing it into our spiritual makeup.

This is the difference between building our house on sand that shifts and has no foundation, and building our house on a rock that is immovable. Those who build upon the rock are those who hear, take in, and do according to the Word of God.

Throughout the Bible, we see statements regarding having ears to hear and eyes to see, which refer not to our natural senses but our spiritual senses. When we ask for our daily bread, we are asking for a heart to hear His Word, sit at His table, eat His bread, and dine with the Father. At the family dinner table is where many significant conversations and interactions occur. This is our spiritual family dinner table where we partake and interact with each other.

It is at the family dinner table where we learn of our family's identity, history, lineage, and heritage. We learn about our family members and what they do. We learn about our identity and position in the family. All of this ties together the points in the sections of this book on the Word of God and identity, position, and faith in God. The Word of God has everything you need to know about your position before God, your identity, and who He says you are. The more you eat of the bread of life, the more your faith in God grows. To ask for our daily bread is a simple but profound prayer.

> *Father, help us to hear Your Word and understand the truths of Your Word. Let Your Word dissect us, transform us, and help us to be all that we can be. Amen.*

## The Lord's Prayer: Part 4

> And forgive us our debts, as we also have forgiven our debtors...For if you forgive others for their transgressions, your heavenly Father will also forgive you. But if you do not forgive others, then your Father will not forgive your transgressions. (Matthew 6:12, 14-15)

This is a section of the Lord's Prayer that we need to meditate on and commune with God continually for, because it is core to a Christian's growth and experience with God. The answer to prayer is a lifelong growing experience with God.

I have not delved into the subject of forgiveness in prayer previously because I have found that you can never have a prayer life without walking in forgiveness. The subject of forgiveness is core to God's nature and to the essential message of the gospel. It is something that God always draws our attention to. When we are coming into the presence of a holy God to worship Him, then we are presenting ourselves to Him in worship with the commitment of our living sacrifice. We then ask to hear His Word and receive His daily bread. Somewhere in there, if we have not forgiven someone else, or ourselves, or even God, it will be addressed by Him.

In Psalm 103, David talks of the wonderful compassion and lovingkindness of God, forgiving our iniquities, not dealing with us according to our sins, or recompensing us according to the debts we incur. He says that God has removed our sins from us as far as the east is from the west. Paul said the wages (payment) of sin is death, but the gift of God is eternal life through Christ Jesus (Romans 6:23). I could write many pages on the subject of forgiveness and sin, but that is not the overall purpose of this book.

When it comes to prayer, Jesus made the point that if we are going to pray in faith, we need to forgive anyone who has sinned against us. If we do not, then there will be hindrances between us and God. If Jesus died for everyone and could forgive them for what they have done, why can't we do the same? Paul said it so well in his epistles when he talked about forgiving one another. He instructs people to be kind, tenderhearted, and forgive one another. Forgive just as the Lord forgave you. If we cannot forgive someone for their shortcomings or failure of duty, how can we commune with God? The issue is not just between us and the other person; it is between us and God. God loves them and has forgiven them. Just like us, they too are God's beloved. When we do not forgive, we sin against one of God's beloved children. We have two major categories of relationship: first, with God, and second, with our brothers and sisters in Christ. The two great commandments—love God and love one another—are tied together. By loving God, we will learn to love one another. God is love, and He imparts a kind, merciful attitude that allows us to see one another the way He sees us. God will forgive us our sins *in proportion to how* we forgive those who have sinned against us. The word "forgive" here means to forgive for failure of duty or failure to do what is right before God and others. We all fall into this category in life knowingly or unknowingly at times. If we are quick to forgive someone for an actual or perceived fault, and we do it consciously, God will forgive our failures and faults that are known and unknown to us. Jesus mentions forgiveness in prayer a number of times. The first is at the end of the Lord's Prayer as recorded above. In the Gospel of Mark, we read that He mentioned it in the prayer of faith as well. Jesus talked about having faith to move mountains if we do not doubt and waver. If we say it and believe it in our heart, we can command the mountain to be removed and cast into the sea. That is an immensely powerful prayer concept! But right after Jesus said that, He repeated the exact statement He made in the Lord's Prayer. The best way to send our communication and prayer life downhill is to allow unforgiveness to enter our heart and mind and have a hold on us. How can we have faith to move mountains if we do not have faith to forgive?

I want to end this chapter with a practical understanding of how this works in our life. This spiritual principle is recorded throughout the Bible. It is the subject of how mercy and truth work together. In the Old Testament, there is the word *hesed*. It is translated as mercy, kindness, lovingkindness, or goodness. It is the essential character and nature of God. This is what Jehovah is filled with, and He used the word "hesed" when He passed by Moses and proclaimed His glory.

> Abounding in lovingkindness (hesed/mercy) and truth; who keeps lovingkindness for thousands, who forgives iniquity, transgression, and sin. (Exodus 34:6-7)

We should act in the same manner:

> Do not let kindness (mercy/hesed) and truth leave you; Bind them around your neck, write them on the tablet of your heart. So you will **find favor (grace) and good repute in the sight of God and man.** (Proverbs 3:3-4)

Mercy and truth bring together the true knowledge of God in our heart and mind. God is full of mercy and truth. When we are merciful to people and forgive them, and combine that with the truth of God's Word, it releases the grace of God in both our life and those we forgive. Now, whether the person you forgive receives that or not is up to them. But its effect in your life will be the abundant favor and grace of God working in you and through you. God's grace brings favor to us in all aspects of our life. God's grace and favor cover us even in situations where we unknowingly sin or do something against someone else. This is because we have a heart that does not see people's sins and shortcomings, but forgives them and sees them through their calling—by the work of the cross and by what God has destined them to be.

When we walk in this manner, it leads to transformation in our life and the lives of others. God is a God of truth, and His truth has a good mix of mercy and lovingkindness. It does not condemn and bring people to the point of hopelessness, but to a point of understanding and acceptance that there are shortcomings and sin. There is a sense of personal responsibility, but there is hope through God to be forgiven and changed. That is why we come to the throne of grace to receive mercy and forgiveness, and grace to change. We can receive mercy at any time, but we need to find grace. Grace comes by humility and acceptance of the truth that only God can change us.

> **By lovingkindness (hesed/mercy) and truth iniquity is atoned (covered) for**, And by the fear of the LORD one

> keeps away from evil. **When a man's ways are pleasing to the Lord, He makes even his enemies to be at peace with him**. (Proverbs 16:6-7)

Bringing the mercy and lovingkindness nature of God, and mixing it with the truth of the Word of God, results in forgiveness. Living our lives with mercy and truth guiding us brings pleasure to God, and the promise associated with this is peace, even with those who do not like us. This is finding grace and favor in the sight of God and man.

The application of this, with regard to our prayer life, is to communicate to God our heart's desire to live in forgiveness by exercising mercy and truth in all of our relationships. When we practice this application, we engage in open communication with God, and we ask Him to show us areas of unforgiveness and sin of which we are unaware. As He reveals these to us, we act appropriately from there. We keep moving forward with our communion and fellowship with God.

God will show us who we need to forgive and the things we need to ask forgiveness for, whether they are acts of commission or omission.

> *Lord, help us to walk in mercy and truth so we can forgive and ask forgiveness from others. Please help us to stay in a place of communion and righteousness with both You and those around us. Amen.*

## The Lord's Prayer: Part 5

> And do not lead us into temptation, but deliver us from evil. (Matthew 6:13)

This section of the Lord's Prayer needs some meditation and communion to experience what Jesus is getting at. It is a relational prayer statement which requires continual communion and communication to bring answers.

It is a prayer of communication that needs discussion, meditation, and waiting on the Lord.

Let us consider various translations of this verse:

> And don't let us yield to temptation, but rescue us from the evil one. (NLT)
>
> Keep us safe from ourselves and the Devil. (MSG)
>
> Rescue us every time we face tribulation and set us free from evil. (TPT)
>
> And do not lead us into temptation, but deliver us from evil. (AMP)

This is a prayer for wisdom, discernment, and understanding that comes from communion and intimacy with God. In order to understand what is evil, we need to define what is evil. In order to do that, we need to understand what is good. We read in the Bible that God is good. He is good all the time. What does that mean?

One day in prayer, God asked me why I thought He was good. What a question to be asked by God! I thought about it for a few minutes and then realized that if God asks a question, there is a reason. Rather than blurting out all that I thought I knew, I said to the Lord, "There is obviously something I do not understand that You want to share with me, so please tell me." The Lord said, "I am good because whatever I do is for the benefit of others, even when it is at My own expense." Wow, what a profound statement! It is the opposite of selfishness. Whatever God does for us is always for our well-being. The epitome of a demonstration of God's goodness is the offering of His Son on the cross to die for our sins. God so loved us that He gave us His only Son, and if we believe in Jesus, He will impart to us forgiveness, transformation, and eternal life.

If goodness is doing something for the benefit of others, even at our own expense, then evil is doing something for our own benefit at the expense of others. It is selfishness when the satisfaction of self is more important than anything else. Selfishness can be very deceptive, and many times, we can fall into it very quickly without realizing it. God always intended for man to walk in goodness. In the garden of Eden, He told man that they could eat of every tree, except for the Tree of Knowledge of Good and Evil.

The devil will play on the string of selfishness and try to deceive us into taking the bait, thinking it is a good thing. But it never is. Adam and Eve were already like God in every way. The devil deceived them into thinking that God kept something good from them, and that if they just ate of the tree, it would help them be more like God. As usual, the devil provides half-truths in order to manipulate us and get us to do what he wants us to do. That is what evil does. It manipulates us into doing something that will bring about adverse consequences. The consequence of what Adam and Eve did was spiritual death—separation from God—and the giving away of their authority to rule the earth the way God wanted. The devil's deception brought him power and authority over this world, and the ability to further manipulate God's wonderful creation. The devil knew that if Adam and Eve ate of the tree, they would die spiritually and taste evil, and they would be subject to his influence and dominion as long as they lived in the flesh.

We read in Genesis that Eve looked at the tree and saw that it was good for food, a delight and desire to the eyes, and could make one wise. John, in his first epistle, refers to this as the lust of the eyes, the lust of the flesh, and the boastful pride of life. Adam and Eve had a stronger desire to please themselves than to please God. The benefit to us becomes more important than the hurt and pain it may cause others. Adam and Eve died spiritually and separated themselves from God. They found themselves in a place of knowing evil and its ongoing results, which is stealing, killing, and destroying. They could easily be influenced by evil because it became their nature. After they ate from the tree, they failed to discern the difference between good and evil, they yielded to evil, and they were forced to live with the consequences of it. Later, in Genesis 6:5-6, notice what the Lord spoke of man:

> Then the LORD saw that the **wickedness of man was great on the earth, and that every intent of the thoughts of his heart was only evil continually**. The LORD was sorry that

> He had made man on the earth, and He was grieved in His heart.

When we become self-centered and not God-centered, our understanding becomes cloudy, and we fail to understand truth as God does. We can easily be deceived when we do not see the way God sees. The New Testament says that although we are saved by the work of the cross, we will all be judged for the deeds done in our body, and judgment will be based on whether they were good or evil. Judgment for believers is for receiving rewards in heaven for works done on earth. That kind of judgment should be what motivates us. Are we motivated to please God and do what is good and for the benefit of all, or are we more interested in what gives us more benefit? Are we concerned about notoriety, power, influence, and satisfying the strong desires of the flesh, or are we interested in building up and edifying one another?

The writer of Hebrews says it well as he exhorts people to move on and grow up from the base principles of spiritual growth—which he calls "milk"—to the "meat" of the Word of God:

> Solid food is for those who are mature, **who through training have the skill to recognize the difference between right and wrong**. (Hebrews 5:14, NLT)
>
> But solid food is for the mature, **who because of practice have their senses trained to discern good and evil**. (Hebrews 5:14)

Growing up and maturing is an ongoing practice. It is not any different than practicing intensely for years to become a top athlete in any field. A person may have the natural ability to become a great athlete, but there are a number of factors that separate the great ones from the rest. There is preparation and practice, which means a continual discipline to study and to practice—whether anyone is watching or not. For a basketball player, it is the hours spent in the gym practicing shooting, dribbling, proper defensive posture, and lifting weights. I can promise you that when you compete after all that challenging work, people will notice.

Mental toughness and concentration to accomplish the task are also important. This especially comes into play during tough times when there seems to be more failure than success. Failure is just a bump on the road to success. The focus should always be on the goal.

Being teachable, humble, and always willing to learn is key. Understand that there is always something to learn, and that we can learn from the most unseemly or unlikely people and circumstances.

These practices also train our spiritual senses. Back in the day, the word used for "exercise" in the context of athletes training in a palaestra—school of athletics—means to exercise naked. That is exactly how they trained; they would take off their clothes and exercise naked so there would be nothing to inhibit their muscles.

Similarly, in the spiritual race, when we continually take in the Word of God, endeavor to live it out, apply it to our lives, and walk by faith through the different trials that come our way, we learn to discern the ways of God. We learn to discern the true motives and intentions of our heart as well as those around us.

I do not care how powerful your spiritual gifting is or what office in the church you have grace for—spiritual gifts do not determine your spirituality. Your life of faith and your personal walk with God—allowing Him to transform you—will determine how well you run your race and the quality of the fruit that comes from it. This is actually fulfilling the first and second commandment: loving God and loving one another.

The description that James put together in chapter 3 of his epistle gives us a good concept of those who are self-aware and aware of good and evil. James 3:13, 17-18:

> If you are wise and **understand God's ways**, prove it by living an honorable life, doing good **works with the humility that comes from wisdom**...But the wisdom from above is first of **all pure**. It is also **peace loving,**

> **gentle (meek) at all times, and willing to yield to others. It is full of mercy and the fruit of good deeds. It shows no favoritism and is always sincere. And those who are peacemakers will plant seeds of peace and reap a harvest of righteousness.** (NLT)

James also describes the wisdom that is not from God, which is evil.

> But if you are **bitterly jealous and there is selfish ambition in your heart**, don't cover up the truth with boasting and lying. For **jealousy and selfishness are not God's kind of wisdom**. Such things are earthly, unspiritual, and demonic. **For wherever there is jealousy and selfish ambition, there you will find disorder and evil of every kind**. (James 3:14-16, NLT)

Where jealousy and selfishness exist, you will have disorder, confusion, and evil. That kind of evil will cause a person to steal, kill, and destroy. It will bring broken relationships and church splits. Evil will cause us to focus more on what divides us than what unites us. It will deceive us into believing that our actions are justified. We are most deceived because of our self-centeredness.

Peter writes that the divine power of God has granted to us everything pertaining to life and godliness (2 Peter 1:3). But, in order to attain that, there is a measure of continued diligence that we need to apply. He exhorts us to apply diligence to our faith, good character, knowledge, self-control, perseverance, godliness, and brotherly kindness. This is our workout regimen that trains us to walk out our faith and to discern good and evil. We do not just get this from memorizing scriptures. We get this through practically applying the Word of God in faith in our daily lives.

Where does all of this lead us when praying this part of the Lord's Prayer? It is a prayer of meditation and waiting for God, asking Him to search our heart, and listening to Him as He shows us the true thoughts and intents of our heart. Psalms 51 and 139 are wonderful prayers that put this part of the Lord's Prayer into perspective and can be used in our own prayer life with faith-filled, heartfelt words. David ends Psalm 139 beautifully, asking God to search his heart to see if there are any wicked, hurtful, painful, or evil ways in him. He then goes on to ask God to show him His everlasting way. That means to expose evil motives and actions in our heart, lead us to the ways of God, and change our motives and actions by His grace, into the same as His. Just as a rigorous physical workout is not easy, so is this process. If we want to walk and experience God, we have to be ready for a God-workout at any time.

This part of the Lord's Prayer is a prayer of intimacy, submission, and communion with God that sometimes needs to be waited on in His presence, and often needs to be spoken aloud. One way or another, this type of communication and discussion with God is what brings a divine spiritual substance into our life that comes from God alone. This leads to intimacy and an enjoyable prayer life that will be foundational for our godliness and conformity to His image.

## Intimacy, Prayer, and Supplication

The Lord's Prayer is s a blueprint to help us structure our prayer life. It is by no means all-encompassing of what is contained in an intimate prayer life. This structure is helpful for those who are seasoned and have a consistent prayer life, as well as for those who are just starting out. Every time we pray, we do not have to go through each section of the Lord's Prayer. We could do just one section. If you ask me, worship is the only section I would do all the time. But there are days when I just go through a couple of statements and commune through them. One can make the order and process their own. The point is to start praying and be consistent.

Supplication is the most common type of prayer. It is when people ask God for things for themselves or others. But the type of prayer the Lord is concerned with is more relational—both with Him and with others. It is about intimacy, communion, fellowship, and transformation. Asking God to reveal His Word to us, forgive us, and help us discern good and evil, all point to relational harmony with God and one another.

Does this mean that we should never ask God for anything else? Not at all. Jesus, in His upper room discourse with His disciples, talked about praying and asking the Father for all things in Jesus's name. It is much easier and more effective to ask for things in intimate prayer. That prayer comes from a place of intimacy, understanding, and faith, and not from a place of just throwing up a prayer to Someone you do not know or have a relationship with.

Moses asked God to show him His ways so he could find more favor (grace) with God. He asked God to show him His glory. That was a bold prayer! God consented.

How could Moses make such a bold supplication? He could because he had just come back from spending time in God's presence, learning about Him, and God showed him more of His character. Moses could be so bold because of his knowledge of God and his relationship with Him. Moses knew his position before God, and God's desire for man. We ask our most intimate friends for the biggest favors, don't we? Why? Because of our close relationship with them.

In the Gospel of John, we read that Jesus talked about supplication and intercession that proceeds out of intimacy and relationship with God. These scriptures are commonly quoted to encourage us to be bold and confident before God when we ask for things in prayer.

> If you abide in Me, **and My words abide in you, ask whatever you wish, and it will be done for you**. (John 15:7)
>
> No longer do I call you slaves, for the slave does not know what his master is doing; but I have called you friends, for all things that I have heard from My Father I have made known to you. **You did not choose Me but I chose you, and appointed you that you would go and bear fruit, and that your fruit would remain, so that whatever you ask of the Father in My name He may give to you**. (John 15:15-16)

> Truly, truly, I say to you, if you ask the Father for anything in My name, He will give it to you. **Until now you have asked for nothing in My name; ask and you will receive, so that your joy may be made full**. (John 16:23-24)

Reading these chapters in context of what was going on in Jesus's life makes these statements more meaningful. This was His upper room discourse, knowing that He was going to the cross shortly. Jesus told His disciples, "*If you abide in me, and My word abides in you, you can ask whatever you wish, and it will be done for you.*" This points to intimacy—God in you, and you in God. When supplication comes out of intimacy and prayer, it is powerful, confident, and full of faith.

God chose His disciples, and He chose us; it is He who initiates. We are no longer slaves; Jesus calls us friends. Before this, only Abraham was called the friend of God. He was the father of our faith. Now we are all close friends of God, just like Abraham. Friends tell each other secrets and trust each other with essential information. That is why Jesus said that all things He heard from the Father, He made known to us. The Father wants to make things known to us, and He wants us to be sure that we can walk in faith, ask anything in His name, and receive what we ask. Asking and receiving are parts of the overflow of our friendship with God.

We are friends of God. We are children of God. We are the bride, and Jesus is our big Brother. All these things point to confidence in prayer. Jesus said that answered prayer brings fulfillment of joy. As I was thinking about how joy comes into this, I realized that joy is the overflow of our relationship with God.

Joy is a catalyst to faith. A "catalyst" is something usually used in insignificant amounts to cause a reaction. It is something that provokes a meaningful change or action. Joy is an agent that causes meaningful change and action in the effectiveness of our faith. When I read about my joy being made full because of answered prayer, I thought about the time my dad promised to buy me a bike. I was a little boy then, and I knew I would get that bike because my dad promised me. Even though I did not have it and had to wait for it, it did not stop me from telling my friends that I was going to get a bike and keep talking about it like it was already mine! Why would I do that? Because I had confidence in my father and who he was; if he promised me something, he would do everything in his power to make it happen. Both of my parents were like that. Now, I understand that not everyone is blessed with a natural father like that. Even if you did not have natural parents who were like that, you have been adopted into a new family with a Father who wants to be like that to you.

The day the manifestation of my bike happened, my joy was made full, or complete. My joy from asking to receiving was an agent to help sustain my faith until the day came. That is why the joy of the Lord is our strength. That is why we should count it all joy when we encounter trials and tribulations in life. It is that joy that will add to your faith to make it unmovable and unshakeable. It will help us stand in faith, even when it seems like we have nothing to stand on, or when every ounce of physical or mental energy leaves us.

The waiting period produces another substance, or agent, called patience. It is through faith and patience that we will inherit and receive all that God has for us. When patience works in us, the end result is maturity. We become spotless, without sin or blemish, and lacking or wanting nothing. Joy is the catalyst to our faith that leads to maturity, wholeness, contentment, and entirely lacking and wanting nothing.

Intimate prayer and fellowship with God lead to a confidence to ask Him for things—without guilt or shame—knowing that He will do what He said He would do. There is a confidence that will grow in us, which comes from intimacy with God. We proceed down a path of increasingly knowing the will of God. Then, in knowing the will of God, we will receive whatever we ask, just as 1 John 5:12 tells us:

> This is **the confidence which we have before Him, that, if we ask anything according to His will, He hears us**. And if we know that He hears us in whatever we ask, we know that we have the requests which we have asked from Him.

Is what we ask for always the will of God? The will of God is outlined in His Word, but we do know that we can twist truth, especially when our motives are out of sorts. Motives are very important, and that is where patience comes in. Patience is the perfect motive purifier. James writes about this.

> You lust and do not have; so you commit murder. You are envious and cannot obtain; so you fight and quarrel. **You do not have because you do not ask. You ask and do not receive, because you ask with wrong motives, so that you may spend it on your pleasures**. (James 4:2-3)

There is friction that lives within us that needs to be conquered in order to bring our asking and will in line with God's will. This is when intimacy and prayer work within us. I love what David says in Psalm 37:4-5. It brings everything into perspective.

> **Delight** yourself in the LORD; And He will give you the desires of your heart.
>
> **Commit** your way to the LORD, Trust also in Him, and He will do it.

In the beginning of this book, we talked about desire and delight in prayer. Delight has a number of connotations; it means delicate, sensitive, to be soft, or to be pliable. I like the thought of a person being soft and delicate with another, so much so that the person is willing to bend and change for the other because of their deep love for them. When we are like this with the Lord, He gives us the desires of our heart. The Amplified translation phrases this as "*the desires and secret petitions of the heart.*" The heart is the source of the motives that drive us. That is why the first commandment is to love the Lord your God with all your heart. When you are in this type of relationship with God, your desires become His desires. We are in union with Him; He abides in us, and we abide in Him.

When we commit our ways to God, we are actually giving our wants and desires to Him, exercising faith, and trusting Him to bring to pass our petitions. This friction and interaction is well-penned by David in Psalm 84, which we previously read: It is better to have one day in the presence of God than a thousand anywhere else. It is better to just be a gatekeeper who lets everyone into the palace than having a luxurious life with sinners. He then states that God does not withhold any good thing from those who do what is right. God wants to give us good things and bless us with the things we want and need on this earth.

We go through a process while we grow with God. Union with God blends patience and faith. Patience and faith bring an understanding and unity with God, and they bring His promises to fulfillment and manifestation in our lives.

So we see now how intimacy with God in prayer results in a powerful prayer life, where God answers our supplications. Hopefully, this excites us even more to hunger and thirst for Him in prayer and communion, so we can experience the joy of asking and receiving from our Father.

## Intimacy, Prayer, and Intercession

Another subject on prayer that I have not touched on much is intercession. I have written about supplication and intercession toward the end of my book because both of these types of prayers will be more meaningful to you by understanding and walking in the truths revealed in the previous chapters.

One of the most quoted scriptures on intercession and prayer is recorded in 2 Chronicles 7:14 (NLT):

> **Then** if my people who are called by my name will **humble themselves and pray and seek my face** and turn from their wicked ways, **I will hear from heaven and will forgive their sins and restore their land**.

Most often, people quote this scripture without looking at its context. The context brings a deeper and more powerful meaning to intercession. Let us take a look at what was going on in the beginning of 2 Chronicles. This will help us better understand the subject of intimacy, prayer, and intercession. Intercession is when you stand in the gap between a person or a cause and God, and you ask for that person's or cause's need to be met. Moses was a great intercessor who stood between God and the children of Israel, asking God to lead them into the promised land. Jesus is our greatest of intercessors. He intercedes for us before the throne of God. His death and resurrection were intercession for us. He entered the heavenly holy of holies and poured His blood on the mercy seat for the redemption of our sins.

Second Chronicles begins with Solomon taking the throne after his father, David. Solomon calls all the leaders of Israel together and has a massive worship service, where they sacrifice one thousand animals to the Lord. God appears to Solomon and asks him what he wants. God says that He will give him whatever he asks. So Solomon asks God for wisdom. He did not just ask for wisdom for himself; he asked for wisdom to govern God's people. To get deeper insight into Solomon's prayer, read 2 Chronicles 1 and 1 Kings 3.

> "Now, O LORD my God, You have made Your servant king in place of my father David, yet I am but a little child; I do not know how to go out or come in. Your servant is in the midst of Your people which You have chosen, a great people who are too many to be numbered or counted. So give Your **servant an understanding heart to judge Your people to discern between good and evil.** For who is able to judge this great people of Yours?" It was pleasing in the sight of the Lord that Solomon had asked this thing. God said to him, "Because you have asked this thing and have not asked for yourself long life, nor have asked riches for yourself, nor have you asked for the life of your enemies, **but have asked for yourself discernment to understand justice**, behold, I have done according to your words.

> Behold, I have given you a wise and discerning heart, so that there has been no one like you before you, nor shall one like you arise after you." (1 Kings 3:7-12)

Solomon asked for wisdom so he could rule, judge, and discern between good and evil (right and wrong). This is not about how man sees good and evil, but how God discerns good and evil. This also speaks to the subject that we discussed in the Lord's Prayer about delivering us from evil. God's response was that He was delighted that Solomon was more interested in discernment so he could understand justice and administer it to the people of God. God is a God of justice; He always wants justice to reign on earth and over the hearts of men. What a prayer for any leader to pray. God answers Solomon's prayer and gives him wisdom along with riches and fame, which he did not ask for, and promised him long life if he kept the commandments and decrees of God. Solomon's wisdom and riches were known throughout the world, and his fame grew.

Solomon set his mind on building the Temple of God. His father, David, wanted to build the Temple, but it was not ordained for him do that. However, he collected offerings and got all the financial needs ready for Solomon to build the Temple. The Temple was the dwelling place for God, where people could come and worship and interact with Jehovah. It was the place that set Israel apart because they had the living God dwelling in their midst. The plan for the Temple was designed by God and given to Moses. In that plan, the Temple had the holiest of places, where God would dwell. He called it the holy of holies. Solomon finished the Temple and brought the ark of the covenant into the holy of holies.

When the Temple was dedicated, all the priests, singers, and musicians gathered together and worshipped God. The presence of the Lord came down, and they were overcome with the power and glory of God. All of Israel was rejoicing because the presence of God was in its designated place. Israel was prospering in peace, and God's promises were fulfilled. It was a time of great celebration in Israel.

Solomon acknowledged that God heard the prayers of His people in the Temple, which was the place of God's dwelling, and then he prayed through a litany of things:

> Nevertheless, listen to my prayer and my plea, O LORD my God. Hear the cry and the prayer that your servant is making to you. May you watch over this Temple day and night, this place where you have said you would put your name. May you always hear the prayers I make toward this place. May you hear the humble and earnest requests from me and your people Israel when we pray toward this place. Yes, hear us from heaven where you live, and when you hear, forgive. (2 Chronicles 6:19-21, NLT)

Solomon listed numerous sins that caused separation between God and man, and the consequences of those sins. He told the people that if they came to the Temple and prayed and asked God to forgive them, He would hear their prayer and forgive them.

When Solomon finished praying, **fire came down from heaven and consumed the sacrifice that was made at the altar, and then the glory of the Lord filled the Temple again**. After that, the people of Israel had an even more massive worship service and celebrated for seven days.

> When Solomon finished praying, fire flashed down from heaven and burned up the burnt offerings and sacrifices, and the glorious presence of the LORD filled the Temple. **The priests could not enter the Temple of the LORD because the glorious presence of the LORD filled it.** When all the people of Israel saw the fire coming down and the glorious presence of the LORD filling the Temple, they fell face down on the ground and worshiped and praised the LORD, saying, "He is good! His faithful love endures forever!" (2 Chronicles 7:1-3, NLT)

Solomon sent everyone home, and then the Lord appeared to him in a vision at night and told him that He had heard his prayer.

> I have heard your prayer and have chosen this Temple as the place for making sacrifices. At times I might shut up the heavens so that no rain falls, or command grasshoppers to devour your crops, or send plagues among you. **Then if my people who are called by my name will humble themselves and pray and seek my face and turn from their wicked ways, I will hear from heaven and will forgive their sins and restore their land. My eyes will be open and my ears attentive to every prayer made in this place. For I have chosen this Temple and set it apart to be holy—a place where my name will be honored forever**. I will always watch over it, for it is dear to my heart. (2 Chronicles 7:12-16, NLT)

Notice the order of what God said: We as a people must humble ourselves, pray, and seek His face, meaning, seek the presence of God and mourn for His presence.

First, I want to highlight our dependency on God. Humility comes from a place of complete dependence on God. It is a place where we know that God is our only Source, Supplier, and Joy. Prayer is communication with God. When we talk about seeking His face, we talk about seeking to know who He is, His ways, and His thoughts. The result of this is intimacy, honor, and respect for God. We can never express humility before God without a continual, intimate prayer life with Him. Humility lifts us up to a place where we experience prayer from our position and calling. It is the highest form of prayer.

This leads us to seek God's face, and not His provisions or His hand. It is not just a one-time situation, but a continuous way of life where you are interacting and nurturing the most desired relationship in your life.

Did you ever want to achieve something in life like a particular job, relationship, or goal? If so, your thoughts will continuously be on how you can attain those things, and you will center your actions and days around whoever can help you attain those desires. This is the word picture!

How long should we seek His face? It should be a lifelong and consistent part of our life and being. It should be the most desirous habit we practice.

This is the attitude, passion, and desire that God is looking for from us. When we learn God's ways, we become more able to understand what is evil in His sight. What is the root of those evil acts? Pride and the lack of dependence and faith in God. Evil comes because of selfishness. We are more concerned about our own well-being, and we do things at the expense of others for our benefit. When such desires enter our heart, they cause us to exalt our will and ways above God. John calls it the lust of the flesh, the lust of the eyes, and the pride of life. Many times, these evil acts find their way into our lives, and we cross that fine line between dependence on God and dependence on ourselves.

Resting in God's presence and communion with Him result in transformation. When we truly seek God's face, our hearts are purified, and the spiritual strength that comes upon us leads us to change. From deep longing for His presence comes the revelation of God, and along with it comes transformation. God wanted Israel to keep remembering that He blessed them with His presence, and as a result, other blessings followed. What God said to Solomon about humbling himself, praying, and seeking His face is very relatable to "*blessed are those who mourn.*" In the end, we all get comforted by His presence. The Comforter reveals to us anything that is separating us from Him and brings us back into the place of communion and fellowship.

This type of prayer creates an open, continual communion with God who simultaneously lives in our heart and in heaven. His heart's desire is to bring healing to our spirit, soul, and body. The word in the New Testament for being made whole is *sozo*: to be healed, saved, and made whole.

There are many similarities between Solomon's prayer and the Lord's Prayer. When we worship, we are seeking God's face. When we pray, we are humbling ourselves and learning to depend on God. We are asking for His kingdom to come and His will to be done in our lives. By this, we are submitting to His will and letting go of our own. God reveals His Word to us, helps us, and delivers us from our evil ways. Then, He heals our land, and His kingdom's glory manifests on earth.

Prayer and communion are dear to God's heart. We read about the Temple made with human hands and dedicated to Him. Jesus reiterated this after He turned over the money changers tables around the temple, saying, "*My House shall be a house of prayer*," quoting Isaiah 56:7.

In the New Testament, God made a new temple to dwell in. It was not made with human hands, but by the hand of God. When Jesus died on the cross, there was an earthquake, and the man-made temple veil, which was a giant curtain separating the holy place from the holy of holies, was torn from top to bottom. This signifies that God does not dwell in man-made temples anymore. He dwells in and with men. When we are born again, our spirit is recreated in the image and likeness of God. There was an adamic explosion when God split the old Adam and the second Adam (Jesus), who released us from the death nature of man. Our spirit becomes born again, and now, God dwells within man once more. The Spirit of God lives in us and flows out of us. We are the living temple of God.

We all are houses of prayer, both individually and corporately. The body of Christ is corporately being built as a dwelling place for God. His eyes and ears are attentive to the prayers made in our temples. He is always listening to our prayers. As the temple is holy, so are our prayers holy to God. He is perpetually watching for our prayers, and He counts them dear to His heart. We need to say that aloud: Our prayers are dear to God's heart.

In conclusion, it is the deep desire for God's presence and interaction with Him that feeds continual spiritual growth and communion. God also seeks those who seek Him. He continually looks throughout the earth for the heart that hungers after Him (2 Chronicles 16:9). He promises that He will meet us and commune with us. This is the place of intimacy in prayer, where inspired and faith-filled intercession happens.

How is your prayer journey? If you have never started, let us go! If you are stalling, let us restart! If you are well on your path, keep going!

Now that you have finished this book, please go back and re-read sections and chapters as an inspirational prayer devotional. Prayer can and will be the most enjoyable part of your life!

## *Return to Prayer* Model By Pastor Lance Bane

I want to add another practical prayer model that encompasses many of the truths you read in this book. I heard Pastor Lance preach about how the Lord was leading and guiding him into a closer and more intimate relationship. They were some of the most anointed and passionate messages I have heard him preach. I could see the Lord's hand all over the teaching as Lance explained how the Lord revealed the *Return to Prayer* model to him. The practical approach to prayer and intimacy is outstanding, and I thought it would be a wonderful addition to have practical steps on learning to make prayer the most enjoyable part of your life. Please use the truths learned in these pages, and the practical steps laid out here, to enjoy an intimate and fulfilling prayer life.

Be Blessed,

**—Scott Tavolacci**

## Welcome to a Return to Prayer

The origin of this prayer guide is from my own times of praying with open hands and a lifted heart. It is called ***Return to Prayer*** because of my hope that you will develop a joyful, confident, consistent, and effective prayer life. This guide will help you stay aware of important themes and topics during times of intentional prayer.

Use this prayer guide in the order it is published, or enter into any of these themes as applicable in your moments of purposeful prayer. The more comfortable you become using this prayer guide, the more you will experience a joyful rhythm between each theme. You may pray in one area and find yourself seamlessly praying in another.

On each page, you will find suggested instructions and thoughts to help you maximize each step as you journey and pray with God's Spirit.

Praying Together,

**—Lance Bane**

## Remain Quiet

Be still, and know that I am God! (Psalm 46:10)

- Find a place that is free from distractions.
- Set a time to be silent before God.
- In silence, we can hear God, which is the need of our spirit and soul, and we realize how noisy our internal world is.
- When you experience distraction, be gentle with yourself and return to the Lord.

What did you learn about King Jesus during your silence?

What did you learn about yourself during your silence?

"Silence and solitude are the two most radical disciplines of the Christian life."
- Dallas Willard

## Revere God

You must worship the Lord your God and serve only him. (Matthew 4:10, NLT)

Utilize the following covenant names of God to inspire your worship:

- Jehovah Elohim - The Supreme God (Genesis 2:4)
- Jehovah Jireh - The Lord Provides (Genesis 22:14)
- Jehovah Rapha - The Lord Heals (Exodus 15:26)
- Jehovah Nissi - The Lord is My Banner (Exodus 17:15)
- Jehovah Shalom - The Lord is My Peace (Judges 6:24)
- Jehovah Raah - The Lord is My Shepherd (Psalm 23:1)
- Jehovah Sabaoth - The Lord of Hosts (Psalm 24:10)
- Jehovah Shammah - The Lord is There (Hebrews 13:5-6)
- Jehovah Tsidkenu - The Lord Our Righteousness (Jeremiah 23:6)

To revere is to regard with awe, reverence, to worship.

---

"Worship springs from amazement."
- G.K. Chesterton

---

## Remember His Goodness

Let all that I am praise the Lord; may I never forget the good things he does for me. (Psalm 103:2)

- When you are struggling to hear God or see Him at work in your life, choose to remember His goodness.
- Remembering the goodness of God and His faithfulness is an active decision that clarifies the reality of God's presence in your life and circumstances.

What was the last thing you remember God doing in your life?

As you bring these to remembrance, specifically give thanks to God for the moments He has worked for you.

*God wants us to live in remembrance because it strengthens our faith for today.*

## Repent

Repent of your sins and believe the Good News!
(Mark 1:15, NLT)

- Ask the Holy Spirit to show you the sins you have committed since your last prayer time. We cannot repent for what we do not see and know.
- Acknowledge your sins and declare with repentance, "I repent of ___________."

Repentance is a change of heart, mind, and action.

---

"For you alone know each human heart."
- 2 Chronicles 6:30

---

## Renounce

To renounce is to formally declare one's abandonment of; to reject; to stop using; to refuse or resign a right or position.

- Once you know the sins you have committed, declare, "I renounce all agreements made with sin and darkness."
- Heaven looks for our agreement, so we break agreements with sinful behaviors, habits, and lifestyles.

We exercise our authority and rights as children of God by renouncing agreements.

If you need more need ministry time and help in this area, talk to a pastor or trusted, mature friend who can guide you.

---

*"So humble yourselves before God. Resist the devil, and he will flee from you."*
*- James 4:7*

---

## Release

To release is to set free; to allow something to move.

- This prayer theme is to encourage you to release control of people, situations, and circumstances that are not going the way you want.
- Declare your trust in King Jesus.
- The only control we are given is self-control. (2 Timothy 1:7; Galatians 5:23; Ephesians 4:23-24; 2 Peter 1:6)

---

"On your best day you can only manage yourself. You can't control the wind, but you can control your sails."

- Dr. Bob Chope

---

## Relinquish

To relinquish is to voluntarily give up.

- This prayer theme is to encourage you to relinquish the emotional burdens that do not belong to you, such as worry, fear, resentment, and bitterness.
- Imagine giving to King Jesus the situations, circumstances, and emotional burdens you are carrying around.

"Come to me, all you who are weary and carry heavy burdens, and I will give you rest. Take my yoke upon you. Let me teach you, because I am humble and gentle at heart, and you will find rest for your souls. For my yoke is easy to bear, and the burden I give you is light."
- Matthew 11:28-30

## Request

Keep on asking, and you will receive what you ask for. Keep on seeking, and you will find. Keep on knocking, and the door will be open to you. (Matthew 7:7)

Suggested categories for requesting:

- Family
- Friends
- The lost
- Church leadership
- Government
- Missionaries
- Nations
- Finances
- Circumstances

---

"God is looking for people to use, and if you get usable, He will wear you out. The most dangerous prayer you can pray is this: 'Use me.'"
- Rick Warren

---

## Receive

Since He did not spare even His own Son but gave Him up for us all, won't he also give us everything else? (Romans 8:32)

- Ask the Father, "What will you give me today that will help me faithfully, expectantly, and obediently live for King Jesus?"
- Be a good receiver. This means to receive by faith and allow yourself to feel the emotions associated with receiving. These emotions may be joy, weeping, thanksgiving, humility, excitement, etc.

## Rejoice

"Always be joyful." (1 Thessalonians 5:16)

Rejoice is to return to joy; to return to the source of your joy.

- Conclude your time with King Jesus by rejoicing in His goodness and with the confidence that He will hear and answer your prayer according to His will (1 John 5:14).

"Joy is the serious business of Heaven."
- C.S. Lewis

# Well Done!

Thank you for using this prayer guide. As a simple tool designed and purposed to help people pray and commune with King Jesus, I hope it serves you well for years to come.

If you have any feedback on how we can make this prayer guide more useful, please email gatewaylance@gmail.com or visit www.lancebane.com/connect.

Remember, love is the greatest reason to spend consistent time with King Jesus.

You are loved.
You are valuable.
You have a purpose.
Live, Love, and lead as a much-loved child of God.

Praying Together,

**— Lance Bane**

# About the Author

Scott was ordained in 1985 and has worked in various ministerial roles in churches and other Christian organizations for the past thirty plus years—leading, teaching, organizing, and training believers in the kingdom of God. Scott has operated in various five-fold ministries and has a strong prophetic, teaching and healing anointing, often challenging people to know God and fulfill their God-ordained destiny. He has written many prophetic teachings and courses such as Understanding Divine Healing through The Ministry of Jesus; Paul's Spiritual Secret; Revival; Kingdom Leadership and Authority; Prayer, His Presence, and Intimacy with God; The Person, Gifts, and Ministries of the Holy Spirit; and Releasing the Power of the Heart and The Soldier of Christ. Scott is a pastor at Gateway Christian Fellowship in West Haven, and the founder of Kingdom Master Builders.

For additional information and teaching from Scott, please go to KingdomMasterBuilders.com, where many more of his teachings and other material can be obtained. Kingdom Master Builders is all about what is written in the book, building the Kingdom and dominion of God in the hearts and minds of mankind. If interested in contacting Scott for Ministry opportunities, please email him at Kingdommasterbuilders@gmail.com.

# Other Books By Scott Tavolacci

**Kingdom Master Builders**

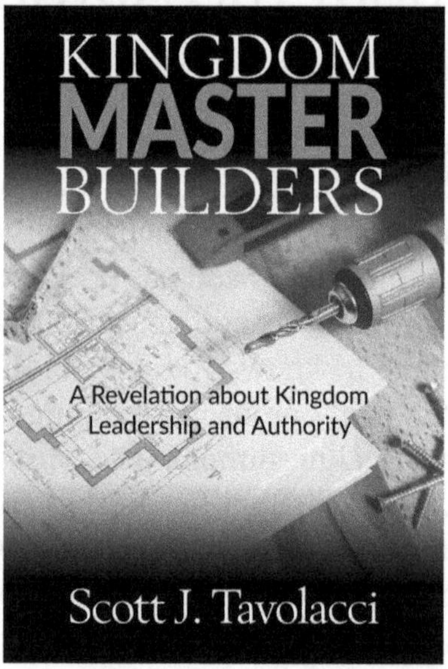


To be a wise Master Builder you need to be a kingdom leader. And to lead in the kingdom and walk in kingdom authority, you need to know how to use the keys to the kingdom that Jesus gave us. The Lord disclosed to me what I would consider to be the "key of keys" for kingdom leadership. He said, "If My leaders want to walk in the authority of the Lion, they need to walk in the meekness of the Lamb."

> "I love this book! My friend Scott Tavolacci has given us a comprehensive approach to building God's kingdom on earth, as it is in heaven. *Kingdom Master Builders* will bring you into God's revelation of who God entrusts with His master plan for changing the world. This book can change your life and change the planet!"
>
> — **Brian Simmons**
> *The Passion Translation* Project
> Passionandfire.com, ThePassiontranslation.com

# Other Books By Scott Tavolacci

**Understanding Divine Healing and the Ministry of Jesus**

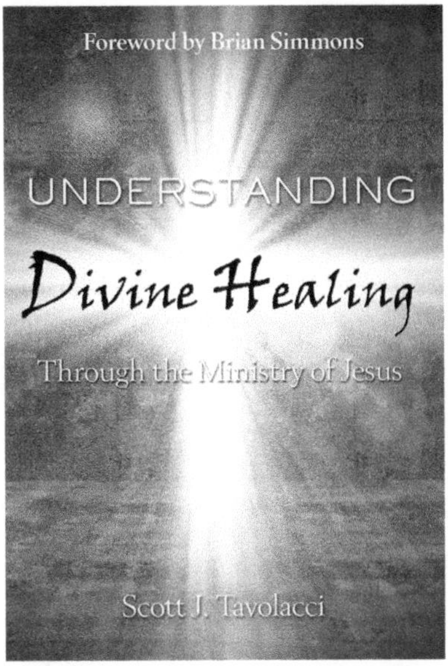


Is healing real for today? After studying divine healing intensely for ten years, Scott Tavolacci thought he had a reasonably good understanding of the subject. He had read or listened to numerous well-known—and not so well-known—teachers on healing, studied and memorized almost every passage regarding the topic, and prayed over many people for healing. But then God led Scott into a very intense, year-long study about the ways Jesus ministered healing in the Gospels. God started opening up the relational side of how Jesus led people to interact with Him and receive healing. What Scott discovered is that healing is not about formulas or doctrine, but relationship.

There are not many books on divine healing like this one; it is a revelation for this day and age. Take time to meditate on what is being said as you read these pages. Let the Holy Spirit bring you into a greater understanding of Jesus the Healer.

Printed in the USA
CPSIA information can be obtained
at www.ICGtesting.com
JSHW010716281123
52635JS00009B/8

9 781734 005349